Revealing Antiquity

· 7 ·

G. W. Bowersock, General Editor

Prophets and Emperors

*Human and Divine Authority
from Augustus to Theodosius*

DAVID POTTER

HARVARD UNIVERSITY PRESS
Cambridge, Massachusetts
London, England
1994

This book is printed on acid-free paper, and its binding
materials have been chosen for strength and durability.

Library of Congress Cataloging-in-Publication Data
Potter, D. S. (David Stone), 1957–
Prophets and emperors: human and divine authority
from Augustus to Theodosius / David Potter.
p.   cm. — (Revealing antiquity; 7)
Includes index.
ISBN 0-674-71565-9
1. Divination—Rome.   2. Oracles, Roman.   3. Sibyls.
4. Prophets—Rome.   5. Astrology, Roman.
6. Rome—Religion.   I. Title.   II. Series.
BF1768.P67   1994
133.3′248′0937—dc20
94-25982
CIP

Acknowledgments

THIS BOOK began to be formed in the delightful atmosphere provided by the senior common room of New College, Oxford, during a term as visiting fellow in Michaelmas 1989. I am indebted to the Warden and Fellows for this opportunity. It was written in Ann Arbor during the academic year 1992–93 in the equally congenial atmosphere provided by colleagues in the Department of Classical Studies at the University of Michigan. An early version of Chapter 5 was delivered at a colloquium here and at the University of Toronto in March 1993, and it is a pleasure to thank my audiences on both occasions for their comments. Portions of Chapter 3 have adapted earlier work on Sibylline Oracles that appeared in the *Journal of Roman Archaeology* and *Prophecy and History in the Crisis of the Roman Empire*. With some minor variations, references to ancient works follow the system in H. G. Liddell and R. Scott, *A Greek-English Lexicon*, 9th rev. ed. with supplement, and P. W. Glare, *Oxford Latin Dictionary*. The maps were designed by Brian Harvey, to whom I am extremely thankful for his generous donation of much time and ingenuity. I am equally grateful to Peg Fulton for her advice on a number of problematic issues and her support for this project. Ann Hawthorne made many improvements through her careful editing of the manuscript.

Throughout my work on this subject, I have benefited from the advice of many friends. My debts to Glen Bowersock, George Forrest, Robin Lane Fox, and John Matthews are of long standing, and it is a pleasure to acknowledge them once again. So too are the debts I owe my colleagues Sue Alcock, John Cherry, John Dillery, Ann Hanson, Sara Myers, Brian Schmidt, Traianos Gagos, and, above all, Ludwig Koenen, for the vast learning that he has put at my disposal with enormous tolerance and unfailing generosity.

Most of all, it is a pleasure to thank my wife, Ellen, who vastly improved this book, and our daughter, Claire, who contributed in her own way.

This book is dedicated to the memory of a scholar and friend whose learning was matched by his humanity in the broadest sense of the word—Antony Andrewes.

Contents

Prophets and Emperors

[1]

Prophecy and Cult

PLUTARCH OF CHAERONEA, philosopher, biographer, and—by his own admission—cultural icon, cared deeply about oracles. He held a number of offices at Delphi in the early first century A.D., including the most important, and he wrote several works depicting the sort of conversations that he felt should occur at this shrine. These Delphic dialogues are not merely discussions of the source of prophecy, the quality of Delphic air, and the nature of the universe. They are also crucial testimony on what people thought was important about prophecy, and on its traditions. Plutarch's discussants and the tourist Pausanias, who left the most important description of the site in his mid-second century guidebook to Greece, see Delphi as a centerpiece of their cultural heritage. It was a place where Apollo had spoken for centuries, and where it was appropriate to think about other great prophetic feats in the past. It was valued not so much for the prophecies that were uttered there in the present (there was some feeling that they were not as interesting as those given in the past) as for its historical role. Both Plutarch and Pausanias shared the belief of their contemporaries that a person could know if a prophecy was authentic only if it had been proved to have come true. Plutarch's dialogues and Pausanias' description therefore provide accounts of numerous prophets and their accomplishments in the past: prophecies of the Sibyl, of Musaeus, of an inspired individual who could be found on the shores of the Red Sea, of other shrines in Greece, and of Apollo himself at Delphi—all of which are treated as being equally valid and important.[1]

In a sense, it is not surprising that a Plutarch or a Pausanias could be more interested in prophecies about past events than in contemporary prophecies concerning the future. The fact that the Athenians could produce oracles of both the Sibyl and Musaeus to prove that their fleet had been betrayed to the Spartans in 404 B.C. was far more interesting than the possibility that a person's runaway slave was going to be found, or that the god was suggesting that the boor whom one might have met that morning was going to make a fortune in the Black Sea.[2] One could not be sure that these remarks were really authentic utterances. Prophecy concerning the future was interesting because of the possibility that it would offer a new marvel that could be added to the cultural treasure house. Until such time as it was proved true, a prophecy could still be interesting if it seemed to reflect contemporary circumstances: this reference offered a sort of guarantee that it really was inspired by a divinity.

In antiquity, as now, prophecy was only rarely concerned with the future. Most prophetic interpretation was concerned with isolating moments in the present that had been foreseen in the past, interpreting the symbolic meanings of prophecies, making venerated texts relevant in the present. Prophecies could describe and validate current conditions. They could provide confirmation that the current state of affairs was part of some sort of divine plan. Inspiring confidence through the picture they provided of the present, they offered a socially valid suggestion about the way in which problems could be resolved. For a Christian or a Jew, these forces were described in the canonical books of their faiths, interpreted in accordance with accepted standards of allegory. For an ancient polytheist, these forces were described by a local system of cult or the common heritage of classical culture. A contemporary American who accepts the statements of economic forecasters, implicitly assumes that there are "laws of economics" that can be divined, and, like the ancient polytheist, does not seem to be too greatly disturbed by persistent or obvious failure. The fault lies with the practitioner rather than with the practice.

Prophecy is implicitly connected with power. In a society that attributes great power to the supernatural, the language of cult is intimately connected with the expression of ideas about earthly authority. The consequences manifest themselves in official and unofficial contexts. Prophecy may be used to support an existing order by demonstrating that the current state of affairs has divine sanction. It may defuse conflict by introducing a divine referee, or incite it by introducing an independent line of communication between human and divine.

Millenarian movements founded upon novel interpretations of prophetic books were but one form that this independent line could take. The crafty man or the witch of the seventeenth-century English village offered cleric-free avenues to all sorts of knowledge derived from age-old wisdom. Today faith healers offer an alternative to practices that are sanctioned and supported by agents of social control. Astrologers can still vie with the agents of a society's intellectual elite to guide the lives of the troubled or curious at even the highest levels of government.

This book explores the role that prophecy played in the power structure of the Roman empire during the first four centuries of the Christian era. It proceeds from a very broad definition of prophecy—divine revelation about past, present, or future situations—without drawing semantic distinctions between prophecy, divination, and apocalypticism. These distinctions were not drawn in antiquity, so there seems little purpose in imposing them upon the evidence now.[3] The overwhelming impression conveyed by the evidence is that people were deeply concerned about the truth or falsity of divine communication. Each individual made a choice as to what, if anything, could be believed. The issues that concern me are connected with the evolution of different ideas about individual forms of divine communication, and individual prophets. The explanation for these different forms and ideas is to be sought in the nature of ancient religious practice.

At some point in the mid-second century, a plague struck the city of Hierapolis, located near the modern resort of Pammukale in western Turkey. The people of Hierapolis recognized this disturbance as a sign of divine anger and sent an embassy to an oracle of Apollo at Claros asking him how they might be freed from their troubles and saved from further suffering of the same sort.[4] The Hierapolitans had their own gods, of course, with their own cults, but the divinities worshipped through these cults could not help them because these rites celebrated traditional solutions to previously recognized problems. This did not mean that these cults were without their own value, only that they could not be expected to provide people with aid in the face of a new crisis. Clarian Apollo could, and he duly prescribed a regimen of "solemn libations and hecatombs of full-grown animals" as a cure. They were to sacrifice a "common ox" to Gaia (goddess of the earth) in a huge precinct, then turn their devotions to Aither and the gods of the sky, and conclude with offerings to the divinities of the underworld—being mindful throughout of Apollo Kareios. The pattern of sacrifice reflected Apollo's view that the entire cosmos was in disarray, and that the gods connected with its three regions all needed to be propitiated. In return for his help, the Hierapolitans were to erect statues of him at all the gates and send choruses to his temple, where they would sing hymns and offer sacrifices. The text that records these instructions is but one of a number of inscriptions commemorating the intervention of the gods through their oracles to help Hierapolis survive various times of trouble.

The interaction between Apollo and the traditional cults of Hierapolis is of tremendous importance for explaining the continuing vitality of "classical paganism" for centuries after the conversion of Constantine.[5] Traditional cult did not simply vanish into the back alleys, basements, and mountains of the Mediterranean world when Constantine crossed his spiritual Rubicon and became a Christian. Traditional cult was not at this point suffering any noticeable decline that can be attributed to any factor other than lack of the money necessary for its celebration in the wake of the economic catastrophe of the early third century. Christianity did not triumph over a "degenerate" adversary, and, as Gibbon argued long ago, there is a great deal to be said for the notion that the needs met by traditional cults reformed Christianity every bit as much as Christianity reformed pagan practice.[6] When the young Theodore of Syceon, a future saint from a village near Ancyra, went to visit an area that was "inhabited by Artemis and her demons," he was going there to test his holy power, not to wipe out what must have been the survival of the old cult in the late sixth century (*V. Theod.* 16). The holy man whom his mother, a prostitute, visited to ask about a vision she had experienced after sleeping with an imperial emissary (a former acrobatic performer with camels in the hippodrome) was clearly there to fulfill a function that would have been filled by a pagan in the past (*V. Theod.* 4).

A successful religious system, as was traditional polytheistic cult in the Mediterranean world, must have an implicit medium for change, so that it is able to adapt to developments in the society that it serves. In other words, it needs an "active" aspect in order to keep up-to-date the "passive" side of worship that is defined by the celebration of cult.[7] In religious terms, the distinction between "active" and "passive" is the distinction between the acceptance of old knowledge and the search for new. Oracles and other media of divine communication were the essential vehicles of "active" religious experience, while cult ritual, which confirmed and celebrated the existing relationship between human and divine, was the essential public feature of "passive" experience. Such experiences celebrated the past and the present, the order of things as they were. Even mystery cults such as that of Demeter at Eleusis, or that of the god Mithras commemorating, on the one hand, the ancient gift of the goddess or, on the other hand, the ancient battle of good and evil, provided their initiates only with the information that they needed to understand the implications of these acts for their own lives. In a "passive" religious ceremony, an individual followed a script that had already been written; an "active" religious experience could provide an entirely new one. In the case of the people of Hierapolis it was clear that their own cults were not adequate to solve the new crisis caused by the plague. The seeking of the oracle was thus, quintessentially, an "active" experience that served to update the existing "passive" system. The continuing validity of these old cults is specifically stressed by Apollo's stricture that the Hierapolitans be "mindful of" their own cult of Apollo Kareios.[8]

Though intellectually "passive," the actions of civic cult often demanded significant personal involvement, and their celebrants showed obvious emotional attachment to their rituals. There is perhaps no better evocation of the life connected with such cults than that contained in a letter that the great ancient historian Michael Rostovtzeff wrote to the Russian historian George Vernadsky from India in 1937:

> What struck me above all in India is the life of . . . what I have studied all my life as a destroyed, ruined past. The life of the pagan religion and cult. In the Indian temples, especially in South India, it is all alive. Enormous temples—just like the temples of the Syrian cities—with hundreds of Brahmans, temple servants, dancing girls, musicians, temple prostitutes, beggars, pilgrims of both sexes. Temples where incense is burning, where flowers, fruit and all sorts of food are presented to the gods and goddesses, where the deities are rubbed in with oil and the symbol of blood (red paint), and where sometimes bloody sacrifices are made. Temples where religious ceremonies are carried out each day. Temples where religious processions and celebrations constitute an important event. Where thousands draw the colossal chariot of the god, when he, parched due to heat, leaves for a few days to his summer residence. The classical cult is re-enacted before my eyes. I *see* it, and for me seeing is identical to feeling and understanding.[9]

These rituals provided a model for the order of society, and for a human being's relationship with the vast, uncontrollable forces of nature. Human existence in a preindustrial society was extraordinarily tenuous. Life expectancy at birth was somewhere around twenty-five years; the world was full of dying children (roughly half the children born did not live to see their fifth birthday), and those who survived had to confront mortality, hunger, and chronic injury or illness on a daily basis.[10] The extraordinary number of medicinal remedies that have survived in sundry works are testimony to humanity's virtual impotence in the face of illness of any sort. The ritual of passive cult provided psychological reassurance that there was help and reason to hope in the face of all this. The urge to control the uncontrollable manifested itself in devotional exercises of all sorts. But the cults of the Roman world were often more than this. Classical polytheism existed on a plane beyond that of simple grunt and sacrifice in an effort to control the weather. Although the ancient world produced intellectuals of all sorts who laughed at the idea that the gods took an interest in human affairs, or that they could be influenced by the slaughter of animals at their altars, by far the greater number of intellectuals in this world believed profoundly in the gods. They might, and did, evolve their own, complex explanations of the way in which humans could deal with the gods, and complex models of the way in which the divine world was ordered, seeking to explain the multitudinous manifestations of divine action that they perceived. But they did so in terms of the existing "passive" structure.

A community's cults represented its historical success in the face of nature, its special relationship with the powers that controlled the earth. The celebration of these cults offered a very clear illustration of propriety and power. Public sacrifice in celebration of these cults was intended to bind the community together; the distributions of food and other gifts on the occasion of these celebrations were meant to reflect the order of the state. The priests of these cults were guardians of tradition and social order. The basic Greek word for priest is *hiereus,* someone connected with cult acts, *hiera;* the basic Latin words are *flamen* and *sacerdos* (the former of obscure Indo-European origin, though obviously connected with a root meaning "priest" while *sacerdos* is a formation from *sacra,* rites).[11] They are depicted in works of art as overseers of the ritual, mediating the existing relationship in a socially acceptable fashion.[12] Their actions represented the idea that nature and society were under control. A civic priesthood was embedded within the nexus of wealth, family, and civic administration that defined a respectable person's place in society, and that society's place in the wider world. Such people were not to be innovators.

"Passive" cult was practiced on several levels. Cities had their gods, groups within the city could celebrate other gods who were specially relevant to their activities or identities, and individuals celebrated cults that they felt were important to their own lives. Ordinarily there was no reason why there should be any conflict between these different forms of cult activity, for cults simply defined a community's or group's or individual's own way of dealing with the natural world. So long as personal religious predilections did not offend a community's notion of the natural order, and thus, by implication, the gods who were the active overseers of that order, there was no need to take offense. Put most simply, there was "no nation without gods, just as there is none without kings. Different people honor different gods, but the worship of all is directed toward the same power" (Art. *On.* 1.8).

The definition of what accorded with nature and what did not lies at the heart of much religious controversy in the ancient world.[13] Christians who were thought to practice incest and cannibalism offended just about everyone's sense of nature, and disturbances in the natural order were often thought to be the result of the presence of individuals whose actions were offensive to the divine guardians of that order.[14] Murderers, desecrators of temples, oath breakers, and other offenders against the natural order incurred gross personal impurity that could infect society as a whole if it were not removed. In antiquity pollution, impiety, and error were all defined as actions that broke the proper relationship between mortals of their gods, they were actions that were quintessentially unnatural.[15] Atheism, the simple refusal to show proper respect for a community's gods, was equally plainly an offense against the natural order represented by the cults of those gods. But beyond these obvious cases, the definition of natural and unnatural was remarkably fluid, for, despite the thin veneer of cultural homogeneity that was imposed on urban life by the Hellenized culture of the ruling classes of the Roman world, the Roman empire embraced an enormous range of cultural attitudes.

The greatest ostensible divide in this world was between the urban and the rural. In the Roman empire, as in other preindustrial European and Mediterranean societies, roughly 80 percent of the population was directly engaged in agriculture.[16] This was an ecological imperative: crop yields from average land in most parts of the empire could offer a surplus of only some 20 percent beyond the needs of the cultivators.[17] But the impact of this division between town and country varied a great deal. In areas where high-intensity agriculture was possible and where there were ready means of transportation, urban centers might be so densely packed together that rural inhabitants would be in close contact with city dwellers, while in other areas they might live in virtually complete isolation, joined in effect by little more than the tax collector.[18] The cult structure of the countryside, which is often extraordinarily difficult to glimpse through the lenses of the urban literature of the empire, could therefore be, in some places, radically different from that of the cities, in other places remarkably close, and at all times subject to change as the balance between urban and rural life shifted. It is sometimes extremely tempting to take the evidence of late antique Christian writers as a guide to these behaviors, as traditional polytheism was forced from its urban environment, and Christians combated their surviving rivals in the countryside. But this is a temptation that should be succumbed to only with great caution, because neither urban nor rural cult remained static: the "active" aspect of religious experience—the seeking and receiving of new information about humankind's relation with the natural order—was a consistent force for change.

The paradigm of nature held in the evaluation of "active" experience as well as it did in the "passive." But here the questions raised were all the sharper, and the range of debate even broader, and in this case it is necessary to be all the more conscious of the analytical baggage that western scholars, myself included, carry with them. Ever since the Reformation the divide between "magic" and "religion," and even between "magic," "religion," and "science" has provided a powerful tool for describing the efforts of human beings to control their environment.[19] The Christian tradition, as refined in early modern Europe, provided firm criteria for dividing "approved" religious activity from "magic," or "occultism." If something is arguably approved by the example of scripture it is "religious"; if not, it falls into the category of "subreligious" or "magical" conduct. Non-Christian conduct that roughly parallels "approved" Christian conduct is therefore "relig-ious" as well, while that which fails to measure up must be some-thing else.[20] In these terms, prophecy is conventionally restricted to "inspired speech at the initiative of a divine power, speech which is clear in itself and commonly directed to a third party," or, more generously, "the fortelling of future events," because this is what good prophets do in Christianity's sacred books.[21] The stress in these definitions on "speech," and the concurrent image of the prophet as a person, almost always male (often with a long white beard and a staff), who delivers a prophecy at divine initiative simply fails to account for much of the activity that was regarded as "prophetic" in the ancient world.

The English word "prophet" derives from the Latin word *pro-pheta*, which in turn derives from the Greek *prophetes*, a compound of the verb *prophemi*, to speak forth, and the suffix *–tes*, denoting a person who performs an action. The parallel formulation, *hypo-phetes*, is someone who speaks under compulsion. Greek has a word, *mantis*, connected with the verb *mainomai*, to rant or rage, and Latin has *vates*, a word of Italo-Celtic origin connected with the ideas of singing and divine possession. Greek also has *chresmos*, oracle, connected with the verb *chrao*, to proclaim, and its nu-merous further formulations, including *chresmologeo*, to utter an or-acle; *chresmologeia*, the uttering of an oracle; and *chresmologos*, a person who utters oracles or expounds them. Finally, there are formulations such as the verbs *thesphatizo* and *thesphatoomai*, de-riving from *theos*, god, and, again, verbs connoting speech. Thus we have an abundance of words linking the idea of divine com-munication with speech, but the content and manner of that speech are much more complicated matters.[22]

There is no implication in these words that they are connected with the future, they are simply connected with the idea of com-munication. Further examination of the way in which the words connected with the idea of divine communication are used shows that there was an important distinction drawn between the provi-sion and interpretation of this communication. A fragment of Pindar offers a good illustration of this difference: "sing, Muse [*manteueo*], and I will speak [*prophateuso*]"; the Muse creates the speech, and the poet interprets it.[23] Theocritus draws a similar distinction when he writes, "Tell me, goddess, for you know; I am the interpreter [*hypophetes*] for others."[24] Plato asserts that those who are in direct contact with the gods could not speak clearly about what they had learned and needed a second person around to interpret the messages that they received.[25] The same view recurs throughout Greek literature.

The terminology used to express the division between the revealer and the interpreter of divine knowledge is not, however, consistent. *Mantis, prophetes,* and *chresmologos* are the most common words in Greek for a person connected with the business of divine communication; *haruspex, augur, ariolus,* and *vates* occupy a similar position in Latin discourse. But the use of the words alternates, and the actual techniques of communication vary greatly. Thus Pausanias, in describing an oracle near Corinth, wrote, "there is an oracle there [*mantike*] and it gives oracles [*manteuetai*] in this fashion even today: there is a woman, barred from sexual intercourse with men, who gives prophecies [*prophetousa*]. Every month a lamb is sacrificed at night, and the woman, tasting of the blood, is possessed by the god" (2.24.1). At Amphicleia he records that the people say that "the god is their prophet [*mantis*] and savior when they are sick; the diseases of the Amphicleians and their neighbors are cured by dreams, the agent of the god [*promantis*] is a priest who speaks when he is possessed by the god" (10.33.11). A recently published Hellenistic inscription from Claros shows that a man described as a *chresmologos* was brought from Smyrna to act as the interpreter of the god's responses at the oracle, while an inscription of the third century B.C. tells of an embassy from Akraiphiai was sent to "speak with the priest [*hiereus*] and the prophet [*prophetes*] about the cities in Boeotia."[26] Artemidorus, whose book on dream interpretation offers a wealth of detail about social attitudes in the second century A.D., notes that if a person dreams that he is a prophet *(mantis)* (and here he clearly means someone not connected with a shrine) and his predictions are well thought of, he will have experience in many areas and take the anxieties of others upon himself.[27] His prophet "is concerned not only with his own troubles but also with the troubles of others" and, like a rich man, is in great demand (On. 3.21). The failure to develop a precise terminology to distinguish between receivers and interpreters of divine communication is a result of the great range of techniques available and underlines the basic point that definitions that insist upon direct divine contact as a feature of prophecy or simply specify speech will not do for the Greek and Roman world. The important issues in this world were those connected with truth and fraud, honesty and dishonesty, reliability and chance.

The debate over what form or forms of divine communication were true, honest, and reliable was conducted in terms of the division between nature and magic. In theory, magic was bad; it was the effort to influence the natural world by unnatural means, to control forces that no human should seek to control in order to hurt someone else.[28] The Greek word *magike,* whence the Latin *magica,* is a formation based on the word *magos,* a Persian priest, and thus intrinsically connected with the notion of wisdom that was foreign. Sometimes this could be a good thing, but more often than not, it was evil. The other Greek word for magic, *goeteia,* was less ambivalent. It is derived from a root (*go–*) implying sad noise, and the practice of *goeteia* was one that brought sorrow. In practice, *magike* or *goeteia* acted as an explanation of unexpected success or failure, prosperity or ruin.

The rhetoric of magic is almost always tied to results, results with a negative implication for someone else.[29] It is interesting therefore that the *haruspex* who offered to secure Augustine victory in a poetical contest spoke in terms of a positive action rather than a negative one (making Augustine's opponents look like fools), while the people who accused Libanius or Apuleius of magic accused them of doing harm.[30] Most people could agree that tossing a lead token inscribed with a curse into a well in the hope that a demon would do some harm to someone else was magic, and bad if it worked.[31] Carrying an amulet around for good luck was entirely another matter. Uttering incantations to harm crops in the field was certainly magic (and defined as such by the twelve tablets upon which Roman law was first codified). The utterance of incantations to make the crops grow was even approved by Constantine.[32]

Summoning the spirits of the dead to a conversation was the province of Thessalian witches, and horrific. But it was also the province of epic heroes, and a service provided by the magi (pages 65–70 below). Summoning a divinity to speak through a statue was a cheap magic trick to some, a demonstration of philosophic power to others (pages 203–204 below). And what about the boy at Tralles who was consulted through "magical interrogation" *(magica percontatione)* about the outcome of the Mithridatic war, and who uttered 160 verses on the subject while gazing at an image of Mercury in a bowl of water (Apul. *Apol.* 42)? Was this evil? There was a perfectly natural explanation for it, for "the human soul, often the simple soul of a child, is able, when called by certain incantations, or under the impulse of certain perfumes, to be brought out to forgetfulness of the present, and briefly removed from the memory of the body, to be returned and reconnected with its true nature, which is immortal and divine" (Apul. *Apol.* 43). The technique could even be used by the respectable Nigidius Figulus to find out what happened to 500 denarii that had been lost by Fabius (Apul. *Apol.* 42). The very fact of this kind of discussion is crucial for understanding prophecy in the Roman world.

The enormous variety in the cult system of the polytheistic world did not lend itself to ready organization or rationalization. Civic cults were an expression of community identity, and leeway given in ordinary circumstances to individuals to worship in their own way meant that they were free to make their own personal arrangements with the gods. The connection with local identity and personal taste may also help explain the vast diversity in divinatory practice that is attested at the oracular shrines of the Roman world and among individuals. Each place had its own technique, sanctioned by long practice, and there was no point in an established shrine's trying to bring itself into line with other places. It was the reputation of antiquity that would draw visitors. Thus the future emperor Titus was drawn to the shrine of Aphrodite at Old Paphos because it was old, and because it followed a mantic tradition hallowed by antiquity. The specialty here, as at the shrine of Apollo Lakeutes at Kition, was reading the future by observing the way in which victims burned on an altar.[33] The consultant of the oracular

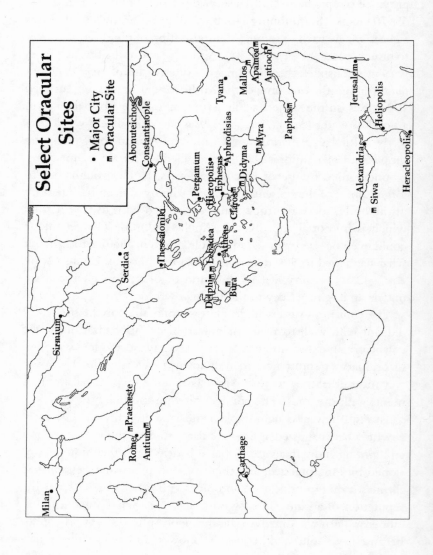

Select Oracular Sites

- Major City
- ɯ Oracular Site

Milan

Sirmium

Serdica

Thessaloniki

Constantinople

Abonuteichos

Pergamum

Hieropolis

Ephesus

Clarosɯ

Aphrodisias

Tyana

Mallosɯ

Apameaɯ

Antioch

Jerusalem

Heliopolis

Myraɯ

Didymaɯ

Paphosɯ

Alexandria

Siwaɯ

Heracleopolisɯ

Delphiɯ

Lebadea

Athens

Buraɯ

Praenesteɯ

Romeɯ

Antiumɯ

Carthage

spring at Daphne near Antioch learned the future by dipping a laurel leaf in the water; the consultants at Myra in Lycia and Hierapolis in Syria watched fish; while at the shrine of Allat near Emesa, the betyl (stone) that housed the divinity is said to have talked.[34]

As there was such a wide variety of ways to consult the gods at oracular shrines, so too there were numerous ways for individuals to find out what was in store for them even if they were not able to visit one of these shrines. These techniques were not necessarily in conflict with one another; a decision to consult the oracular fish at Myra would not rule out the consultation of an astrologer. But this openness does not mean that there was no room for dispute. In fact there was a great deal of room for it. The diverse practitioners of the different prophetic arts had reason to condemn the efforts of their competitors, and too much information from on high could be a dangerous thing if it were disseminated in the wrong place. Hence, too, the ready acceptance of the notion that the gods might not always speak very clearly, "since they are wiser than we and do not wish us to accept anything without a thorough examination" (Art. *On.* 4.71). The gods were manifestly not under human control, and it was this simple fact that made prophecy a vehicle for social disturbance and social commentary as well as one for social order.

Inductive and Subjective Prognostication

In general terms, the different techniques for making contact with the gods were either inductive or subjective.[35] The primary characteristic of inductive divination was that it did not depend on direct divine inspiration, but was founded upon facts known from previous experience; it was "for those who have learned what happened in the past by observation, and pursue the future by conjecture" (Cic. *De div.* 1.18.34; cf. 1.56.127; Iamb. *De myst.* 3.3.12, 15). It was no less highly regarded than subjective divination, divination that was based upon direct contact with a divinity.

The basic problem that most people had was not whether prognostication was possible, but rather with the meaning of a prophecy (did it mean be careful or that there was no hope?) and with the form. Tacitus seems to have been willing to leave the question open: as a *quindecimvir sacris faciundis* (the board of fifteen for making sacrifices) he was a member of the college responsible for the collection of sibylline oracles at Rome that were used as a guide to human relations with the divine; as a historian he suggests very strongly that human beings are largely responsible for what happens to them. At points, Tacitus was willing to concede that there might be some truth in astrology (*Ann.* 6.21–22); in the oracle of Apollo at Claros that predicted the death of Germanicus, the nephew of Tiberius, the year before his death in A.D. 19 (*Ann.* 2.54.2–3); and in the oracle of Aphrodite at Paphos, which predicted greatness for the future emperor Titus in A.D. 69 (*Hist.* 2.3). On the other hand, he felt that Scribonius Libo Drusus, who was executed for treason in A.D. 16, was a fool for consulting with people who claimed, among other things, that they could raise the spirits of the dead (*Ann.* 2.27–28). Similarly, the Celsus who in the second century wrote a stinging attack on Christianity clearly revered the traditional oracles of the gods, while despising the contemporary prophets who wandered around Palestine—people whom he imagined to have resembled Christ (Orig. *Contra Cels.* 7.9). In both cases the attitude appears to have been that a prophet who was old and well established deserved respect, but one who lacked these qualities should be treated with contempt. Another view is set forth by Artemidorus in a passage about people whose words are and are not believable when they speak in dreams. In his view prophets *(manteis)* are to be believed, but only those who do not lie. His list of liars includes Pythagoreans, physiognomists, necromancers, and diviners from dice, cheese, sieves, forms and figures, palms, and dishes. Those who are to be believed include sacrificers, diviners from birds, some astrologers, observers of strange phenomena, soothsayers who examine livers, and, not surprisingly, dream interpreters.[36]

The emperor Vespasian was clearly so concerned about the prophetic and magical powers of the German priestess Veleda that he sought reassurance from Apollo that she really was not a significant spokesperson for the divine;[37] earlier in his life he had given credence to the prophetic powers of the future Jewish historian (then Jewish rebel) Josephus.[38] The emperor Hadrian rewarded the prophet Pacrates for getting him a particularly powerful dream,[39] and the emperor Marcus Aurelius was willing to credit an oracle in Pontus where a "New Dionysus" in the guise of a snake gave responses, as had been his adoptive father, the emperor Antoninus Pius.[40] Marcus Aurelius may also have been influenced by the word of the distinguished senator Rutilianus, who claimed to have had a good experience with this oracle (Luc. *Alex.* 30). Two members of the imperial house of the Severans, the empress Julia Domna and her son, the emperor Caracalla, evinced considerable interest in the first century holy man Apollonius of Tyana.[41] Ammianus Marcellinus, writing about the disastrous campaign of the emperor Julian against the Persians in 363, dramatically portrays the emperor's refusal to heed the plain warning of the Etruscan hauruspices who accompanied the expedition because fate had decreed that he must fall in battle, all the time depending upon the advice of philosophers who appear to have claimed that they could alter fate for him.[42]

ASTROLOGY

Pride of place among the various forms of inductive divination available in the Roman world must go to astrology. The development of this discipline was complex. In the Roman empire it was often coated with a veneer of eastern wisdom, the province of the Chaldeans. But in reality, like so much else, this eastern wisdom was Greek in origin, and Greek doctrine obscured most real connection with the ancient art of Mesopotamian astrology (see Chapter 5 below for similar problems). In practice it has been described as an amalgam of a seductive philosophic doctrine, and absurd mythology and learned methods employed in a bizarre fashion.[43] The philosophic doctrine was the idea of the unity of the cosmos and the interdependence of all its parts. The cosmos was believed to be formed of a series of concentric spheres, with the earth at the center. These spheres were in constant interaction with one another. Such ideas seem to have been purely Greek and to have been in line with the paradigm of interpretation whereby a system of prediction based upon natural phenomena must be good. Babylonian astrology worked by analogy: if event X had occurred to person Y under the following planetary signs, then person Z, if he was in the same position as person Y, had better be careful. This was the same principle that governed other forms of Babylonian divination, and while it has obvious connection with Greek horoscopy in technique, the absence of the philosophic component is significant. Even more important in this regard is that Babylonian astronomers did not describe heavenly spheres. Therefore, although Babylonian mathematics had some influence upon the most important developments in Greek astronomy in the Hellenistic world, astrology as it was practiced in Roman world was essentially a Greek development.[44]

Once the heavens could be described, the principles of astrology were straightforward. The astrologer observed the location of the seven planets that were known in antiquity (the sun, moon, Mars, Jupiter, Venus, Saturn, and Mercury) in the zodiac at a given time and compared them with the Horoscopos (the ascendant sign) at the time of the consultant's birth.[45]

Among believers in this system, there were two views as to just how much astrology could predict. Both however, started from the premise that the position of the stars at the time of a person's conception determined future relationships with humans and with the stars themselves. A person who was conceived with the stars in a certain position would be liable to profit or peril as the stars moved through the heavens. The main question that remained was whether the person's fate had thereby been determined in detail throughout his or her life, or whether the stars could influence only the outcome of the life; these were, respectively, the fatalistic and catarchic schools of thought.[46]

A number of literary texts have survived offering theoretical discussions of the art and giving practical illustrations of its efficacy. In addition, several horoscopes have survived on papyri that enable us to view the practice in its pure form. Literary horoscopes, that is, horoscopes preserved in the works of specialists who wrote to demonstrate their craft, seek to show the reader how it is that the signs that they read accurately determined the life of a human being.

They are always given anonymously to convey an impression of scientific detachment. One form, beginning with the signs at birth and then those that were relevant at a particular moment in a person's life, is as follows:

> Sun, Mercury, Venus (and) moon in Taurus, Saturn in Sagittarius, Jupiter in Scorpio, Mars in Leo, Horoscopos in Pisces, clima 2. In the 22nd year he had a crisis: Leo 19 and of moon 25, making 44, half of which is 22. In addition 36 of Scorpio and 8 of Taurus are 44, the half of which is 2[2]. These six men on a voyage, with many others, encountered a violent storm and, the rudder being lost, were in danger of death by drowning as the ship took in water. By the draft of the blowing wind and the steersman's management of the sails they escaped; and they encountered other dangers at the same time from a roving pirate [ship].[47]

The principle is explained in another case preserved in the work of the fourth century astrologer Vettius Valens:

> and we will explain nativities by way of an example for quick understanding of those approaching the theory. As sun, moon, Venus, Mercury (and) Horoscopos in Scorpio, Saturn in Sagittarius, Jupiter in Capricorn, Mars in Leo. In the 20th year the paradosis [transmission of rulership from one planet to another](takes place) from Jupiter in Capricorn to Mars in Leo via 8 (signs). Hence Jupiter gave over to Mars from the 3rd to the 10th sign (counted from H), that is, to Midheaven. A petition for honor to the king's (court) was made but did not succeed, for Jupiter giving over to Mars was grievous . . .[48]

The typical horoscope that a person could expect to receive from an astrologer on the street was, not surprisingly, less detailed. In some cases they explicitly stated that the stars indicated danger or good fortune (for example, *P. Oxy.* 804, *P. Oxy.* 2556);[49] otherwise they ordinarily gave only the position of the stars, suggesting that the astrologer would take a reading for the consultant and explain its implications in terms of the other available information.

Literary texts also provide some stunning criticism of the basic tenets of astrology. Some argued that the universe did not work like a human body and thus that the principle upon which the science depended was based upon a false premise. Others claimed that destiny or fate was a false premise, and still others said that if the premises were correct, then the science of astrology was useless, for a prophecy was valuable only if a person had a chance to avoid it. For astrologers to claim that they could predict things that would happen by chance was stupid, since chance happenings were, by definition, beyond prediction; and to claim that they could predict what would happen through human action would render their predictions useless, insofar as an action that was under human control could not be predetermined.[50] Sextus Empiricus pointed out that accurate observations were impossible anyway (*Adv. math.* 5.42–106).

DREAMS

A person who did not trust the stars or the local astrologer could always have recourse to, among others, interpreters of dreams. Perhaps the best known example of their craft is Artemidorus' *Interpretation of Dreams,* a specialist handbook in which the author sets forth a particular theory of dream interpretation that is somewhat different from that of his contemporaries.[51] The "mainstream" philosophic view of dream prediction, enunciated most clearly in Stoic thought was that in sleep the mind might travel free of the body to make contact with the divine. Artemidorus divides dreams into predictive and nonpredictive varieties (*On.* 1.1), and argues that predictive dreams result from a movement of the mind, which is able to predict everything that will happen in the future. The mind does this "through images of its own, called elements, which are natural products" (*On.* 1.2 trans. White).[52] Dreams themselves are either direct or allegorical and are as accurate as a direct vision of a god or an oracular response. A typical treatment of a dream of the allegorical variety follows.[53]

In my experience, the most dangerous dream of all is to have been fellated by one's mother; the significance is the death of children, the destruction of wealth, and terrible disease for the one who dreams it. I know of a man who after having had this dream lost his private parts; it was appropriate that he should be deprived in the part of the body where he had committed the wrong.   (*On.* 1.79 trans. White)

Artemidorus admits that there are those who doubt that dreams can be used at all, but he claims that he has reached his conclusions through extensive consultations with countless practitioners of the art who have provided him with the examples that he uses in his book. Among them, he says, are "much-despised diviners in the marketplace" (*On.* pref.). It is fair to say that these dream interpreters had very different views about how dreams might be obtained or viewed, and that one of his contemporaries, Aelius Aristides, certainly thought that the many dreams that he experienced throughout his career were a sign of the direct interest that the god Asclepius took in his career.[54] Others might take an even more active role in obtaining a predictive dream. Dream oracles were extremely common, and there are numerous prescriptions in the extant corpus of magical papyri that give advice on just how someone who wanted a predictive dream, and either could or did not want to visit such an oracle, might make certain that one came.[55]

There could be as many ways to procure and interpret dreams as there could be interpreters. The same is true of another art, physiognomy.[56] Here too there was a specialist literature to help people discover the evil natures concealed behind various physical features; and there were guides to all sorts of other natural phenomena. An example of one of these is preserved on a papyrus of the late second or early third century from Oxyrhynchus in Egypt. It runs as follows (*P. Oxy.* 885):

[If the statue of a poor man should be struck by lightning and it should not fall] it will be the beginning of happiness for him; but if the statue when struck by the thunderbolt falls down, it indicates the destruction of his whole family. The poor man should therefore purify the statue and sacrifice to Zeus Wielder of Thunder and Hercules and Fortune the Preserver in accordance with his means and appropriate to the former portent; but the portent of the fallen statue he should expiate and avert by sacrifice to the same gods . . .

A significant feature of this text, as of many others, is the implicit assumption that the observer of the phenomenon can do something to stave off the evil that is portended. It is suggested that there is no immutable fortune, but rather that the gods have indicated that some great misfortune will befall a person if the latter does not take some action to prevent it. In a physiognomic text, the reader is taught to recognize the outward signs of deep-seated personal failings, so as to be warned off dealing with such a character. As such, the ostensible promise of a text like the papyrus just quoted, or the objective divinatory practices that developed in early Rome, *haruspicium* (divination on the basis of events in nature and the innards of sacrificed animals) and *auspicium* (divination by bird watching), mesh badly with the notions that the human experience was ruled by the caprice of fortune or was determined by immutable fate.

Oracles and Prophets: The Agents of Subjective Divination

Subjective divination depended upon divine impulse, actual contact between a god or his messenger and mortals. As Cicero put it, "those who lack art sense the future not through reason and conjecture on the basis of known and observed signs, but through a certain excitement or loose and free movement of the soul" (*De div.* 1.18.34). Subjective divination provided the answer to questions such as "Which of two possible options should I take?" "What is going to happen to me next?" "How am I going to get out of the mess that I am in?" or even "What is the true nature of god?" As a general rule, the agent from whom such information was demanded should be, to some degree, apart from the society of the inquirer. On the grand scale, it is significant that the most ancient oracular shrines of the Greek world were physically removed from cities; on a lesser scale, holy people were invariably felt to be marked out from ordinary mortals by the peculiar qualities of their lifestyle.

Subjective divination could be carried out in a number of different ways. A person could go to an oracular shrine where there might be an inspired prophet, or an object or animals whose prognostic movements could be interpreted by a local specialist. If a person did not go to a shrine he or she could consult a wandering specialist who could predict things on account of his or her own special qualities or who had access to sacred books; or the consultant could role dice or cast lots.[57] The curious could even seek a revelation from the divinity in person by going to a holy place and waiting for an apparition, by performing certain special actions, or even by getting very sick. In the face of this variety, it is reasonable to inquire if there was a specific hierarchy of methods. In asking this question it must also be recognized that one person's hierarchy might not be remotely interesting for another.[58] Although any and all methods were called into question at times, there does not, on the whole, seem to have been any generally accepted ordering in terms of efficacy: individuals ranked the various methods as they saw fit, and the criteria might vary from social standing to psychological preferences.

LOT ORACLES

At one point Cicero singles out oracles that worked though lots as being particularly worthy of contempt. They might retain the affection of common people, but "what man of reputation ever consults them?" (De div. 2.41, 86–87). In the same dialogue he has his brother Quintus assert that the lot oracles (such as that at Praeneste) that were sanctioned by age might work (De div. 1.34); and an inscription from Forum Novum near Parma preserves a text that appears to have been a lot oracle, and was plainly inscribed in a public place by people who might not have taken the view of either Marcus or Quintus seriously. Other texts provide ample evidence for the lot oracles at Tibur, Antium, and Ostia.[59]

Members of the lower classes can have had no direct access to a god such as Apollo at one of his great oracular centers. This fact was recognized at Delphi itself, where an alternative form of consultation, by lot oracle, was provided for those who could not approach the inspired prophetess.[60] Apollo spoke to cities, emperors, members of the senate, and the sort of people who might be expected to be found in their company. He did not have any interest in speaking to peasants at these shrines, or even to the more ordinary sort of townsman. His more general exhortations to decent behavior on the part of the rich are in keeping with the political

1. "Shall I get my pay? Am I to be sold as a slave? Shall I go on an embassy? Am I to become a town councillor? Shall I be separated from my wife? Am I under a spell?" These are some of the questions preserved in this portion of the *sortes Astrampsychi* (*P. Oxy.* 1477; photo courtesy of the British Library).

literature which advised members of the local aristocracies of the empire to maintain social peace so that they would not find themselves in trouble with the imperial authorities.

The demand for divine contact was too great to be channeled solely through inspired oracles. There were numerous handy devices for making information readily available at all levels of society, and several proved to be readily transferable to a Christian context.

The *sortes Astrampsychi* was one such form of prediction. It was based upon a secret book allegedly composed by a sage named Astrampsychus, who was thought to have flourished in the age of the Ptolemies,[61] and preserved on a number of papyri and in several medieval manuscripts.[62] The wide range of the book's attestation is testimony to its popularity as a form of prognostication and the ready acceptance of this particular book after its composition in the third century.[63] The book has two parts: the first contains ninety-two questions numbered 12–103; the second consists of a series of answers (arranged in groups of ten) to the questions. The use of the book is explained in a "letter of Astrampsychus" at the beginning of several of the manuscripts:

> taking the number of the question chosen by the customer and keeping it in mind, ask him to choose by lot any number he wishes from 1 to 10 and tell him that God will put the number in his mouth. Taking this number, add it to the number of the question. Proceeding then, you will find a table with numbers in black starting from 13 and continuing in order, and against them other numbers in red in no consecutive order but indiscriminately arranged to match the answer to the question.[64]

The customer therefore picked one of the questions that had been numbered from 13 to 102 and added a number between 1 and 10 to the number of the question. This put the customer in the right group of ten answers, and the number that he had selected was the number of his answer within that group (the organization of these answers was not as indiscriminate as the letter implies).[65] Thus, if the consultant was worried about continuing in office he would select question 16, "Am I to advance in office?" and then, for instance, pick the number 5. The oracle-monger would go to group 21 and see what red number it was matched up with. He would then go to the group of ten answers whose number he had obtained from the red number and look down the column to that number, where he would find the answer, "You will advance after a while as you wish."

The theory behind this method of consultation was that the god's action put the proper number in the mind of the consultant. The actual oracle-monger had only a very small role: he acted as the god's agent interpreting the wisdom of the sage Astrampsychus. In so doing, this book filled a need for relatively easily obtainable information about the future, and it is also clear from the range of questions that the anticipated consultants came from all levels of society. Questions such as the one mentioned in the preceding paragraph could have been of interest only to members of the upper class, as would also be the case with, for instance, question 41, "Am I to be a sophist?" or numbers 87 and 88, "Shall I be an ambassador?" and "Am I to become a member of the town council?" On the other hand, question 46, "Am I to be reconciled with my master?" and question 74, "Am I to be sold?" clearly concern slaves. Questions such as number 47, "Shall I have a baby?" clearly concern no one social class or gender in particular.

The dice oracle was a form of consultation that was similar to the *sortes Astrampsychi*.[66] A number of examples of these oracles have survived on stones from southern Asia Minor, and, interestingly, eight of the texts that we have were copied from the same original: all of them may have been derived from verse responses that were given at various oracular shrines. This was a process that Theon, one of the interlocutors in Plutarch's dialogue on the oracle at Delphi, thought brought oracles into disrepute (*Mor.* 407C)— although the existence of these texts makes it obvious that a great number of people would have regarded Theon's view as eccentric. This particular version had fifty-six entries containing the following elements: a statement of the sequence of numbers in numerals on the die, the sum total of the dice, also given by a numeral; the name of the god in the genitive whose oracle will follow; and four lines in hexameter verse. The first gives the number rolled on the dice and the next three give the oracle. The fifty-fourth oracle in this sequence reads as follows:

66663   27   of Aphrodite
of Aphrodite
four sixes, one three, thus she spoke to you
the child of heaven, Aphrodite, powerful mistress of love
sends a good oracle, give yourself to the road
be free of sickness and of grievous thoughts. (*TAM* 31.1 no. 33)

It is of great significance that this particular group of oracles was set up in a public place in several southeastern Anatolian cities, as were all the other examples of this form of prognostication. This fact shows that these were texts for everyone who could throw the dice. But it was not a "lower-class" oracle, even though members of the lower classes could certainly use it. These texts were civic monuments erected with the full knowledge and quite probably the active encouragement of the town councils in the several cities that had them. Indeed, it is said that before he became emperor, Tiberius consulted the lot oracle of Geryon at Patavium, where he was told to seek an answer by throwing golden dice into the spring of Aponus. It was also said that the very dice that he threw were on display there in the early second century (Suet. *Tib.* 14.3). Although there were other forms of prophecy available to people like Tiberius, they clearly thought that it was worth the effort to have this form available to them as well (see pages 158–160 below for some of Tiberius' other interests).

Perhaps the most vivid account of such an oracle is provided by Pausanias. He describes a cave in the valley of the river Buriacus in Achaea where there was a small statue of Hercules, who was "surnamed Buriacus, and here can divine by means of a tablet and dice." A person "who inquires of the god offers a prayer in front of the image, and after the prayer he takes four dice, a plentiful supply of which are placed near Hercules, and throws them on the tablet; for every figure made by the dice there is an explanation written on the tablet" (7.25.10). Pausanias' mention of a large supply of dice at the shrine shows that the people of Bura, who administered the oracle, expected that there would be a regular stream of visitors, as well as that the town council very probably had some role in overseeing the operation of what was clearly something of a local attraction. It is reasonable to infer that the simple ceremony recorded here was repeated with some variations countless times and in countless places throughout the Mediterranean world.

The forms of consultation that have been treated so far were somewhat more elaborate than that which appears to have been employed in connection with a number of papyri from Egypt that range in date from the Middle Kingdom to the sixth century A.D. The texts of these documents consist of an application to a god, whose name appears in the dative; sometimes the applicant's name;

2. "Mistress Isis, if my illness has come from you, and you will give me my healing, make this chit come out for me." This is a typical lot oracle from Egypt. Such requests would be submitted in pairs; the other papyrus would have put a negative proposition such as "if my illness does not come from you, and you will not be the source of my healing . . ." (*P. Mich.* 1258; photo courtesy of the University of Michigan; the text is published by A. Henrichs, *ZPE* 11 [1973], 117).

and a statement of the problem in a conditional clause.[67] A standard example follows:

> To my lord Scopnopaeus, the great god, and the associated gods. Etrenias asks you: if it is not granted that my wife Ammonous would return to me spontaneously but that I should go out so that she comes back, give me this.[68]

This petition would then be placed in an urn with another slip, which might be blank or might have the same question phrased differently—in this case, "if it is granted that my wife . . ." The consultant would then draw one of the papyri out of the urn and thereby obtain his answer. This form of consultation, so simple, so flexible (the consultant was not limited by a series of predetermined questions or answers), and evidently so satisfactory that it continued to be used well after the demise of the worship of the traditional gods as was also the case with the *sortes Astrampsychi,* was adapted into a Christian context. In fact, we have two papyri, cut from the same roll, which give us the positive and negative questions that were asked on one occasion in a very Christian context. The texts are as follows:[69]

> O my Lord God Almighty and Saint Philoxenus my patron, I beseech you by the great name of the Lord God, if it is your will and you are helping me to take the banking business, I beseech you to bid me hear this and speak. (*P. Harris* 54)

> O my Lord God Almighty and Saint Philoxenus my patron, I beseech you by the great name of the Lord God, if it is not your will that I speak either about the bank or about the weighing office, to bid me hear this, in order that I may not speak. (*P. Oxy.* 1926)

The extensive attestation of all three forms of divination shows that they acquired a good track record and were thought to be reliable. The consultant could feel reasonably certain that he would get good advice whenever he used them, and they were simple to operate, which may explain why various forms of lot oracles were among the most important kinds of prognostication available in the ancient world.

HOLY PEOPLE

Reliability and simplicity were very important, but it must be admitted that the various oracles that have just been examined were rather dull, and there was clearly a demand for more lively sources of information. Holy men (and women) were everywhere, predicting all manner of things and obtaining various levels of acceptance at all levels of society. It was well known that some mortals in the past had become gods,[70] and that the gods themselves had once walked the earth. At the Letoon in Lycia and on the island of Delos in the Aegean, people could point to the very spot where

Leto had given birth to Apollo and Artemis.[71] Nor were they alone; the people of Tegyrae in Boeotia also claimed that Apollo had been born among them (Plut. *Mor.* 412A); throughout Thrace and the Troad people could point to the bones of monsters that the gods had killed;[72] and the people of Cyprus could point to the very beach where the goddess Aphrodite first set foot on land after her birth among the waves. There was always a chance that a new god would be encountered.[73]

Even if a "new god" were not available, there were still mortals who were endowed with special powers and wisdom. Such people had a real and very important function in society, and, aside from various acts such as feeding multitudes, healing the sick, and raising people from the dead, they could be called upon to predict the future. The only problem that a person might have was in telling a fake from the real thing. But for this there were simple tests.

The best evidence for the sort of routine that a prophet could be called upon to perform is provided by a spell preserved on a papyrus that was to be spoken to Helios:

> I will not let god or goddess give oracles until I, NN, know through and through what is in the minds of all men, Egyptians, Syrians, Greeks, Ethiopians, of every race and people, those who question me and come into my sight, whether they speak or are silent, so that I can tell them whatever has happened and is happening and is going to happen to them, and I know their skills and their lives and their practices and their works and their names and those of their dead and of everybody, and I can read a sealed letter and tell them everything [in it] truly. (*PGM* V.256–269)

The ability that this spell was to confer is precisely what Alexander of Abonuteichos had to supply when he was establishing his cult of Glycon in the first half of the second century, and it is clearly the knowledge that would be sufficient to answer any doubts about his competence. As early as Homer, it is clear that the ability to range freely from the past to the future was a sign of divinity or of divine inspiration. The seer Calchas is described in the *Iliad* as he "who knew the things that were, the things that were to be, and those that had been before" (1.70). Homer's own leaps backward and forward in time may have provided the grounds, quite early, for claims that he was theologizing, for this was the sort of knowledge that could be expected only of a god.[74] In order to claim divine inspiration, the prophet thus had to act like a god.

Purveyors of divine knowledge could take a number of forms. Dio Chrysostom records that he met an inspired shepherdess in the hills of Arcadia during the late first century, and Luke records that Paul silenced a slave woman who possessed prophetic ability and was evidently rented out to provide prophetic services (Acts 16:16). A similar arrangement appears to be attested on a papyrus that was written at Side in southern Turkey. This mentions a Phrygian slave girl named Sambathis, whose name was changed to Athenais— both names of Sibyls—and several inspired women appear in significant political contexts at various points in the history of the principate (page 169 below).[75] Others were considerably more freewheeling, and in these cases the best impression of their activity may be that, despite its hostile tone, which is conveyed by Celsus in his *On True Doctrine:*

> There are many obscure men in that region [Palestine] who, with great facility and on the least occasion, either in the temples or outside them, and others begging for their bread, wandering the cities and the military camps, shake as if giving oracles. In the mouth of each one of them is the commonplace formula, "I am God, the Son of God, or the holy spirit. I have come. The world is already destroyed, and you mortals will perish for your injustice. But I wish to save you. You will see me coming again with a heavenly power. Happy is the man who pays me cult today! I will throw an eternal fire upon the rest, upon the cities and lands. Mortals who do not know the punishments to come will repent too late and groan. I will protect those who trust in me forever." (Orig. *Contra Cels.* 7.9 trans. Chadwick)

The most extensive descriptions of such activities are provided by the Gospels and the Acts of the Apostles, where it is clear that such traveling holy men could make quite an impact upon their countrymen and be a major force for change.

It could be objected that all the instances cited above are connected with Palestine, where there was a long-standing and significant tradition of conflict between established religious authorities that were primarily urban and inspired prophets who were associated primarily with rural areas. In general, though, the situation in Palestine was typical of the eastern Mediterranean world. The careers of Apollonius of Tyana, Proteus Peregrinus, and, indeed, the earlier career of Alexander of Abonuteichos all appear to fit the pattern of the holy man/prophet who deliberately placed himself beyond the fringes of city life and then sought to impose change upon the city from the outside. In the case of Apollonius, one of his revelations led to the foundation of a new cult at Ephesus, and the foundation was the principal act of Alexander of Abonuteichus after a youth spent wandering the empire. Plutarch tells of a man whom he met near the Red Sea who held meetings with humans on only one day a year, and explained that he spent all the other days of the year in the company of nymphs and demons. He was extraordinarily handsome (good looks were also characteristic of Alexander and Apollonius), and he was also a prophet:

> He was practiced in the use of many tongues; but with me for the most part he spoke a Doric that was almost music. While he was speaking, a fragrance overspread the place, as his mouth breathed forth a most pleasant perfume. Besides his learning and knowledge of history, always at his command, he was inspired to prophesy, and one day every year he went down to the sea and told the future. Dynasts and the agents of kings come each year and then depart. (*De defect. orac.* 421B Loeb trans.)

His information would include "new views" as to the true nature of cults—in this case the cult of Apollo at Delphi. Although this story may be literary fantasy, it is still an important illustration of the principal points that were recognized as making a person sacred: separation from society and special physical conditioning. In doing what they did these characters could recall some of the great wandering prophets of the past: characters such as Musaeus, Orpheus, and various Sibyls.

Although the great majority of wandering wonder-workers came from, and operated in, the lower echelons of society, this was not a hard and fast rule. Paul, who filled this niche in a Christian context, came from a respectable family in Tarsus and sometimes moved among well-educated people. He was able to impress Sergius Paullus on Cyprus with a demonstration of his superior magical powers, and although he was unable to convert the Areopagus at Athens to his beliefs, he was allowed to speak there and to defend his views before three high imperial officials, Gallio, Felix, and Festus (all of which is somewhat more than the Savior himself could have done—in attacks upon the faith pagans often harped upon his low social status).[76] A *martyria* (testimonial) shows that Apollonius was able to impress contemporaries with his philosophic discourse, as well as with the magical powers that are attested by the Ephesian cult of Hercules Alexikakos. Indeed, this *martyria* makes specific reference to Apollonius' philosophic expertise, stating: "Apollonius, your fellow citizen, the Pythagorean philosopher, has made an honorable stay in Greece and benefited our young men who truly pursue philosophy, and we wanted our goodwill to be made clear to you by letter."[77]

In the centuries after his death, as is now becoming increasingly clear, Apollonius was readily admitted to the company of sages, and revered for being able to combine philosophy with his miracles—so much so that in dealing with a figure like this, the distinction between wonder-worker and philosopher is quite irrelevant: the question really is how to balance the two aspects of the individual. This point is made especially plain by the inclusion of Apollonius among the "sages" who were honored in the fifth-century "philosopher's school" that has come to light at Aphrodisias, as well as by interest, centuries after his death, in a book about sacrifices that Apollonius is supposed to have written (Eus. *Praep. Ev.* 4.12).[78] The epigram in his honor from the area around Mopsuestia in Cilicia lays particular stress on the miracles that Apollonius was continuing to work after his death.[79] Ammianus Marcellinus, who was clearly uncomfortable with the theurgic pretensions of a contemporary like Maximus of Ephesus, was able to speak respectfully of Apollonius as a man whose "genius" made him great (see especially 23.6.19).[80] The miracles of Apollonius were presumably a subject of much interest to Sossianus Hierocles when he composed his comparison of Apollonius and Christ (much to the detriment of the latter) in the early fourth century, and they must have been of some interest to the distinguished Nicomachus Flavianus when he translated Philostratus' life of Apollonius into Latin at the end of that century.[81]

The late antique Apollonius (miracles and all) was marginally acceptable to Jerome (*Ep.* 53) and Augustine (*Ep.* 102.32, 136.1), while on the pagan side both Eunapius and Libanius regarded him as a truly great figure.[82] The miracles were certainly interesting to the author of the *Historia Augusta,* who records that it was a vision of Apollonius that convinced the emperor Aurelian to spare Tyana when he captured it in 272 (*HA V. Aurel.* 24.3). His story that the image of Apollonius was cultivated by Alexander Severus suggests that he also knew of him as a character who was revered for his wisdom (*HA V. Alex.* 29.2). The miracles were still of interest in the mid-sixth century, when the Antiochene chronographer John Malalas included a long account of "the most learned Apollonius of Tyana, who traveled around making talismans everywhere in the cities and their territories" (*Chron.* pp. 263–264), and especially of the talismans that he made for Antioch. He was also held responsible for the creation of talismans for Constantinople that kept away floods, storms, invasions of rats, savage beasts, and storks.[83] In the west, when Sidonius Apollinaris in 476–77 sent a copy of Nicomachus' translation of Philostratus' life to Leo, an adviser to the Visigothic king Euric at Toulouse, he recommended the work as morally improving (*Ep.* 8.3.3–4). In the east, Isidore of Pelusium, who disapproved of Philostratus' life, praised Apollonius for the talismans, and one late Christian text records that Apollonius was a prophet of Christ (Ps. Justin *Quaest et resp.* 24)![84]

The later reputation of Apollonius is of such interest in part because it clearly had to survive in the face of a certain amount of negative publicity that was produced very soon after he died (and, no doubt, a certain amount in his lifetime as well). Thus Lucian referred to him disparagingly as a proto-Alexander (*Alex.* 5),[85] while Origen and Philostratus preserve references to a lengthy work by a man named Moeragenes, who wrote a book in the early second century that presented his magical powers as good: just the sort of thing that was embarrassing in many educated circles. Philostratus regarded Moeragenes' book as "the last thing to listen to" and "very ill-informed on important matters" (*V. Apoll.* 1.4), while the third century Christian philosopher Origen noted that if Celsus thought that philosophers were immune to the blandishments of magicians, he should look to the pagan world, and there he "had only to read the memoirs of Moeragenes on the magus and philosopher Apollonius of Tyana; the author, who was not a Christian but was a philosopher, says that certain worthy philosophers, influenced by the magic of Apollonius, had come to regard him as a sorcerer [*goēs*]" (*Contra Cels.* 6.41). Philostratus presumably disliked the work of Moeragenes because it made such statements possible by laying stress on Apollonius' magical powers, whereas Philostratus wanted to present him as a completely respectable philosopher whose achievements stemmed from his innate perceptiveness and knowledge, not from wizardry.[86]

A debate similar to that concerning Apollonius surrounded the figure of Peregrinus, whose followers wished to believe that he had become a god, and whose home city of Parium in Asia Minor claimed that a statue of him gave oracles.[87] Again, despite invective such as Lucian's *The Passing of Peregrinus,*[88] his reputation endured and, indeed, flourished. Menander Rhetor, who was probably writing in the mid-third century, recommended his work, *The Praise of Poverty;* and Ammianus referred to him with admiration.[89] In the case of Peregrinus we even have the positive witness of a contemporary member of the Roman aristocracy: Aulus Gellius attended his lectures in Athens and wrote warmly of him after Peregrinus threw himself onto the pyre at Olympia (*NA* 12.11.1).[90] Another survivor was Alexander of Abonuteichos, whose cult of Glycon flourished long after his death: it was clearly of interest to people in the Balkans in the third century, and to the people of Tomis in the fourth.[91] These instances are important because they provide a living parallel to the reverence that was shown toward the memory of other, by then long-dead, independent religious figures (such as the Sibyl) in the second and third centuries. This did not stop with the coming of Christianity.

In the life of Saint Anthony that was composed in the first half of the fourth century,[92] the holy father is found sitting on his mountain outside Alexandria answering precisely the same sort of questions that were once put to oracles, and performing the various other functions (frightening demons, healing the sick, and the like) that were attributed to Apollonius. From time to time he went into Alexandria to support the cause of the embattled orthodox bishop Athanasius in his struggle against the Arian heretics. In another case, the emperor Theodosius called upon an Egyptian monk named John to predict the course of the imperial campaign against the usurper Eugenius in 392 (Aug. *Civ. dei* 5.26). Another Egyptian monk, John of Lycopolis, needed a hall that could hold a hundred visitors to his hermitage (Pall. *HL* 35.4); and it has been observed that "[t]he lonely cells of the recluses of Egypt have been revealed, by the archaeologist, to have been well-furnished consulting rooms,"[93] an observation that could equally easily have been made about the pagan shrines that these characters were replacing. The emergence of multifunctional holy people in a Christian context is of particular interest because, in the second century, the faith had been deeply shaken in some places by the prophetic urge of Montanism, which threatened the emerging power structure of bishops and presbyters, as well as the authority of the developing canon of gospels.[94] Montanism did this by proclaiming that the spirit of God was roaming the earth, providing fresh inspiration, and providing a guarantee of salvation to anyone who lived a particularly harsh existence. This inspiration was even provided to women, who came to be quite prominent in the movement. Montanism failed, and in the course of the debate the Christians appear to have sought to find a distinction between appropriate visions, visions that aided individuals in their understanding of scripture, and bad visions, deceitful revelation that was passed off as new information that was supposed to be relevant to the church as a whole. This solution seems to have worked in the third century, and the principle that true knowledge of the future for all Christians was to be found only in scripture triumphed. In the fourth century, when the church was drawn into the center of power, old tendencies began to reappear; the wisdom of holy people had once again to be admitted as relevant to the whole community.

The most important change that Christianity ultimately introduced was one of scale rather than thought. While the pagan holy man might be considered a god, or a man who was realizing his divine potential so as to become a god, the Christian holy man could hope only to imitate Christ. By adopting the old pagan notion that the human body could become more susceptible to the divine through an ascetic lifestyle, the aspiring holy person could bring himself closer to God and become the vehicle through which God's power worked. In the non-Christian world—and here it needs to be stressed that there is a continuum of belief that runs from the humble peasants of Pontus to some of the most refined schools of philosophy—a mortal could actually become a god. Porphyry not only makes it clear that he believed Plotinus was equal to a god, but provides a sufficient amount of evidence to make it clear that Plotinus believed this as well.[95] These "new gods" were constantly active in solving the problems of mortals and in introducing great changes into their lives.

INSPIRED ORACLES

Continuity between the pagan and Christian empires was lacking in the consultation of oracles at centers where the prophet was thought to be directly inspired by a god at the moment of the consultation, or where the god appeared in a dream or influenced the behavior of some divinatory substance. In the case of "inspired" oracles, the prophet's inspiration could occur either because the prophet's mind was especially prepared to receive images placed in it by the god, or because the god took actual physical possession of the prophet and either spoke through the prophet's mouth or compelled the prophet to speak.[96]

The principal feature of such shrines was that the god was thought to be in a given place at a given time so as to speak through the prophet to the consultant, or to provide the answer to written questions. This was also the principle behind the dream oracle, for the consultant (or priest) slept in a spot where experience had shown that the god would appear to him and answer questions. Dream oracles are, in principle, very much the same as the healing shrines of Asclepius at Pergamon or Epidaurus, insofar as there was believed to be a special connection between the god and those places and that this explained why his power was manifest there. The inspired oracles appear to have been a feature of religious life that was peculiar to the eastern Mediterranean: their like appears on tablets from Mari and Assyria, and from records of the earliest periods of recorded Greek history. But they did not exist in Egypt, and they do not seem to have existed in the Italic or Celtic worlds.[97] Furthermore, although there were a number of places where people could go, the temples of Apollo at Claros, Didyma, and Delphi essentially had no rivals in the Roman empire: they were places whose inspiration was sanctioned by time and the experience of generations.

It was the essential feature of the "inspired" oracle that the god was actually present, or, if not the god himself, then at least a suitable deputy in the form of a "good demon." There was very often little difference between the sort of question that was put to the god under these circumstances and the sort that were put to the gods or holy men under other circumstances. Both Plutarch (*Mor.* 408C) and Porphyry remark that the gods were bored by the banality of inquiries about marriage or the prospects of a marriage, and could not be held responsible if they did not answer, or answered incorrectly, alhough Porphyry did add that an incorrect answer could be the result of an "evil demon" or the "adversary" taking possession of the prophet in the absence of the god (Eus. *Praep. Ev.* 5.10). But the inspired oracles could also deal with questions that were far more complicated, and they were flexible enough to be able to change their tones so as to be in touch with changing literary tastes; it has been noted, for example, that the Platonic tone of many "theological oracles" that were delivered in the second and third centuries was well in keeping with the dominant intellectual trend of the time.[98]

If a city was in need of relief from a plague or contemplating some major new step such as making a treaty or sending out a colony, it tended to ask the god directly. The city fathers entrusted with decisions took this step not because they felt that other methods did not work (many of them undoubtedly used them), but rather because they knew that the inspired oracles had a very good record, and that by consulting them they were placing the decision that they were contemplating in the context of others that the gods had similarly sanctioned for their ancestors. Furthermore, the high status of these oracles meant that civic leaders who had obtained their support could speak with more authority when addressing political problems within a community, such as whether to admit new citizens, as happened at Miletus in 223/22 B.C., or even how to build a theater (an event also recorded at Miletus).[99] The god was also the best source to consult directly when there was a problem such as was confronted by the priestess Alexandra in the second century A.D. when she wanted to know why many people were having visions of the gods (she was told that the gods could do anything they wanted),[100] or when the elderly widow Setorneila wanted to be a priestess of Athena, or when any new cult was to be established.[101] The gods could even be called upon to give their blessings to Apollonius (Phil. *V. Apoll.* 4.1).

Another reason to consult an inspired oracle was to confirm that the interpretation of a message a person believed a god had delivered through another medium was in fact correct. A very good example of this sort of reasoning is provided by Aelius Aristides in his spiritual autobiography, *The Sacred Tales* (3.10–12). He says that he fell ill in the city of Lebedus and decided to take a drug that a doctor had given him. As the symptoms grew worse (including a bout of lockjaw), "it occurred to me to consult the god at Colophon concerning both my present troubles and general weakness. Colophon is not far from Lebedus, and the sacred night happened to be near. Since it seemed best to do this, I sent Zosimus." Zosimus, Aelius' adoptive father, obtained an oracle to the effect that Asclepius would cure him. The most important feature of this story is that Aelius, who was constantly having dreams of Asclepius that offered him guidance about his career and general health, still thought that it would be a good idea to consult an oracle. He does not imply that the oracle was better than the dream, only that it was a useful supplement.

As Aelius' story shows, the consultation of an inspired oracle was not a completely straightforward operation, and the various rites connected with consultations should be seen as strategies devised by the operators of the shrine in their dialogues with consultants to enhance the credibility of responses. This does not mean that the operators of the shrines were engaging in self-conscious fraud—no more so than does the ordinary worshiper of a divinity who defines the role that the divinity is to play in his or her life. The rites and practices connected with consultations should instead be seen as culturally conditioned representations of the relationship between the human and divine planes. The gods, being far more powerful than mortals, could not be expected to be at human beck and call: they were distant, powerful beings who demonstrated their concern for mortals by agreeing to speak to them at all. The limitation on the number of days in a year that the god would speak through the prophet represented the notion that this kind of special contact with divinities could happen only under special circumstances. The ceremonies accompanying the consultation served to emphasize the point that something remarkable was about to happen. The quite considerable cost of such consultations prevented the poor from taking part, and the evident provision for the most important consultants to get closer than others to the prophet while the god was present merely reinforced the hierarchical divisions of society.

CONSULTATIONS

The rites that preceded the actual consultation of an oracle varied considerably in detail from shrine to shrine. At Delphi, for example, the process would begin a little before dawn on the seventh day of the month (the priestess would speak only one day a month, nine months a year), when the Pythia would go down to the Castalian spring and take a ritual bath.[102] She would then purify herself at the temple hearth, upon which laurel leaves and barley meal had been placed to burn. While the Pythia was preparing herself, the priests would offer a goat to Apollo, sprinkling it with cold water until it began to shake, for only if the goat shook, as the Pythia would shake when the god was present, could the ceremonies begin. If the goat gave the proper signs, it was then sacrificed and the Pythia would enter the sanctuary to take her seat upon the tripod. While she did this, the priests would perform a ceremony of purification for themselves at the Castalian spring. The consultants of the oracle would also purify themselves before approaching the oracle in an order that had been determined by lot for all those who did not represent states that had been given the privilege of "first consultation," *promanteia,* by the Delphians in return for favors that they had done them in the past. As each consultant approached the temple, he would make an offering of the sacrificial cake that he had bought from the Delphians at some expense, and when he entered the temple he would offer an additional sacrifice of either sheep or goats. In the classical period he would have to be accompanied through all of this by the local Delphian representative of his city, the *proxenos,* and a portion of the sacrifice would go to the Delphians.

After he had completed his sacrifice (and made his contribution to the Delphians) the consultant, who had to be male—no woman other than the Pythia was allowed into the temple—entered the inner sanctuary, where he was warned to think pure thoughts and speak well-omened words. In effect, he was being told to be silent during the actual consultation; for he would already have given his question to the prophet, who would read it out to the Pythia. The Pythia's answer would probably have been fairly incoherent, as it was uttered in a trance, and it is likely that whatever she said, if she said anything beyond a simple yes or no, would then be interpreted for the consultant by the prophet. The consultant, if acting on his own, might then ask to have it written down; if the consultant was acting for a third party, the answer would definitely be written down and sealed, and he would be warned of dire consequences if he opened it before he had returned to his principals.

Although the details of consultations of Apollo at Didyma and Claros are more obscure, basic outlines can be reconstructed, and when all the uncertainties are taken into account, they reveal a number of formal parallels with Delphi. At Didyma there were only a limited number of days upon which oracles could be given. The absolute minimum interval would be four days, and it is probable that the interval was far greater—Menander Rhetor observes that there were noticeable Apollonine absences from the shrine (Men. Rhet. 336)—possibly some months at some times of year.[103] The

3. The *adyton* of the temple of Apollo at Didyma. The structure in the middle of the *adyton* is the *naiskos* over the sacred spring where the oracles would be given (photo by author).

session itself began with a three-day fast by the prophetess, during which time it appears that she resided in the *naiskos* (a small building) of the god that was built over the sacred spring in the temple, or in another structure within the temple walls (Iamb. *De myst.* 3.11).[104] On the day appointed for the actual giving of oracles the prophetess would take a ritual bath and go to the building above the spring while those who wished to put questions to her sacrificed outside and choruses sang hymns to the gods. These consultants might all then have been allowed down into the central shrine, or, more probably, some of them would be let in to witness the consultation and others would give their questions to the priests and wait outside the central shrine for an answer.[105] In the *naiskos* itself, the prophetess would be sitting on an axle that was suspended over the sacred spring, and when a question was put to her she would dip her foot (or her dress) into the spring, but not drink from it, before giving her answer.[106] These answers would probably have been in prose and would then have been turned into verse by the priests.

At Claros, we know that there were "sacred nights" upon which the consultations would take place, and on those occasions there would be a procession of consultants to the temple of Apollo with many sacrifices and much singing of hymns. They would then hand over questions to the priests who would descend into the *adyton* (the sacred chamber beneath the temple), through the blue marble-faced corridors, to a place outside the room in which the divine spring flowed. In this room the *thespiodos,* who was a man, would drink from the spring and utter his responses to the questions that each consultant had in his mind. These would then be written down in verse by the *prophetes* and delivered to the consultants.[107] Special visitors, it may be assumed, would be allowed down into the area beyond the *adyton,* but since the space was very small it is a safe assumption that only the most important people could get this close to the place where the god actually spoke.

The clearest account of an oracular consultation that we have does not involve an inspired oracle at all, but rather the "dream oracle" of Trophonius at Lebadia in Boeotia, where the consultant underwent such an extraordinary series of experiences that he evidently felt that he had encountered the hero Trophonius.[108] Pausanias, who consulted the oracle himself, described a period of purification by the consultant in which elements of both the preparations of oracular prophets and the consultants of their shrines appear to have been joined together. He said that when a person had made up his mind to descend into the shrine he lodged for several days in a building that was sacred to the Good Demon and Good Fortune and consumed a great deal of meat from the sacrifices that he offered to Trophonius, the children of Trophonius, and a large number of divinities while abstaining from hot baths (he had also been told that a bodyguard of Demetrius, presumably Demetrius the Besieger in the late fourth century B.C., had not followed these rites and he had died when he descended into the oracular chamber). At each sacrifice a priest inspected the entrails of the animals to make sure that the process could continue. The final chance to halt the operation did not come until the actual night of the consultation, when a ram was sacrificed over a pit, "and even though the previous sacrifices have appeared propitious, no account is taken of them unless the entrails of the ram indicate the same" (9.39.6).

If the sacrifice was propitious, the consultant was taken to the river Hercyna by two thirteen-year-old boys (of citizen birth) who washed him and anointed him with oil. After this the priests took him to a fountain, where he was given a draught of the "water of forgetfulness" and was shown an image made by Daedalus, the architect of the Labyrinth, before being led to the oracle in the special clothes that he had donned. He then descended into the shrine, which was in the form of a circular pit of white marble, and:

> after going down he finds a hole between the floor and the structure . . . the consultant lies with his back on the ground, holding barley cakes kneaded with honey, thrusts his feet into the hole, and he himself follows, trying hard to get his knees into the hole. After his knees the rest of his body is at once swiftly drawn in . . . those who have entered the shrine learn the future, not in the same way in all cases, but by sight sometime and at other times by hearing. (Trans. Loeb)

When he had done this, he emerged from the hole feet first and was taken by the priests to the "chair of memory," where he would tell the priests what he had learned and then was turned over to his relatives (in Pausanias' case it appears that he was "paralyzed with terror and unconscious of both himself and his reply"; 9.39.13) and taken to the building where he had stayed before his experience.

The whole procedure at Lebadia was clearly designed to ensure that only the "right sort" of person got near the hero: the expense of the journey was increased by the large number of sacrifices and would have been enough in and of itself to dissuade most. Furthermore, the arrangement of the sacrifices gave the priests every opportunity to make sure that the consultant was not being frivolous, and if he appeared to be so the priests could just call the whole thing off. The process (stories about the ancient founder, Daedalus, and cheaters who had died hundreds of years before) gave the rites an aura of great antiquity. Thus those who participated in the whole experience would not only be in the best possible position to report on the oracle; they would also be most inclined to feel that they had had a truly great experience with the divine. The result, in this case, is that Pausanias' narrative is perhaps the most remarkable firsthand account of an "active" religious experience to survive from the classical world.[109]

The cult of Glycon, founded by Alexander of Abonuteichos in the reign of Antoninus Pius, offers the best example that has survived of the connection between social level and degree of participation in the mantic session. In his early years, when he was still very much a local phenomenon, Glycon, who was kept in an *adyton* at the temple of Asclepius, responded only to questions that were submitted on sealed slips of papyrus (Luc. *Alex.* 19, 23). When the oracle became famous enough to attract the attention of distinguished Romans, Glycon began to give "autophones," oracles spoken directly by the god to his consultants—an operation that may have been arranged by attaching speaking tubes to the mask that Glycon (who was a large snake) wore over his head (Luc. *Alex.* 15, 26).[110] There is also some evidence to suggest that some consultants were allowed to sleep in the temple in the hope that the god would appear to them. This is the easiest explanation for the birth of a son of Glycon to a woman from Caesarea Trochetta.[111] Two other features of this cult are also important. The first is that Alexander kept records of all questions and answers that could be used to provide evidence of Glycon's excellence as a prophet (Luc. *Alex.* 27); the second is the creation of an annual festival on successive days to commemorate the birth of Apollo and Asclepius, the birth of Glycon, and the birth of Alexander himself along with his daughter (Luc. *Alex.* 38–40).

The record of responses, like the record of miraculous cures, worked to provide a history of the oracle, and was certainly not unusual. The earliest attestation of such a record appears in Herodotus' account of king Croesus, and a shrine that rose to prominence in Syria during the second century, the shrine of Bel near Apamea, was conveniently located near an important military base and appears to have been active in the consistent updating of

4. Statuette of Glycon. Small images of cult objects, *hieromata*, of this sort
were used as protective amulets throughout the Greco-Roman world. On
these objects see especially L. Robert, *OMS* 5.747–769 (*Greek, Etruscan and
Roman Bronzes in the Museum of Fine Arts, Boston* [Boston, 1971], no. 128,
Francis Bartlett Donation; photo courtesy of the Museum of Fine Arts,
Boston).

the record of its responses to important people. By the end of the
first quarter of the third century it could claim to have predicted
the deaths of Trajan, Caracalla, and Macrinus with stunning accuracy. It is difficult to believe that any of these prophecies were
made before the deaths in question (see page 170).

There was clearly something for everyone here. Written questions (which were taken for a nominal fee) provided access to those
who were lower down on the social scale and thus kept physically
farthest from the god, various forms of incubation (either in person
or with Alexander as a proxy) for the wealthier, and autophones
for the most important, who could stand in the presence of the god

himself. It was the very model of the oracular shrine, and like others it played an important role in civic self-identity.

The Nature of Prophetic Inspiration

Given the wide range of ways in which the gods could be consulted, it is not surprising that there was a considerable range of opinion as to just what actually happened. The issue underlying these debates was whether or not it was reasonable to think that the gods really took the sort of interest in the world that believers in divination thought they did, and whether the form of contact that people believed they were using was accurate. In other words, was divination in accord with nature, or was it a fraud?

Stoicism was perhaps the single most important philosophic movement in the Roman world, and the arguments used by Stoics in favor of divination are given a full airing in Cicero's *Concerning Divination*. Here Cicero's brother Quintus expounds the theory, borrowed from the Stoic philosopher Posidonius, that divination derives from three sources: God, Fate, and Nature. Nature teaches men how great the power of the soul is when it is divorced from bodily senses, which happens particularly during sleep or during a frenzy. At such times humans see things with their souls that they cannot perceive when their souls are mingled with their bodies (*De div.* 1.57.129). In other words, the soul of an inspired prophet will encounter the order of events to come when, in a frenzy, it is released from the body to encounter the future. The experience does not involve the human body's being taken over by the god, but only a meeting between the soul and Fate. Plutarch's Theon puts it quite differently, but still resists the notion that the god entered a human body. He observes that the voice of the prophet is not the voice of the god, nor is the utterance, nor the diction, nor the meter. All of these belonged to the Pythia. What happens is that the god puts visions in her mind and a light in her soul with regard to the future—the god provides the impulse, but not the words (*Mor.* 397B–C).[112] In another dialogue on the oracles at Delphi, Plutarch reasserts this point when he has Lamprias say that it is foolish and childish in the extreme for people to think that the god acts like a ventriloquist, entering into the bodies of prophets and using their mouths as instruments (*Mor.* 414E). Tacitus, Plutarch's contemporary, also appears to have accepted this view when he writes that the *thespiodos* at Claros gave forth his oracles on the basis of what the consultants had "conceived in their minds" (*Ann.* 2.54.3). In his account of Claros and Didyma, Iamblichus says that the god placed images in the mind of the prophet (*De myst.* 3.11).

A slightly different point appears in Porphyry's work on philosophy from oracles; he writes that a godlike spirit, an emanation from the heavenly power, enters a human body and uses the soul as a base and speaks through the body as if it were an organ—a view that clearly stands somewhere between the notion that the prophet was solely responsible for the words and the view that the god was.[113] This view is, however, somewhat more restrained than that which emerges from some of the texts that he goes on to quote, such as "Now release the King, the mortal can no longer hold the god," or "Why, praying, do you torment this mortal?" The readiest interpretation of these lines is that the god (or in the latter case possibly the god's messenger) was in full physical possession of the prophet, that the divinity was there in person and that this was no mere emanation—precisely the point that Eusebius himself draws from these passages (Eus. *Praep. Ev.* 5.9).[114]

The point of Glycon's autophones was that the god himself was speaking, and the case made by Plutarch's interlocutors was evidently developed to answer criticism of the poetical style of the oracles, which was so bad that an educated man could not believe that such words were actually those of a god. Indeed, Theon expressly says that his opponent "speaks for Epicurus" when he suggests that anyone but the priestess made up the words (*Mor.* 397D). But these arguments were probably beyond the ken of most mortals. Inscriptions recording oracular responses tend to begin with the words "the god said," and this is presumably what most people thought happened: the god entered the prophet and spoke. In this respect the Christian critique of oracles, that they were the work of demons who spoke through prophets, was probably much closer to the perception of the average person than were the arguments of these intellectuals.

The spoken responses of the gods were essentially the words of the gods for the rich. The procedures for consulting the gods mirrored the social stratification of society as a whole. Only the very richest could get in to hear the god speak at some places; at all places only the rich could get into the temple; certainly only the well-to-do, or cities, could afford the cost of having the answers that they had received inscribed on stone. But the tastes of a dominant social and economic class go a long way toward conditioning the tastes of others, and it appears that public records of oracles had an important place in forming popular views of divine concern for their cities. Few would have disagreed with Celsus' statement that "the oracles given by the Pythia, the priestesses of Dodona, the god of Claros, the god among the Branchidae or at the temple of Ammon, and by a thousand other prophets under whose impulse, without a doubt, the whole world was colonized" (Orig. *Contra Cels.* 7.3 trans. Chadwick) were decisive proof of the existence of the immortals and their favor toward men. Indeed, this same argument was described by Cicero several hundred years before Celsus as "the citadel of the Stoics" (*De div.* 2.6) in their arguments in favor of the gods. Simply put, "if there is divination, then there are gods; if there are gods, then there will be divination" (*De div.* 1.10). It was a very empirical, simple style of proof—and very effective. Christian frustration with it is perhaps best illustrated by Eusebius in *The Preparation for the Gospel,* where he observes that if by some stroke of luck an oracle comes true, "you would find them [the pagans] most loudly boasting and carving inscriptions on columns and shouting to the ends of the earth, choosing not to remember that so many persons, it might chance, were disappointed" (*Praep. Ev.* 4.2).

Christian critiques and, indeed, a number of pagan critiques raise the further question of what a person who received an oracle could do with it. This person's options ranged from simple belief, through a desire to test the authenticity of the prediction, to simple disbelief. Oracles could be disbelieved by people who thought that the whole notion of divination was absurd, or by people who thought that, although oracles could predict the future, a particular oracle or holy man was a fraud or a particular soothsayer incompetent. Even as staunch a believer in the accuracy of oracles as Quintus Cicero in *Concerning Divination* had to admit that those who practiced divination by "art" were apt to make mistakes (*De div.* 1.55.124); and Plutarch's pious Theon observed that oracles were brought into disrepute by the common crowd of lower class soothsayers (*Mor.* 407C).[115] Someone who wanted to test an oracle could look around for other prophecies from the same oracle or ask for further information on the spot. In a case such as that of Apollonius, it is clear that his image improved as people came to think that time had proved that his prophecies were correct. Furthermore, it is also clear that the people who operated oracles themselves realized that there could be problems and that they evolved strategies to enhance their credibility. According to Theon, when powerful men consulted oracles, it was not to the advantage of those who controlled them to provoke and annoy people by overt unfriendliness: it was better to couch such predictions in obscure language (*Mor.* 407D–E). Observers could point to the famous oracle that was given to Croesus of Lydia around 545 B.C., telling him that a great empire would be destroyed if he crossed the Halys river to fight the Persians, and how the kingdom turned out to be his own; or to the notorious obscurity of the oracle that urged the Athenians to seek safety in their wooden walls when facing the great Persian invasion of 480 B.C. Given the nature of the ceremonies that preceded consultations, it might not even be necessary to go that far: if the goat did not shake, nothing could happen for at least another month.

Inquiry into the credentials of oracles took place at various levels. The surviving evidence for such debates is often difficult to evaluate because it tends to derive from a very small class of highly sophisticated authors, often using difficult literary forms, and writing for a small reading public. It would therefore obviously be wrong to assume that a work like Cicero's *Concerning Divination* could have much direct impact upon opinion in antiquity and, indeed, that the skeptical arguments of book 2 were meant to be decisive. The dialogue form may have been employed to set issues before the reader and let that reader make up his own mind.[116] The best that can be done is to assume that a work such as this represents the sort of questions that were in the air—quite an easy proposition in light of the extremely derivative nature of the work. It is also the case that some members of the aristocracy may not have attained even this level of comprehension, and that they thought in ways not very much more sophisticated than their lower-class contemporaries; and it has already been seen that on a number of occasions the evidence of inscriptions and papyri flatly contradicts the impression that can be gained from literary texts. In addition to this, we have very little record of the most important form of communication about the divine, the oral diatribe. Such public harangues, which were characteristic of Greek cities, could have some effect in the transmission of ideas and terms among the less sophisticated, as Christian hymns and sermons were later to do. But no speaker could be certain that his auditors cared particularly for his ideas. Paul certainly found that this was the case when he spoke before the Areopagus at Athens (Acts 17:16–34), and it is fairly certain that Diogenes of Oenoanda's great epigraphic diatribe, his massive inscription of the principles of Epicureanism on a stoa in his own city, had very little impact on the thinking of his contemporaries (or even upon members of his own family, one of whom seems to have taken a very un-Epicurean interest in athletics). We cannot even be certain whether Ofellius Laetus, who was honored for his philosophic poem at both Athens and Ephesus in the early second century A.D., impressed people more with his style or with his arguments.[117] Certainly one philosopher of the first century, the younger Seneca, thought that the people who came to listen to philosophers were more interested in their performance than in their doctrine (*Ep.* 108.6).

Ordinarily, arguments both for and against divination tended to the severely practical.[118] "In my opinion, even though many things deceive those who are seen to practice divination by art or nature, divination exists; although men in this as in other occupations are able to make mistakes" (Cic. *De div.* 1.55.24). The errors that could be used to attack divination are not, therefore, the errors of the gods or any sort of proof that divination per se should be challenged, but are only indicators that some men need to be scrutinized with care. The thrust of the argument is that if a prophet at one time can be shown to have been correct about something that he said would happen at another time, he should be believed at a third time when he says that something else will happen, and therefore that it is correct to believe in the power of the gods—a position that is still considered to be an intellectually respectable proof of the existence of a divinity,[119] as it was also of the authority of a prophet when the existence of a divinity was not in question. Josephus wrote that Vespasian decided to spare his life after he had predicted that Vespasian would become emperor because Josephus had "proved a veracious prophet in other matters" (Jos. *BJ* 3.405).

On the negative side, it was possible to argue that it was all chance and nonsense.[120] If all is ruled by Fate, then why bother with divination? After all, it cannot change a thing: could the great Roman disaster at Lake Trasimene in 218 B.C. have been avoided even if the consul Flaminius had observed the signs that indicated he should not give battle (*De div.* 2.8.20–21)? In many cases knowledge of the future could only have made people unhappy: how could Cnaeus Pompey, the most successful Roman of his generation, have have enjoyed his success "if he had known that he would die in an Egyptian waste after losing his army" (*De div.* 2.9.22)? Tiberius is said to have despaired when he learned that he could not prevent Caligula from being his successor (Jos. *AJ* 18.218). It is significant that Ammianus Marcellinus employed this argument to justify Julian's continuation of his invasion of Persia in 363 despite a great number of bad signs that had been observed, on the grounds that no one can change the decrees of Fate—but Ammianus certainly did not think that divination was silly or that it made him particularly sad (23.5.7), indeed, he explicitly subscribed to the view that traditional divination worked, even though the interpreters might make mistakes (21.1.7–14).[121] It might in fact be a comfort to be able to think that failures could not be prevented—and the signs merely confirmed that Julian was doing what he had to do. Signs could then offer confirmation that great events took their shape in heaven—or, in the words of Theophylact Simocatta, a Christian writing in the early seventh century, after recording prodigies in Constantinople, "the appearance of portents to cities does not signify good" (*Hist.* 6.11.2). Cicero noted that for Stoics of his own time to reply that evil was made less by the observance of religious rites was stupid: if everything happened on account of Fate, it was not possible to make any evil less (*De div.* 2.10.25). In the case of natural divination, the whole notion that the gods were so interested in the offerings of humans that they would lead a slave to a specific sacrificial beast, was bizarre (*De div.* 2.17.39). The response to this line of argument would be that experience showed that the gods worked this way. The notion that the stars could give a clue to a person's fate from their position at his birth was equally absurd, Cicero argued (*De div.* 2.44.93). Even natural divination was silly; oracles were so obscure that they could apply to anyone (*De div.* 2.55.110–114); oracles that came true did so by chance, and so on (*De div.* 2.56.115). It is clear that purely skeptical arguments could not do much to convince a person whose belief was founded on empirical observation of the sort outlined above: the answer in each case was that experience had shown that such doubts were unnecessary.

Pure skepticism was not the only possible approach. Oenomaeus, the Cynic philosopher from Gadara who flourished in the second century, launched a more direct attack.[122] In *The Unmasking of Tricksters* he combined an account of personal experience of what he considered to be a false prediction by Clarian Apollo with examples combed from Greek literature so as to prove that oracles in neither the past nor the present did anyone any good.[123] He himself had received an oracle from Claros that was also given to a merchant from Pontus named Callistratus (fr. 14), and when he went back for more responses, he received more and more gibberish (fr. 15)— an approach that has a close parallel in Lucian's treatment of Alexander (Luc. *Alex.* 53–54; compare 43–44 for Epicurean attacks on Alexander). The form of this attack was straightforward. The inverse of the empirical argument in favor of oracles, it was an empirical argument against them, and Oenomaeus felt that he could answer the argument from history (that is, the successes of the past proved that oracles were good and true) by producing useless responses from the past. One of these examples concerned an oracle that the Athenians were said to have received after the murder of Androgeus, son of King Minos of Crete, which punished the innocent by saying that the Athenians must send sons and daughters to Crete (where they would be given to the Minotaur). In this case, Oenomaeus pointed out, the gods allowed the guilty to go free and punished the innocent (fr. 1).

Another case cited by Oenomaeus involved oracles given to Aristomedon and his son Temnus before the return of "the sons of Hercules" to the Peloponnese, oracles that were both ambiguous and wrong. The oracle that had been given to Aristomedon advised him to invade the Peloponnese through "the road of the narrows"; he took this to mean the Isthmus of Corinth and was killed. He son was advised that the oracle had meant the Gulf of Corinth, but when he reached his destination via this route, after having killed a man named Carnes, he was still defeated. When Temnus complained about this outcome to Apollo, he was told that the defeat was revenge for Carnes' death (fr. 4).

None of these or the other cases adduced by Oenomaeus would have convinced a person who was not already predisposed to be. Even the most fervent believers in oracles admitted that mistakes could be made if the god was bored or thought that the consultant lacked devotion (as would obviously have been the case with Oenomaeus). Certainly such cases could not convince someone who thought, as Quintus Cicero put it, that "if even one instance can be shown when a prophecy has come true, then it must be taken as proved that divination is, in general terms, possible" (*Div.* 1.54.125).

Two other lines of approach were to deny that the entire universe worked the way that people thought—the Epicurean approach—or to claim that oracles might well work but that they had nothing to do with the action of gods, because they were the work of demons—the Christian approach. Epicurus, teaching at the end of the fourth century B.C., asserted that his followers should participate in civic cult out of respect for the order of the community, although the gods took no interest in human affairs. Even an Epicurean would admit that empirical observation was the essence of belief in the gods, and an Epicurean did not deny that people might see them in dreams; but these dreams were merely chance sightings of the atoms that they gave off and, consequently, were meaningless. People might indeed know what the gods looked like from these emanations, but the Epicurean would deny that they had any relevance because the things that men said that the gods did were figments of their imaginations; they were things that had their origin in weakness, fear and despair, not in the blessedness of the gods (Long and Sedley fr. 23c). Indeed, the impious man was not the one who denied the existence of the gods; rather, he was the one who "attaches to the gods the beliefs of the many about them" (Long and Sedley fr. 23b).[124] The world worked by free will; thus, there could be no Fate, no future that resulted from anything but the actions of men. For this reason, all oracles must be false.

The important feature of the standard Christian line that oracles were given by demons rather than by gods is that it did not deny the possibility of divine inspiration. For an Origen, a Tertullian, a Lactantius, or an Augustine, there could be no question but that prophecy was possible. If it were not, too much of their faith would disappear. Many Christians were perfectly prepared to believe that a Sibyl or other traditional prophet could have been inspired on occasion by the Christian God. Tertullian even conceded that the demons sometimes told the truth (*De anim.* 47.1), although he asserted that there was "no divine speech other than that of the one God" (*De anim.* 28.1). In this sense, the Christian approach to prophetic inspiration was far less agnostic than the Epicurean and, formally, very close to that of a person like Porphyry. Their problem—and it was a very serious one indeed—was to distinguish legitimate prophecy from illegitimate, and it seems that definition changed with time. The victorious church of the post-Constantinian era was able to accept visionaries more readily than the embattled church of the second century, which was severely shaken by the prophetic challenge of Montanism. But the emerging church of Paul had offered direct encounters with the divine as one of its special features. Paul is explicit on this point in his first letter to the Corinthians: "It is prophecy that builds up a Christian community" (1 Cor. 14:3). God "chose to reveal his son" to Paul, and it was

God who directed his journeys through revelation (Gal. 1:15, 2:2).[125] The book of Revelation is nothing less than "the revelation given by God to Jesus Christ," made known by his angel to John (Rev. 1:1–2). Because John was relegated to the role of an observer, it could be asserted that all Christians were able to understand the vision of Christ for themselves,[126] that God was willing to make the future known to the faithful and to allow them to participate directly in his wisdom. The fact that his revelation came in book form, and that his symbolic system could be made to conform with the gospels, also made it possible (albeit not without some reservation) to distinguish between the information that he offered and that which individual Christians might obtain on their own.[127]

Instead of denying the possibility of divine revelation, Christians constructed an alternative paradigm for treating revelation that was distasteful. The sacred books of Christianity's parent religion provided a ready model for exclusive prophecy. No less an authority than Moses could be adduced for the picture of "a prophet or dreamer" who called upon the faithful to follow another god, and for the statement that "even if the sign or portent should come true, do not listen to the words of that prophet or that dreamer" (Deut. 13:1–2). The Founder, in the version of Matthew, addressed this question when he told the faithful that "impostors will come claiming to be messiahs or prophets, and they will produce great signs and wonders to mislead even God's chosen" (Mt. 24:24). The Founder here is explicit, as is Moses, in observing that others can do what agents of God can do, but that the faithful must have the faith to reject them.[128] The book of Revelation offers the next logical development, by admitting the necessity of a deceitful "Antichrist" before the Founder's return. The notion of deceit was crucial. It gave Christians a consistent and viable response to the prophetic traditions of their neighbors, traditions that even they had to admit could point to what were felt to be undeniable prognostic successes. The notion that there could still be authentic revelation allowed them to compete.

The success of the Christian adaptation may be taken as a comment on philosophic critics of the pragmatic view of prophetic inspiration. It was necessary to admit that oracles did work. The feelings of the believer are perhaps most eloquently summed up by Porphyry in his work on philosophy from oracles when he writes that the man who placed his hope of salvation in the information gleaned from the oracles in his book is true and steadfast (Wolff, p. 109; Eus. *Praep. Ev.* 4.7). In his view the gods told mortals through their oracles about their way of life, how they were pleased, how they could be prevailed upon to do something, how they could be compelled, what to sacrifice, what to avoid, what cult statues should look like, in what shape they appear, and what they looked like (Wolff, pp. 129–130; Eus. *Praep. Ev.* 5.11). In other words, for Porphyry, oracles provided the information that was necessary to carry on the "passive side" of traditional cult.

[2]

Scholars, Poets, and Sibyls

"THESE ARE THE women and men who, down to the present day, are said to have been the mouthpieces through whom a god prophesied. But time is long, and perhaps similar things will occur again" (Paus. *Per.* 10.12.11). The sentiments of Pausanias would not have been regarded as exceptional by his contemporaries. Books of prophecy gave people some indication as to what would happen in the future, enabled them to understand the present, to see the events of their own time as part of a divine plan, and allowed them to share the experiences of their ancestors. The prophecies that were found in books enabled their readers to travel through time and share, at second hand, the excitement of meeting a divinely inspired individual who had something to say that concerned their own lives. There could always be the thrill of discovery, the chance that one could understand something that others had failed to understand because the incident had only recently occurred, or because it was only recently that a person had acquired the wisdom needed to understand what the god had been trying to say. This argument is particularly familiar in the works of Christian writers who tried to appropriate the sages of the past as prophets of their own faith, but the writings of Pausanias and others reveal that this was anything but a purely Christian phenomenon. "These recent and unusual occurrences near Cumae and Dicaearcheia," says a speaker in Plutarch's dialogue on the oracles at Delphi, "were they not recited long ago in the poems of the Sibyl, and has not time, as if in her debt, duly discharged the obligation in the bursting forth of fires from the mountain, boiling seas, blazing rocks tossed aloft by the wind, and the destruction of great and noble cities?" (*De defect. orac.* 398E).

The relationship between ancient and modern might not always be as passive as that envisaged by Plutarch's speaker. For just as ancient sages had obtained wisdom from divinities, so too could the modern investigator hope to gain access to the gods and do the ancients one better. This is the theme of the introduction to the physician Thessalus' book *Concerning the Virtues of Plants*.[1] Here Thessalus tells of his long studies in Alexandria, where, "furnished with a large amount of money, I frequented the most accomplished philosophers, and they praised me for my love of learning and the rapidity of my comprehension" (*De virt. herb.* 4). In the course of his education, he was particularly interested by the debates of the physicians and so resolved upon a career in medicine (the ability to engage in public debate like a professional sophist was an important qualification for a successful medical career).[2] Having made this decision, he set about collecting books, and in so doing he "discovered a book of Nectanebus containing twenty-four ways to treat the whole body and every illness according to each sign of the Zodiac with the aid of stones and plants" (*De virt. herb.* 6).

Thessalus was struck by the "marvelous grandeur of the enterprise," but he realized that the king had not known everything that there was to know about astrology and thus that further information was needed. He traveled throughout Egypt looking for a magician who could obtain a divine vision for him so that he could amend the errors that Nectanebus had made. At Thebes he found his man. After a three-day waiting period he entered a room with the magician, who asked him what god he wanted to see. He said Asclepius, and the god duly appeared and greeted him with the words, "O blessed Thessalus, today you receive honor from a god, and, with the passing of time, mortals will tender you the reverence due to a god when they learn of your success" (*De virt. herb.* 25).

Asclepius went on to tell him that he was right about Nectanebus: the man was a powerful magician, but he had not had the aid of a god; although he had been able to appreciate the affinity between stones, plants, and the stars through his native wit, he had not learned the times and places to collect the plants. Thus was a new science born thanks to Thessalus' contest with an "ancient" book.[3]

Just as Greek and Roman terms for prophetic activity often disguise the important distinction between the actual speakers of divinely inspired words and their interpreters, this prophetic terminology also obscures the very great importance of the written word in the development of ideas about the ways that prophets functioned. The encounter between the readers of prophetic books and their texts took place at a number of levels, and with different purposes. The way in which a scholar read a prophetic book might be very different from the way in which a poet read one, and both might in turn be very different from the way in which a professional purveyor of divine wisdom would treat it. None of these groups can be ignored. For this reason it will be necessary to move from the studies of scholars and poets to the streets of the ancient world, to sibylline books of all sorts and the people who sold them.

It is also necessary to note just how different these attitudes toward prophetic books could be from those of Christians or Jews. As Judaism and Christianity became increasingly based upon literary canons, their adherents had to arrive at different ways of treating the revelations contained in those books from those used by their polytheistic neighbors. A polytheist might read one prophetic book against another to decide if one, the other, or both were true; such a polytheist might also read a book as a kind of history or as a literary model. A Christian or Jewish reader, who already knew that the revelation in a canonical book was true, might try to reconcile two different versions, as Bishop Hippolytus did in the early third century when he tried to show that the books of Daniel and Revelation told roughly the same story about the end. If material was outside the canon, this reader would comb it for glimmerings of true doctrine, something that Christians did with sibylline oracles. Such a reader might also be interested in arriving at an additional canon of prophets who could be trusted at a secondary level as guides or supplements to the primary canon. Thus, for the polytheist the touchstone of reliability was function; for a Christian or Jew the touchstone tended to be reconciliation with a canon at either the primary or secondary level.

Scholarship

The bulk of our evidence for scholarly attention to prophecy occurs in the context of paradoxography. This genre, the collection of marvelous and interesting events in the past, is a literary reflection of the authority attributed to antiquity in the ancient world. The fashion for works of paradoxography appears to have developed particularly under the influence of the Peripatetic school in the late fourth century B.C. and to have gained strength in the atmosphere of the Museum at Alexandria in the early third century B.C. The poet Callimachus both contributed to the genre and employed it liberally in his influential poem on origins. An associate, Philoste-phanus, is also said to have written books of this sort, as did a Pergamene scholar of the later third century named Antigonus of Carystus. Such books typically consisted of a series of short sections grouped according to topic and based upon literary works.[4] *Mirabilia,* marvelous events, seem to have been favorite topics, and indeed it is in *Concerning Marvelous Events and People Who Lived for a Long Time,* by the imperial freedman Phlegon of Tralles, that one of the most extensive self-contained examples of scholarly inter-vention in the interpretation of prophecy has been preserved.

The extant fragments of Phlegon's work include three accounts of supernatural events that are of particular interest because they reveal the way in which old prophecies could be written up and dated so as to show that there was nothing further to be feared from them, and in such a way as to make the event into part of a good story—just as the oracles that a city had recorded in the past were not of much help for solving new problems, even though they stood as plain evidence of past favors (*FGrH* 257 fr. 36). The first of these stories is about a young man who is said to have lived in the time of Philip II of Macedon, and thus, by the time that Phlegon chose to include it in his work dedicated to the emperor

Hadrian, about six hundred years old. It tells how a young man named Machetes who was staying with some friends at Amphipolis was visited for several evenings in a row by a young woman.[5] One evening a nurse caught sight of the woman and identified her as Philimmion, the deceased daughter of the house. The next evening Machetes asked her if this was indeed the case, and for a sign. She said that she was indeed Philimmion and gave him a ring. The next evening, when her mother and father burst into the room to see her, she promptly died (again). The account concludes with a description of the rites of expiation that were then performed. The tale as a whole is presented as a report to Philip from one of his officials. It has been traditional to dismiss this story (when it has been discussed at all) as "absurd history." But to Phlegon and his contemporaries, it was not: it was an authoritative and ancient account of a marvelous event, and, as such, the story was worth knowing. This view was certainly shared by the platonic philosopher Proclus, who summarized it, from Phlegon's account, in his commentary on Plato's *Republic* (*Ad Plat. Rep.* 2.118).

A second story, which Phlegon derived from Hieron of Alexandria, tells of an androgynous child born to the wife of Polycritus the Aetolian several months after her husband's death. When the Aetolians met to decide what to do about the baby, Polycritus himself appeared in the meeting and advised his stunned former countrymen to spare it, and then vanished. After considerable discussion the Aetolians decided to kill the child anyway, and when they did so its severed head delivered a prophecy of doom. This prophecy, as Phlegon noted, was subsequently fulfilled when the Aetolians sustained a crushing defeat at the hands of the Acarnanians. The most important feature of this text is thus the last sentence, concerning the Acarnanian victory, because it shows not only that the oracle was authentic but also that there was no need to worry further about the ruin of the Aetolians on its account. It was important that such a prediction be tied to a specific time and place so that no one need worry about the words of this particular talking head in the future.[6]

The same point is true of the third prophetic narrative that has survived from Phlegon's book.[7] This appears to have been constructed from a series of anti-Roman oracles ranging in date from the early second to the early first century B.C., around which a narrative was created that drew bits and pieces from a second-century Hellenistic historian, and a good deal more from someone's imagination. The story opens with an account of Roman operations against Antiochus III and the Aetolians in 192/191 B.C., culminating in the defeat of Antiochus at the battle of Thermopylae and the invasion of Aetolia. It is said that "in the battle that was fought against Antiochus at Thermopylae, an extraordinary portent for the Romans occurred" (*FGrH* 257 fr. 36 III.2). An officer of Antiochus named Buplagos, who had been killed in the battle, rose from the dead on the following day and walked into the Roman camp, where "in a soft voice" he delivered a prophecy to the effect that Zeus would send a mighty race against Italy and put an end to the rule of the Romans, and then dropped dead again (*FGrH* 257 fr. 36 III.3). The Romans, understandably concerned by this turn of events, then sent ambassadors to Delphi, where the Pythia told them to cease their invasion on the spot and return home, for Athena was preparing a powerful army that would destroy their kind.

After receiving the Delphic oracle, the Romans were withdrawing toward Naupactus when an officer named Publius fell into a prophetic fit and predicted that the Romans would suffer disaster on their way home from the conquest of Asia. When asked to explain what this meant, Publius described, in reasonable detail, what would occur during the rest of the war with Antiochus. He also said that the returning army would be attacked by Thracians and lose some of its booty. He then fell into another prophetic fit and predicted, in verse, the destruction of Rome at the hands of an invading army; then, speaking in prose, that a large red wolf would come to devour him, thus proving that he had spoken the truth. The wolf duly arrived and ate Publius, leaving only the head, which once again burst into prophetic song, telling the Romans that Athena hated them, and that she would send a powerful army from Asia that would destroy Italy and drag its people off into slavery. The account ends with the statement that "hearing these words, they [the Romans] were deeply upset and established a temple and altar of Apollo Lycios where the head had lain and got onto their ships and each one went to his own land. All the things that Publius predicted have come true" (*FGrH* 257 fr. 36 III.14).

It is obvious that this story contains several elements, all of which may be associated with anti-Roman propaganda composed at various points between the war with Antiochus and the high tide of Mithridates VI's success during his first war against Rome in 89/88 B.C. This war is the likely time for the composition of the tale that survives in Phlegon's work; and its purpose, when a king from Asia was ranging over the provinces of the Roman east, was to localize various texts that were in general circulation in time and, to place them in the mouth of a prophet whose words could be believed because he had correctly predicted his own death and thus given them credibility. Some two centuries later, in the reign of Hadrian, however, this account could be read by a Roman (although the details do not fit absolutely) as a prediction of the ruin that L. Cornelius Sulla, the conqueror of Mithridates, would inflict on Italy during the bloody civil war that followed his return to Italy in 83/82 B.C. The reader in the second century A.D. could be confident that there was nothing more to fear from these prophecies, for they had already come to pass, and was left to marvel at the extraordinary action of the gods on that occasion. As it stood in Phlegon's text, this story would therefore have lost its anti-Roman meaning.

Prophecy in Literature

The prophetic interests of the reading public were not limited to collections of *mirabilia*. In this regard the Latin epic poetry of the first century A.D. serves as a useful barometer of the kind of thing that members of the upper orders of Roman society were interested in. It can be argued that the prophecies that Vergil's Aeneas seeks on his way to Latium lend some dramatic tension to the tale: when will the tables be eaten, when will someone understand something that a god says? On another level, it is plain that the most important prophetic utterances that are delivered to mortals in the *Aeneid* are connected with Augustus' favored divinity, Apollo, or the Sibyl who is represented as his agent. On yet another level, Vergil's presentation of prophecy after prophecy surely struck a chord with an audience that considered prophecy an important and interesting part of life, and given the fact that prophecy occupies a much more important place in Vergil than it does in earlier Greek epic, the nature of his audience's taste must surely be given a place in the formation of the plot of the poem.[8]

In his poem on the civil war Lucan banished the Olympians from direct involvement (how could they play a role in a tale that was so sad?), but he could not do without prophecy.[9] Oracles are the "guardians of the fates and mysteries of the universe" (*Phars.* 5.198), and it is through his various prophets that Lucan allows the gods to make clear their feelings about events on earth. The process of divine revelation begins in book 1 with his description of three prophets, the Etruscan hauruspex Arruns, the astrologer Figulus, and a Roman matron, acting like a Bacchanal, who predicts the course of the civil wars under the impulse of Apollo. "Now the angers of the gods were clear and the heavens gave clear signs of war" opens book 2, and a few lines later Lucan notes that these portents were the truthful signs of the gods (*Phars.* 2.16–17).

Various prophetic moments mark crucial developments in the tale thereafter.[10] Thus Pompey is treated to a prognostic visit from the ghost of his deceased wife Julia at the beginning of book 3, just as he is on the way to Greece, having abandoned Italy at the end of the first phase of the war. In book 5, Appius Claudius journeys to Delphi to learn the fate of the Pompeian side, and the priestess Phaemone, after attempting to deceive the Roman, is seized by the true prophetic revelation from Apollo and tells Appius, ever so briefly, that he will have no part in the war that is coming as Caesar now sails to Greece (*Phars.* 5.194–196). As the tragedy of civil war deepens, the traditional modes of communication are becoming less useful.[11]

The most horrific event is reserved for book 6, when young Sextus Pompey seeks out a Thessalian witch to learn the course of the campaign. The necromancy that follows takes up nearly a quarter of the book, leaving no reader in doubt of the horror of the combat or of the true nature of Sextus, "unworthy offspring from a great parent" (*Phars.* 6.420), who sought such advice. Better people did not deal in the animation of corpses. Lucan is explicit that this form of consultation is of the most dubious sort as he says that Sextus knew "the mysteries of witchcraft which the gods above abominate, and grim altars with funeral rites; he knew the veracity of Pluto and the shades below; and the wretch was convinced that the gods of heaven are ignorant" (*Phars.* 430–404 Loeb trans.).[12] The witch Erichtho is the civil war's answer to Vergil's Sibyl, and magical animation of a corpse a degenerate substitution for the heroic style of consultation established by Homer in the eleventh book of the *Odyssey.*

There are no winners for Lucan in civil war, but the losers are ennobled by their failures, and this too is brought out with the aid of a couple of prophetic moments. Gnaeus Pompey recognized that he would die if he left his ship in Egypt, but he bowed to destiny, telling his wife to use his head to test the faith of the Egyptian king (*Phars.* 8.576–582). Marcus Porcius Cato is even permitted to speak words worthy of an oracle from Jupiter Ammon, "filled with the divinity whom he bore in his silent mind" (*Phars.* 9.564–565).[13] Virtue can shine in defeat, and the power to see the future on one's own is a sign of moral excellence (see pages 164–167 below).

Silius Italicus has never been regarded as one of the great intellects or literary artists of the Roman world. The younger Pliny judged him competent rather than brilliant (a judgment that could be made with equal justification of Pliny himself), but this is one reason why his poetry is a touchstone for the tastes of his age.[14] It is fair to say that if Silius thought that something was appropriate, his view would be shared by many. Hence it is of interest that prophesies of all sorts dot his *Punic War.* At the end of book 1, the great general Fabius Maximus is presented in a debate at Rome over the response to Hannibal's assault on the Spanish city of Saguntum. He is shown as an explorer of the future with a cautious mind, and foreseeing the future as he speaks (*Pun.* 1.679–686). Hannibal himself looks at the world with the aid of his prophetic soul in book 3 as he foresees the difficulties of the war to come when he invades Italy (*Pun.* 3.73), and the preparations for the battle of Cannae are interrupted by a Roman soldier who in a prophetic fit foresees the ruin of the army (*Pun.* 8.656). The implications of this vision are lost upon the consul Varro, who would command the army on the day of the disastrous battle. Varro's problem, one that he shared with Flaminius, who led the Roman army to destruction at the battle of Lake Trasimene in Silius' fifth book, is that he cannot understand true prophecy. At the same time, readers are reminded that the gods meant this to happen, for the defeat at Cannae was foreseen in the distant past by no less an authority than the Cumaean Sibyl herself.

At the beginning of book 9, the consul Aemilius Paulus begs his colleague not to go into battle the next day, concluding with a reminder that the Sibyl had long ago predicted the disaster: "the Cumaean prophetess once sang these things throughout the world, and, blessed with knowledge of the future, she sang about you and your madness throughout the earth in the time of our ancestors" (*Pun.* 9.57–59). Cannae was not simply the result of an act of human folly; rather, it was one of the challenges that Rome had to overcome on its way to world domination. So too, in book 11, the hero of the poem's end, Cornelius Scipio Africanus, is directed to a Homeric necromancy by a priestess at Cumae and shown a vision of the history of Rome by the Sibyl herself, which ends with a vision of Hannibal's death. The scene is far more literary than Lucan's and the one in Statius' *Thebaid* (see below). Silius could not bring himself to suggest that a hero of the old republic could be closely linked with the practices that raised questions of propriety in his own day.[15] The Sibyl had already predicted Rome's victory, as Silius reminds the reader at the beginning of book 17, the book that will conclude with Scipio's victory at Zama. This book opens with the arrival of the Magna Mater at Rome; she is brought there because ancient oracles of the Sibyl had predicted that the foreign enemy would leave Italy when she arrived from Phrygia. Silius' oracles and prescient mortals serve as reminders of the role of the gods during Rome's struggle with Hannibal, and of the qualities to be expected in great leaders.

Civil war in both the divine and mortal spheres is the theme of Statius' *Thebaid*,[16] and, as he strives to evoke the full range of epic paraphernalia to give his poem a fitting place in the literary tradition, Statius too explores a range of prophetic acts to foreshadow the development of his plot. Like Lucan, Valerius, Vergil and Silius, Statius is very much concerned to make his prophetic moments fit into the literary tradition, to the extent that connections with other epics are far more important than connections with actual practice.

The choice of the Theban narrative provides Statius with a chance to discuss the merits of several of the most famous seers of the mythological past.[17] The first of these prophetic moments is an augury conducted by the seers Amphiareus and Melampus at Argos in book 3. Here it is said that Amphiareus, "to whom skilled care of the future is given," and Melampus, "now old, but thriving with a mind inspired by Apollo," go off to discover the future through exstipacy (Stat. *Theb.* 3.451–455). Why two characters who should have been able to know what was to happen through their own inspiration need to engage in this sort of divination is not discussed, and indeed must have seemed a bit odd to an astute reader. The purpose becomes clear in the next book, where Statius says that Atropos (one of the fates) placed the arms of war in the hands of Amphiareus and "overwhelmed the god within him" (*Theb.* 4.190). It is a clever allusion to the question of what good it could do someone to know the future if there was nothing that could be done to change it.

The situation is obviously bad when neither Melampus nor Amphiareus can find a reasonable sign in the organs of the animals that they have slaughtered. This failure leads them to try to discover the future through augury. Statius supplies particular praise of this Roman craft through Amphiareus' words: "Cirrha cannot more certainly promise the god in her grotto, nor the Chaonian leaves that are said to sing for you in Molossian groves, allow dry Ammon to be envious, and the Lycian lots to contend, and the beast of the Nile, and Branchus, equal in honor to his father, and Pan, whom the rustic inhabitant dwelling near the Pisan waters hears at night in the Lycaonian shadows" (*Theb.* 3.474–480). Despite all this, the augury that follows has nothing to do with the actual techniques employed by an augur at Rome: the vision of birds fighting each other in heaven is pure epic.[18]

In the next book the prophetic scene shifts to Thebes. First, in the hills outside the city, the appropriate venue for an independent, inspired prophet, a Bacchant suddenly breaks into prophetic song. Statius is quite clear about the nature of her inspiration: she is "seized" by the god but speaks with her own voice at his prompting, and when "Bacchus withdraws," she falls silent. This experience is in line with views such as those expressed in Plutarch's dialogues on oracles and seems to have been written quite consciously to conform with contemporary theory (*Theb.* 4.377–405). The same cannot be said of the next prophetic moment, a necromancy. Eteocles, terrified by the signs of divine displeasure that accompany the news that the Argive army is on the march, summons the great seer Tiresias to find out what will happen. After running though a variety of ineffective prognostic techniques, Tiresias sets off with his daughter to consult the spirits of the dead. Statius makes it plain that this is a "good" sort of consultation, combining Homeric techniques, explicit references to other necromantic scenes in Latin literature, and formulae of invocation that may well have been influenced by actual practices in his own day.[19]

The inherent distinction between low-grade necromancy of the sort described by Lucan as a way of characterizing Pompey's son, and "high-grade" necromancy, which could be practiced by respectable prophets, is one that persisted throughout the imperial period. It is clear that there were practitioners of these arts at Rome who could be called upon by people like the exceedingly well-connected Scribonius Libo Drusus in the reign of Tiberius.[20] One indication of the effort to make such necromancy respectable is preserved on a large papyrus of the fourth century containing a variety of magical spells. Here the prescription for questioning a corpse is contained in a prefatory letter to Ostanes from the legendary Thessalian wise man Pithys (*PGM* 4.2140). In the very next section of the papyrus, a person is told how three lines of Homer inscribed on an iron tag will provide assistance in a wide variety of circumstances. Included among these is the suggestion that a person attach the tag "to a criminal who has been executed, speak the verses in his ear, and he will tell you everything you wish" (*PGM* 4.2164–66). In more decidedly polite company, Lucian alludes to the practice, and Pausanias notes a number of sites on his journey through Greece where *necromanteia* once operated as points of interest. The fact that none of them were still operative suggests that there was sufficient ambivalence about this particular form of prognostication to keep local authorities from trying to promote it openly.[21]

Epic poetry was not the only genre in which various poets took advantage of prophetic traditions. It is by now a commonplace that classical Greek and Latin texts are permeated with adaptations of magical practices, and it has long been known that various authors tried their hand at presenting their ideas in pseudo-prophetic form. The most extensive exercise of this sort is Lycophron's *Alexandra,* a poem summarizing the epic tradition about Troy in the form of a prophecy by Cassandra as Paris' ship sets sail to Sparta, where the abduction of Helen will occur.[22] Perhaps the most famous example of such adaptation is Vergil's *Fourth Eclogue,* composed sometime between 44 and 40 B.C. to commemorate some event in the complicated politics of the period as heralding the coming of peace according the predictions of the Cumaean Sibyl. It is perhaps ironic that Vergil's effort to imitate oracular verse is so successful that the poem has been taken to be an actual prophecy.[23] The second poem in Horace's first book of *Odes,* a poem honoring Augustus, is carefully crafted so as to present Augustus as the savior whom readers of prophetic books had come to expect in the wake of the disasters that had beset the Roman state for so long.[24] The sundry prophetic traditions of the ancient world were absorbed into "higher" literature because they were of such interest to the audiences of these works. But did this literature, in turn, exert much influence upon the tradition of prophecy? Here the answer seems to be no, or rather, not very much, until the Christian interest in canonization exalted certain bits of scholarship to positions of significance for the reading of prophetic texts that they had not had in the pre-Christian empire. An examination of the most important of these traditions will suggest the reasons why.

Tradition and Transformation: The Case of the Sibylline Oracles

In a section of his book on marvels concerned with androgynous births, Phlegon preserves what may be the only extant example of a sibylline oracle from the collection that was assembled by the senate of republican Rome (it was destroyed by the fire that burned the temple of Capitoline Jupiter in 83 B.C.). The text, prescribing a series of ritual actions to be taken to mollify the goddesses Demeter and Persephone, may have survived down to Phlegon's time because it had attracted the attention of an earlier commentator.[25] In his section on people who lived a long time he cites two other oracular passages to prove that the Erythraean Sibyl was extraordinarily long-lived. One of these texts is concerned with the *ludi saeculares* at Rome; the other details the Sibyl's relationship with Apollo.[26] The text of the latter runs as follows:

> But why indeed all-sorrowful do I sing divine oracles about other people's suffering, holding to my fated madness? Why do I taste its painful sting, retaining my grievous old age into the tenth century, raging in my heart and speaking things that are not believed, having foreseen in a vision all the unendurable griefs of mankind? Then, envious of my prophetic gift, the son of famous Leto, filling his destructive heart with passion, will loose my spirit, chained in its miserable body, when he will have shot through my frame with a flesh-piercing arrow. Then straightway, my spirit, having flown through the air, sends to the ears of mortals audible omens mingled with the breeze [and] wrapped in complex riddles. My body will lie shamefully unburied on mother earth. No mortal will cover it with earth or hide it in a tomb. My black blood will trickle down through the broad pathways of the earth, dried by time. From there thick grass will shoot up, which, when the herds have grazed on it, will sink into their livers and show the purposes of the immortal gods by prophecies; and birds in their feathered robes, if they taste my flesh, will give true prophecy to mortals. (*FGrH* 257 fr. 37 V)

This story is not unique. Plutarch appears to have known a version of it (including an added detail, that the Sibyl will become the face in the moon), and Lucian appears to refer to it when one of his characters says that he has heard an oracle of the Sibyl.[27] The contents themselves may show the influence of Stoic thought, and these may have contributed to the oracle's appeal.[28] On the other hand, Pausanias, who, like Phlegon, based his account of Sibyls on the texts themselves and on monuments to Sibyls that he had seen, had not heard of it; and it was unknown to Varro, whose first century B.C. list of Sibyls is derived from literary sources rather than from oracular texts. Oracles that reflected local traditions or controversies came piecemeal to the attention of scholars, but when they did, their statements were taken as authoritative.

The evolution of sibylline traditions proceeds at several levels: in the cities of the Roman empire where texts were written and circulated, and in the works of intellectuals who sought to organize and systematize this knowledge. In the end, the scholarly process would result in a reasonably stable sibylline canon in Christian texts as acceptable prophets were catalogued and the unacceptable cast out. Before this happened, however, the Sibyl had a very long history.

Because of the immense variation in the stories about Sibyls, it is probably incorrect to speak of a "sibylline tradition" in antiquity. The oracles are too varied in content, and beliefs about the lives of Sibyls are too confused.[29] The earliest explicit textual evidence for an inspired prophetess named "Sibylla" occurs in the fifth century B.C.[30] From these references, it appears that her words were circulated as books of prophecy and that her name was inserted in these books. This may also have been the case in books attributed to other early prophets such as Orpheus, Epimenides, Bakis, or Musaeus. The inclusion of a name served to differentiate the Sibyl's utterances from those of the prophets and prophetesses at oracular shrines who spoke only as the mouthpiece of a god.[31] The circulation of such collections in Greece may be traced back to at least the sixth century, when the activity of chresmologues, "oracle collectors," is first attested. The earliest story concerns Hipparchus, the son of Pisistratus, who is said to have expelled Onomacritus the chresmologue for inserting a false prophecy into his collection of the works of Musaeus to the effect that Lemnos would disappear under the sea.[32] Given, however, that a sibylline tradition must have traveled to Italy before the end of the sixth century, some sort of corpus must have been circulated by chresmologues at this time, making this development contemporaneous with the others. Aside from this, all that can be said is that "Sibylla" appears to have been less interesting to people in mainland Greece than other prophets, such as Bakis or Epimenides, until the end of the fourth century. The areas that seem to be connected with her activity in the earliest period, Erythrae and Marpessus in the Troad, were in Asia Minor. Like other wandering prophets, she was not associated with a specific shrine and was thought to produce her oracles because she had some sort of special divine knowledge. The form of her prophecies may have been much like that of the surviving books: a series of conditional and final clauses saying that "when certain conditions obtain, something will happen." Her books do not seem to have had any unity other than that they were thought to contain the utterances of a single prophetess.

The early history of this form of prophetic book is difficult to trace. It has been argued that the sibylline tradition developed because there was in fact a famous prophetess of that name who was a representative of an indigenous tradition in the Troad.[33] This may be true (it is impossible to prove or disprove), but it does not explain the currency of the style of prophecy with which the Sibyl is associated. On this point, all that can be said is that there was a tradition of female prophecy in the Greek world, that hexameter poetry was the vehicle for the communication of important ideas, and that there was a tendency in the Greek world to attribute interesting texts to named individuals.[34] Therefore, if men like Bakis could be prophets, it is not surprising that a woman could be as well.

It is not until the time of Alexander that the picture can be filled out any further in the east, but there had already been an extremely significant development in the west: the arrival of the sibylline books at Rome. The earliest literary reference to an Italian Sibyl is in Naevius' *Bellum Poenicum:* called the "Cimmerian" Sibyl, she was placed in the area around Lake Avernus.[35] But this comes long after the Romans had acquired their collection of sibylline oracles, which is first attested in 496.[36] The oracles themselves must have been in Greek (there is no evidence that any Roman ever thought that she spoke in any other language), but the form of the books appears to have resembled that of Etruscan sacred books, which gave lists of prodigies and the appropriate ritual actions that cities should use to expiate them.[37] Their form was evidently the same as that in a text preserved in Phlegon's oracle about the androgynous birth, which lists the actions that Rome should take after the birth of an androgynous child in 125 B.C. (*FGrH* 257 fr. 36 X A). This is a mention of the event, followed by a list of rites in hexameters.[38] It is unfortunate that we cannot know how far these instructions extended in some of the more unusual cases. Did the Sibyl merely say that the most modest woman in Rome should dedicate the image of Venus Verticordia (an image that was to raise the standard of female morals) in 114 B.C., or did she also specify that she was to be chosen by vote of the *matronae* from a list of a hundred aspirants?[39]

We do not know what the Romans thought about the origin of their books in the earliest republic, although Naevius' reference to the "Cimmerian" Sibyl makes it look very much as if they thought that they came from Campania—but they clearly came to a "better" knowledge of the situation quite soon as a result of cross-fertilization between the Roman and Greek worlds.[40] The Greek tradition had no place for a Cimmerian Sibyl, and the Campanian Sibyl had been placed at Cumae even before Naevius. The pseudo-Aristotelian *Concerning Amazing Things That Have Been Heard* reports an underground chamber there of the "chresmologue" Sibylla, whom some believed to have come from Erythrae, even though the people of Cumae said that she was a native (*Mir.* 838). This notice probably derives from Lycus of Rhegium, who wrote around 300 and was clearly considered an authority on the west by the eastern Greeks of the third century.[41] The notion that the Cumaean Sibyl was actually from the east became established in the Roman tradition, as is perhaps best represented by Livy's statement:

Evander was considered more venerable because of the divinity attributed to his mother, Camenta, who gave prophecies before the Sibyl came to Italy (1.8.1).

THE EXPANSION OF SIBYLLINE TRADITIONS

There are some sibylline oracles, quoted by Pausanias and Plutarch, concerning events in the fifth and fourth centuries, which may indeed be roughly contemporary with the events that they predict. To judge from a discourse on Sibyls in Diodorus (4.66), these prophets may have had a place in Ephorus' history, and the cities that were by then most intimately connected with Sibyls, Erythrae and Gergis (which evidently put an image of its Sibyl on its coins),[42] appear to having been making something of their claims. But it was some events during Alexander's campaigns against Persia that seem to have stirred more interest in the subject. The first of these events, in the late 330s, was a poetic outburst on the subject of Alexander's divine birth by a woman of Erythrae named Athenais, who evidently recalled "the ancient Sibyl" to the mind of Callisthenes (*FGrH* 124 fr. 14). The second was the discovery of a Babylonian Sibyl by another of Alexander's companions, Nicanor, who was possibly the son-in-law of Aristotle. We cannot know what it was that Nicanor saw, but we do know that there was a well-established tradition of prophecy in the temples of Mesopotamia, and it seems likely that Nicanor identified this tradition (or, possibly, a representative of this tradition) with the Sibyl, as the Greek colonists in the bay of Naples appear to have done with a native Italic cult.

In the long term the identification of a Sibyl as being of non-Greek origin may have been important, but some questions must be raised about the date of this development. There is no reason to think that Nicanor was widely read (all we have is this fragment, preserved by Varro, and a possible citation in Stephanus), and the tradition about an eastern Sibyl begins to be well attested only in the centuries after the birth of Christ. Pausanias tells us that he knew of a Sibyl named Sabbe who "grew up among the Hebrews around Palestine," and that people said that she was the daughter of

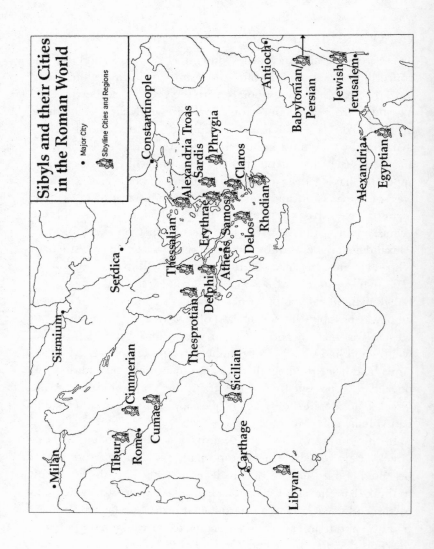

Sibyls and their Cities in the Roman World

- • Major City
- Sibylline Cities and Regions

Milan
Tibur
Rome
Cumae
Cimmerian
Sirmium
Serdica
Thessalian
Thesprotian
Delphi
Athens
Samos
Erythrae
Delos
Sicilian
Rhodian
Carthage
Libyan
Claros
Phrygia
Sardis
Alexandria Troas
Constantinople
Antioch
Babylonian/Persian
Jewish
Jerusalem
Alexandria
Egyptian

Berossus and Erymanthe (*Per.* 10.12.9). In the list of Sibyls in a sixth-century "Sibylline Theosophy," the Babylonian Sibyl appears as the "Chaldean or Persian" who was named Sambathe and was the daughter of Noah. This is obviously a later variation on the fragment of Nicanor in Varro.

Outside Nicanor, there is little independent evidence that the Sibyl was an important Jewish prophet before the Roman conquest of the eastern Mediterranean, and none that she had been adopted by other eastern peoples as a vehicle for their self-expression in the Hellenistic age.[43] Indeed, the only evidence that a pre–Augustan author referred to a Sibyl in a Jewish context at all comes from Alexander Polyhistor the freedman of Sulla, who is said to have attributed an account of the destruction of the tower of Babel to "the Sibyl" (*FGrH* 273 fr. 79). This might suggest that lines on the tower of Babel resembling those in an oracle in the surviving collection (*Orac. Sib.* 3.97–104) were already attributed to the Sibyl, but we cannot be sure even of this: the sibylline passage may have been inspired by Alexander.[44] The fact that he was writing for a Roman audience may have influenced Alexander's choice of a prophet.

Although some Greeks in the generation after Alexander recognized the possibility that there were Sibyls who were born outside the Greek world, and therefore that there was not one Sibyl but several, it cannot be said that the "sibylline tradition" must have taken in much near eastern material at this time. On the other hand, texts of this sort were useful to a people forced to explain the standing of their faith in the face of skeptics. The use of the sibylline form by Jews is just one of a number of instances of the adaptation of Greek literary forms in the Hellenistic age. This said, too much should not be made of it. Judaism had its own books, very powerful books, that remained the most important source of knowledge about their faith. The early translation of the Pentateuch, and then of much other Jewish literature, into Greek and its constant exegesis and discussion were far more important to the spread of Judaism than any imitations of Greek literature.[45]

Most of our evidence for Sibyls comes from writers in the Augustan age or later. This fact reflects the importance of the oracles at Rome and suggests that interest in the subject was enhanced by Rome's political unification of the Mediterranean world. In earlier ages the Sibyl had been but one of a number of similar figures (and probably not the most interesting of them); in the centuries after Augustus she emerged as the preeminent prophet whose words were thought to have survived from earlier times.

The extant books of Livy's history of Rome give us our best evidence for the way in which the official collection was used, a subject to which I will return in Chapter 4. In the generation before Livy, Terentius Varro had assembled the list of Sibyls for the book on the *quindecimviri sacris faciundis,* mentioned earlier. This list mentioned ten: the Babylonian, the Libyan, the Delphic, the Cimmerian, the Erythraean, the Samian, the Cumaean, the Hellespontine, the Phrygian, and the Tiburtine.[46] The Libyan Sibyl may be a creation of Varro or of an earlier scholar, based on Euripides' *Busiris.*[47] The Babylonian Sibyl was reported by Nicanor, the author of a history of Alexander;[48] the Delphic Sibyl was discussed by Chrysippus in his work on divination, and the Cimmerian, as we have seen, was the invention of Naevius. The Erythraean appeared in the work of Apollodorus of Erythrae, the Samian was uncovered by Eratosthenes, and the Hellespontine was discussed by Heracleides Ponticus. Heracleides is known from other sources to have mentioned the Phrygian Sibyl, and he may also be the source for Varro's knowledge of her. Varro does not give a source for his information on the Cumaean Sibyl (who was too well known in Rome to require such annotation) or for the Tiburtine, presumably because she was also too well known. Unlike Phlegon, Plutarch, and Pausanias, Varro has used works of literature rather than oracular texts to compile this list. And just as he did not use primary texts for his study, so too his study had no impact upon oracular poems that either extant oracles, quotations from oracles, or contemporary literature can reveal.[49] In a sense this should not be surprising; for the stories about Sibyls were intimately connected with civic self identity, and they were consequently open to enormous variation.

The claim to be the birthplace (or burial-place) of some famous individual, or the site of some famous event, mythological or otherwise, was of tremendous importance for the cities of the Roman empire. Such claims provided a way for less obviously Hellenic spots on the fringes of the old Greek world to define a place for themselves in the shared urban culture of the Greco-Roman Mediterranean. They could also provide the rationale for asking favors from Rome, as well as giving important tourists a reason to visit. The connection with tourism is made most explicit in an inscription from Erythrae commemorating the construction of a new sibylline shrine there in time for a visit by Lucius Verus in A.D. 162 (*I. Eryth u. Klaz.* no. 224.15–16). It also appears, a century and a half earlier, when Strabo intimated that the only famous people who had ever lived there before his own time were the ancient Sibyl and the Athenais who burst into prophecy during the reign of Alexander (14.645); and it is evident on an offering-calendar from Erythrae in the first half of the second century B.C., and on the coins of that city and of Cyme, in the course of the second and third centuries, which occasionally depict a Sibyl.[50]

The expectations of tourists are brought out very well by Pausanias' digression on Sibyls in book 10 of his *Periegesis*. This digression was inspired by his sighting of the "rock of the Sibyl" between the Delphic Bouleterion and the polygonal wall, which provoked a somewhat different but still interesting digression on Sibyls from "Serapion" in Plutarch's dialogue on the Delphic oracle (*De Pyth. orac.* 398D–399E). Pausanias tells the stories that he heard about the Sibyl at Delphi, and then the stories that he heard when he saw the spot on Delos where she had given oracles. The major part of the digression involves a discussion of the claims of the people of Alexandria Troas that Herophile was native to their area. The village of Marpessus, the original home of this Sibyl, was once in the territory of Gergis, and when the city of Gergis was destroyed in the third or second century B.C., the Alexandrians took the Sibyl for their own. The Alexandrians said that Marpessus was the true home of Herophile because the earth around Marpessus was of reddish clay (which is true), hence that she was known as the Erythraean, and the Alexandrians showed Pausanias her tomb in the grove of Apollo Smintheus, with an inscribed tombstone (10.12.3–6). Pausanias was inclined to believe this story because he had read an oracle in which she had proclaimed the place her home. He also reports that he was disappointed by the display put on at Cumae (they showed him a small stone urn; 10.12.8), and that the people of Erythrae were liars when they claimed Herophile as their own on the basis of what he considered an irresponsible emendation of the verses that he knew concerning Marpessus (10.12.7). We can therefore gain a picture of the assiduous tourist in action: he knew of the various claims, and when he came to the appropriate city he would search out the local monument to the Sibyl or check out the claims that people might make about their Sibyl in verses that he knew. He was certainly not impressed when he discovered that he knew more about the Cumaean Sibyl than did the local inhabitants.

Pausanias was not the last word on the subject, and it is evident that people tried to improve on their sibylline displays if they found that visitors were not impressed. The author of the *Exhortation to the Greeks* reports an impressive tour of the Sibyl's cave and the storage of her remains in a bronze urn, all of which may have been a development after Pausanias' visit.[51] The same tendency toward improvement appears at Erythrae, as the remarkable discovery of a sibylline shrine at Erythrae in 1891 reveals. Four inscriptions were found at this time. One is on the base of a statue of the Sibyl, another is on the base of a statue of her mother, the third records the construction of the fountain and the statues in the reign of Marcus Aurelius, and the fourth provides the long elegiac sibylline autobiography that I have mentioned in connection with Lucius Verus.[52] It was clearly the intention of the Erythraeans to respond to the challenge of the people of Alexandria Troas. The Sibyl is explicit on this point when she says: "I have no other homeland, but Erythrae alone, and the mortal Theodorus was my father" (*I. Eryth. u. Klaz* no. 224.3–4); and to judge from a mention of this shrine in the *Chronicon Paschale,* the Erythraeans were successful in making their claim known.[53] This shrine stands as clear evidence of the importance of intercity rivalry in the development of the sibylline tradition, and Pausanias' digression, and possibly also a passage in Tacitus' *Annals,* show that the rivalry was already a long-standing one by the time this shrine was erected.[54] The explicit connection between this structure and the arrival of Lucius Verus may also reflect a link between this competition and the interest that Romans would naturally have had in Herophile, for her oracles were certainly among those taken back to Rome in 76 B.C.

In light of the evolution of local traditions, it is not surprising that Varro's list had little to do with the actual oracles. It is perhaps more interesting that his research also seems to have had nothing to do with two other aspects of sibylline representation at Rome: the physical appearance of the Sibyl, and descriptions of her inspiration.

Readers of Augustan and Silver Latin literature are familiar with the notion of the Sibyl (bottled or otherwise) as the epitome of old age. People who wanted to be flattering might exploit this image to say: "May old age never wish to mar this countenance even if she reaches the age of the Cumaean prophetess" (Prop. 2.2.15–16); the rude might remark: "You were not yet measuring the ages of the Euboean Sibyl; she was older than you by three months" (Mar. 9.29.3–4). Although it is not specific on this point, the *Aeneid* implies that the Cumaean Sibyl was well established in the Italian landscape by the time Aeneas arrived, while Ovid adopts a notion of that Sibyl's age that appears in various Greek texts, including a passage attributed to the Erythraean Sibyl by Phlegon.[55] But this may not always have been the case. We cannot know what the ancient statues of the Sibyl in the Forum looked like, but they are said to have been the oldest at Rome, and thus they may have looked like the archaic *korai* of Greece (assuming that Pliny's statement was based upon the observation that these statues did not look like the work of the later fifth century or later) and thus like young to middle-aged women (Pliny *NH* 34.22). These statues may help to explain why, on coins issued by L. Manlius Torquatus in 65 B.C., the Sibyl (identified thus by the coin's legend) appears as a young woman (*RRC* no. 411). Whatever the appearance of the statues, these coins certainly suggest that the image of the Sibyl

5. A coin depicting the Sibyl. In this case, as in
other pre-Augustan depictions, the Sibyl appears to
be a young woman (*RRC* 411; photo courtesy of
the American Numismatic Society).

as an old woman had not yet become standard in Italy. The adoption of this image may have been the result of the embassy sent by the Senate to the east in 76 B.C., which was to assemble a new collection of oracles to replace the one lost during the fire in 83 that destroyed the temple of Capitoline Jupiter. The most important source for these poems appear to have been cities that claimed to be the birthplace of the Sibyl Herophile, and it may be that her image as a very old woman thereafter came to be the dominant image in the popular imagination. But this had not yet become firmly established in the 60s.

Varro tells us nothing about how he thought his Sibyls were inspired, although it is interesting that he has nothing to say about Apollo. As we have seen, views on this subject were many and varied. So it is perhaps not surprising that in the texts themselves, Sibyls suggest a number of possibilities. The Sibyl whose words are preserved by Phlegon says that the gift of prophecy was hers, and that Apollo, overcome by jealousy, shot her down.[56] The poem about the Sibyl Herophile, inscribed on the sibylline shrine at Erythrae, says that she was the daughter of a nymph and thus able to speak of her own free will (and that she started doing so immediately after her birth).[57] A similar declaration is made for Herophile in verses cited at Alexandria Troas, the other city that claimed to be her birthplace.[58] The Sibyl in the *Third Oracle* of the extant collection says that she repeated the secrets revealed by God to her father, Noah, on the Ark, after God had placed these same secrets in her own mind so that she could prophesy. In other poems, other Sibyls speak as if they were compelled by a divinity.[59]

The variation in beliefs about sibylline inspiration is of some interest for the picture of the Sibyl in Augustan poetry, for Augustus adopted the tradition that she spoke under the influence of Apollo. The point was made very plain when he transferred the oracles from the temple of Capitoline Jupiter to that of Palatine Apollo, and it also seems to be reflected in the relief of an altar that appears to be based upon the sculptural program of the latter temple. It depicts Apollo, Latona, and Diana, with an exhausted Sibyl on the ground before them. The temple of Palatine Apollo was dedicated on 9 October 28 B.C., and the connection very rapidly found its way into literature.[60]

THE ISSUE OF AUTHENTICITY

Given the diversity in sibylline biography, inspiration, and appearance, how did a person know that a text was authentic? Constantine said that the sibylline texts he cited must be authentic because they were morally improving (*Orat. ad Sanctos* 19.1); Varro thought that a specific form of composition, the use of acrostics, was a useful guide; but the question cannot be left there. Very little in the extant corpus corresponds with Constantine's method of authentication, almost nothing corresponds with that suggested by Varro, and the fact of their existence guarantees that many people thought the texts in the surviving collections were authentic. In fact all prophets could say very similar things in terms of content, and they had a tendency to repeat not only themselves but also one another.

The present sibylline corpus offers a number of examples in which words attributed to a Sibyl can be found in verses attributed to other prophets, or to more than one Sibyl. In line 361 of the current *Eighth Oracle* the Christian God claims to know the number of the sands and the measure of the sea. This is exactly the same line that appears at the beginning of a response given by the Pythia to Croesus.[61] In lines 163–171 of the *Eleventh Oracle* the Delphic Sibyl says that her words will instruct Homer. The Jewish Sibyl makes the same claim with many of the same words in the *Third Oracle*.[62] She states that she will be incorrectly known as the Erythraean Sibyl—and this prophecy is known to have occurred in works that were definitely attributed to the Erythraean Sibyl.[63] The same prediction about Samos and Delos—Samos will be sand, Delos obscure—occurs with slightly different wording in the *Third, Fourth* and *Eighth Oracles*.[64] In a somewhat parallel case Zosimus confessed that he did not know if verses he cited on the foundation of Constantinople were those of Phaennis or the Erythraean Sibyl[65]—presumably because the same lines were ascribed to both.

The explanation for the repetition outlined in the last paragraph lies in the method of composition: the long texts that have survived are manifestly compilations of shorter passages. These passages were themselves written by people who tended to draw heavily on other oracular texts for their inspiration, taking lines or portions of lines from these texts to fill out their own prophecies.[66] Readers do not seem to have drawn a connection between the hermeneutic process and the content: they seem to have preferred to believe that different prophets spoke in the same way.

There was a link between the various mantics not only in the ways in which they were inspired and in how they spoke, but also in the nature of the matter they predicted. Although only three examples have survived—one in the work of Zosimus and two in that of Phlegon—the greatest number of the sibylline texts recorded in antiquity prescribed cult activities.[67] This, as we have seen, was also a major function of the various oracular centers and other mantics. Sibyls, the prophets at oracular centers, and other holy individuals could reveal the nature of god and could predict all manner of events. The only reason why answers to more mundane questions about life were not obtained from Sibyls is simply that there usually were none available to give them. Aeneas' visit to the Sibyl, Trimalchio's alleged sighting of the Sibyl, and the Shepherd of Hermas' misidentification of the spirit of the church as the Cumaean Sibyl indicate that there was no questioning of a Sibyl's capacity to give such answers.[68] The way in which sibylline books were consulted at Rome indicates that some, at least, were recorded as answers to specific questions; the texts mentioned the prodigy or problems that would be expiated or solved by the answers that the oracle prescribed.

Given the wide variety of sibylline activity and the inadequacy of Constantine's or Varro's methods of verifying sibylline oracles for explaining the extant evidence, it comes as no surprise to find that many people used less demanding criteria. The main consideration was that the prophet could be found to have been right about something in the past that the reader knew about—but that happened after the prophet's lifetime or prediction. This principle has already been seen at work in connection with established oracles in Chapter 1: why it should be necessary to enumerate all the events that had been predicted by oracles, prophets, prophetesses, and other inspired persons—the legitimacy of such people was obvious from the fact that the things they had predicted had come true (Orig. *Contra Cels.* 8.45). Plutarch twice remarked on the inspiration of the Sibyl who had predicted the eruption of Vesuvius; Pausanias mentioned a famous prophecy of Herophile "which we know came true."[69] Both Constantine and Lactantius argued that the prophecies of Christ's coming that were being found during their lifetimes in the texts of the Sibyls were not forgeries. The problem was simply that these verses had not been previously recognized for what they were (*Orat. ad Sanctos* 19.2; Lact. *DI* 4.15.28).

Many were willing to take oracular texts at face value—if a text read like an oracle, and, even better, if it contained some reference to an event the reader knew had happened, he or she might easily accept it as genuine. Dio relates that Caracalla was so taken by the sound of one verse that he refused to believe it had been forged even after the author had admitted to it (79.16.8). If a person was more interested in the truth than Caracalla had been on that occasion, it was necessary to find out some details of the prophet's life. As Lactantius wrote in the *Divine Institutes,* the discerning seeker after divine wisdom should find out when the prophet lived and how much of what that prophet had predicted had come true (*DI* 4.5.4). This point not only is of great importance for evaluating the historical content of some sibylline oracles, but also recalls the problem set somewhat earlier: how did someone discover which prophet was which and when each lived?

The answer is provided in the first instance by Lactantius, who noted that there were many separate books produced by each Sibyl, but that because they were inscribed only with the name "Sibyl," they were believed to be the work of one person. Only the works of the Erythraean Sibyl could be distinguished, because this woman had included some lines about herself in the poem (*DI* I.6.13).[70] The same answer is provided by Pausanias when he said that he found out about Herophile from what she had written in her poems. It is provided yet again by the attribution of the *Fourth Eclogue,* in both Lactantius' *Divine Institutes* and Constantine's *Oration to the Blessed,* to the Cumaean Sibyl.[71] The clue was provided by line 5: the last age predicted in the Cumaean song has come. In the extant corpus there are a number of passages that are biographical, and, as noted above, there are numerous examples of this kind of verse picked up at various points in scholarly and literary traditions. Some of them relate to community debate; others are evidently connected with discussion of the value of assertions found in other circulating books. Given that most oracles probably came onto the market through chresmologues, these may reflect little more than ancient marketing strategies. An example of this sort of text stands at the end of the *Third Oracle,* where the Sibyl states that people will wrongly say that she is mad and that she is the daughter of Circe and Gnostos (809–829). The point of these lines is to prove that poems in which the Erythraean Sibyl described herself as coming from other parents were fraudulent, and to identify the Sibyl as a prophetess who spoke for the Jews. This and the other passages serve as guides to their readers and, in at least this case, as potential guides away from fakes.

The first indications readers had that their texts were the genuine article were very straightforward: labels on the book saying "Sibyl" or lines within the poems identifying the writer. But this need not have been all. Since readers were concerned that there be things in the poems that could be shown to be correct, it would be helpful if there were past events or points of doctrine that could be recognized. This could satisfy lingering doubts about authenticity.

THE CHRISTIAN SIBYL

Lactantius and Constantine were not the first Christian readers of the *Sibylline Oracles,* and they were certainly not the last. The Sibyl's intimate connection with Rome made her a natural choice for Christians who sought evidence from pagan sources for the truth of their beliefs. Her earliest appearance, in the vision of *The Shepherd of Hermas,* where the shepherd thinks that the old woman he meets is the Cumaean Sibyl (he soon learns that she is the church), is merely a reflection of the Sibyl's general importance. With the development of the apologetic tradition, she begins to appear with more frequency and in her own right.[72] In Clement of Alexandria and Justin Martyr, both writing in the mid-second century, the Sibyl is mentioned as an example of western prophecy to balance the Hebrew prophets and the "eastern tradition" represented by Hydaspes.[73] By the end of the century she is beginning to appear even more prominently. Theophilus of Antioch quotes extensive sections from sibylline oracles in a work addressed to a man named Autolycus, and, slightly earlier, Athenagoras had noted the value of sibylline prophecy in his address to Marcus Aurelius (pointing out that she had been mentioned by Plato, and thus was a suitable character to introduce into a work putatively addressed to a philosophic monarch).[74] On the Latin side, Tertullian gave the Sibyl a prominent place just before the climactic exposition of Christian doctrine in one version of his *Apology,* written in 197.[75] This is evidently no more than the tip of an oracular iceberg.

"If you had put forward the Sibyl, whom some of you use, as a child of God," wrote Celsus, "you would have had more to be said in your favor. However, you have had the presumption to insert blasphemous things into her verses . . ." (Orig. *Contra Cels.* 7.53). Origen, secure in the knowledge that his deceased literary rival could not answer back, challenged Celsus to point to the interpolations, comparing new copies with old (*Contra Cels.* 7.56). As was the case with other examples of polytheistic literature that

they quoted, the intellectual fathers of the church were not necessarily interested in creating a canon (that had already been done
by generations of rhetoricians), but rather in reflecting and con-
densing what was there into a manageable form. The Sibyl gains a
place in their works because she was more famous than any other
seer. Others, even prophets who had once been accorded greater
respect, disappear. We hear no more, for instance, of Bakis, in the
Christian world, and no more of characters like Phaeno, Linus, or
Musaeus, who are all accorded respect by a man like Pausanias.
But, once approved, the sibylline corpus itself could continue to
grow. Indeed, the two extant collections of sibylline oracles in
Greek hexameters, which date to the late fifth and early seventh
centuries respectively, stand as excellent examples of the fluidity of
the tradition. In their present form they contain individual passages
that can be traced back to the Hellenistic period, to Jewish and
polytheistic as well as Christian hands.

There are eight oracles in the first of these collections, which
dates to the reign of the emperor Zeno; the second collection appears to have been assembled after the final Arab conquest of Egypt
in 646 and is extremely fragmentary: parts of only seven texts (numbered 9 through 15) from an original containing at least fifteen have
survived.[76] Of these texts, the *Eleventh* through *Fourteenth Oracles,*
which contain dynastic prophecies, are the most complete, and are
of a very different sort from the eschatological and ethical texts in
the other collection. The *Eleventh Oracle* gives an account of the
history of the world up to the fall of the Ptolemies, the *Twelfth* and
Thirteenth give the history of Rome from Augustus to the victory
of Odaenathus of Palmyra over the Persians in the 260s, and the
Fourteenth appears to contain a number of dynastic oracles that were
compiled to provide background for a prophecy of the Arab conquest. Their value as examples of the use of prophecy as political
commentary will be discussed in a later chapter.

Three oracles in the first collection are overtly Christian. The
remains of books 1 and 2 provide a history of the world from the
Creation to the Last Judgment, organized in a very rough approx-
imation to a scheme of ten generations.[77] The *First Oracle* describes
the first seven generations, the life of Christ, and concludes with

an attack on the Jews. The *Second Oracle* opens with the tenth generation and moves on to describe events connected with the Judgment Day. It also contains a long extract of hexameter *sententia* of Pseudo-Phocylides. The *Sixth Oracle* is a short hymn to Christ. The *Third Oracle* contains some Ptolemaic material, some material that can be dated to the period after Actium, and some material— such as an extraordinary account of the war between the gods and the Titans (105–155) and numerous prophecies against various nations—that cannot be dated with any hope of precision.[78] The preservation of such diverse material indicates that texts with overtly Jewish content were still acceptable to Christians on the grounds that they provided Old Testament material that dated the Sibyl to deepest antiquity, and thus demonstrated the truth of Christian doctrine. A great number of lines appearing in this oracle are also cited by early Christian authors, especially by Lactantius in his *Divine Institutes;* but it cannot be shown that these quotations come from a text directly connected with this one.[79]

The *Fourth, Fifth, Seventh,* and *Eighth Sibylline Oracles* are eschatological texts. The *Fourth Oracle* provides a history of the world in accordance with two quite distinct patterns: one is that of ten generations, with the world ending in the tenth; the other is that of four empires, with the world ending during the rule of a fifth. The two patterns are not reconciled in this text with any ease. The first four empires, those of the Assyrians, the Medes, the Persians and the Macedonians, take up all ten generations; the Assyrians get six, the Medes two, the Persians and the Macedonians one each. There is nothing left for the fifth kingdom, which is Rome. The eschatological pattern is further complicated by the timing of the end of the world after the destruction of an allegorical Jerusalem, itself occurring in the context of the return of Nero.[80] The doctrinal confusion evident in this oracle provides a very good example of how material could be transferred from one context to another by various compilers who did not have a thorough understanding of the contents. The main appeal of this oracle in its final version may well have been no more than that it contained a number of recognizable eschatological motifs. The *Fifth Oracle* opens with a fifty-one-line précis of world history from the end of the pharaohs to the reign of Hadrian. The rest of the text is taken up with a long series of prophecies against various nations, the return of Nero, the coming of a savior, and the destruction of the world.[81]

The *Seventh Oracle* contains a number of prophecies of world destruction, suggestions on the form of prayer, a prophecy of the coming of the Messiah, and a prophecy of the baptism of Christ. It concludes with an autobiographical statement by the Sibyl.[82] The *Eighth Oracle* opens with 216 lines that predict the end of the world in the middle of the second century A.D.[83] The end of line 216 is lost in a lacuna, and there is a sudden change of matter in line 217 to the exposition of Christian doctrine. This includes a long poem on Christ, a further description of eschatological disturbances, a speech by God on the evils of idolatry (containing two echoes of the Delphic oracle's first response to Croesus),[84] a hymn to God, and a discussion of the incarnation of Christ. It concludes with a general exhortation to ethical and ritual purity.[85] Lines 217–250 are the most interesting part of this poem, for they provide an acrostic on the words "Jesus Christ son of God savior cross" that is known in slightly different versions from a number of sources. A section of this acrostic was included by Constantine in his address to an assembly of bishops at Antioch in 325, the earliest record of its appearance. Since Constantine's speech is otherwise influenced by Lactantius' *Divine Institutes,* which shows no knowledge of this oracle, and since the *Divine Institutes* reveal that the sum of its author's knowledge of Christian sibylline texts that were in circulation at the beginning of the fourth century, it may be possible to date the composition of the acrostic precisely to the period between 308/ 9, when the *Divine Institutes* was finished, and 325.

This acrostic then took on something of a life of its own. In *The City of God,* Augustine says that he knew a bad Latin translation of the text, and that he had done a better one on the basis of a text that he received from Flaccianus, the governor of *Africa proconsularis,* in 393 (*Civ. Dei* 18.23).[86] This version nonetheless lacked the final section of the acrostic, based on the Greek word *stauros* (cross). Another translation of this acrostic, a much more skillful one in that, unlike Augustine's text, it gives a viable Latin acrostic, was produced on the basis of a complete Greek version in Britain during the late eighth century.[87] Although Augustine's version of the acrostic had no influence upon this later tradition, his summary of oracles connected with the Passion, an account that was explicitly derived from Lactantius, did take on an independent life of its own, forming the basis of a short text known simply as *The Sayings of the Great Sibyl,* which appears to have been in circulation within a generation or so of the completion of *The City of God.* Two additional bits of Latin sibyllina came into existence at about the same time (late fourth to early fifth centuries). One is a translation of a text resembling the *Eighth Sibylline Oracle;* the other is a poem of 136 lines covering a number of subjects of interest to the pious, with no direct connection with any extant Greek text.[88]

The Latin sibylline oracles mentioned above were not the only texts in that language, and it was certainly recognized that there were sibylline verses for which no home had been found in a Christian context. This is presumably the reason why Stilicho burned the collection on the Capitoline in the early years of the fifth century.[89] But some well-placed Romans appear to have retained an affection for these texts, to have collected some for private consultation, and occasionally to have used them as a basis for advising their Christian neighbors. Not all these texts were sibylline—it would appear that some Etruscans who claimed to have preserved the art of the *haruspices* devised ceremonies that allegedly saved the city of Narnia in 408—but some certainly were, and the cave at Cumae remained a tourist attraction until at least 552.[90] In that year the Byzantine general Narses used the cave as the starting point for his tunnel under a Gothic fort that was located above it (Agath. 1.10). The description of his operations by the historian Agathias makes it clear that the cave was still on display. Procopius says that in 536 "some patricians" provided the general Beliarius with an inaccurate Latin sibylline oracle while he was besieged in Rome. Further inspection of their texts does not seem to have impressed him:

in my opinion it is impossible for a mortal man to discover the meaning of the Sibyl's oracles before the actual event. The reason for this I shall now set forth, having read all the oracles in question.

The Sibyl does not invariably mention events in their order, much less construct a well-arranged narrative, but after uttering some verse or other concerning the troubles in Libya she leaps straightway to the land of Persia, thence procedes to mention the Romans, and then transfers the narrative to the Assyrians. And while again uttering prophecies about the Romans, she foretells the misfortunes of the Britons. For this reason it is impossible for any man soever to comprehend the oracles of the Sibyl before the event, and it is only time itself, after the event has already come to pass and the words can be tested by experience, that can show itself an accurate interpreter of her sayings.   (*BG* 1.24.33–37 Loeb trans.)

Centuries before Procopius penned (or dictated, as was the usual practice for an ancient author) these lines concerning the sibylline oracles at Rome, a new format for sibylline prophecy had already become a fashionable tool for political commentary. This format was connected with the Tiburtine Sibyl. The earliest version of the Tiburtine Sibyl's oracle appears to have come into existence, in Greek, very shortly after the annihilation of the eastern Roman army under the emperor Valens at Adrianople in 378.[91] Soon after this it was translated into Latin, and from that point onward numerous divergent traditions developed. In the Greek version the text is presented as the "record of the Sibyl, who by revelation explained the dream of the hundred judges of the great city of Rome." It is then said that when the Sibyl came to Rome, everyone came to see her, and the hundred judges came to her asking that she interpret a dream that they had all had. She took them up to the Capitol and asked them to report the dream. They told her that they had seen different suns. These, she tells them, represent nine ages of man. The first six ages bring the history of the world down to the accession of Theodosius, the seventh age comprises the first half of the fifth century down to Gaiseric's sack of the city in 455, the eighth age spans the reigns of Leo and Anastasius, while the ninth offers an eschatological vision of the end of the world.

With the passing of time, the sibylline exposition of the first eight ages became much shorter, and much of the detail disappeared as it ceased to be of interest to later generations of authors. So too, the introductory material and the contents of the final generation might expand, contract, and change as readers needed, desired, or lost information about the Sibyl. In the western Latin tradition, a summary catalogue of Sibyls was added to the beginning (based on Lactantius' description of the Sibyls in the *Divine Institutes,*) followed by a brief tale of the Sibyl's wanderings up until the time that an embassy was sent to bring her to Rome. And in one of the two recently published Old French versions of the text (dating to the late twelfth or early thirteenth century), the Sibyl becomes a queen who prophesied in nine kingdoms before delivering her interpretation of nine dreams of nine sages at Rome.[92] In the eastern tradition, represented by texts in Ethiopic and Arabic, there is no sibylline catalogue, and the Sibyl becomes the daughter of Heraclius. In a recently discovered Arabic manuscript, the introduction is as follows:

> An abridged account of the words of the wise, pure Sibyl, daughter of Heraclius, head of the heathens of Ephesus, in Alexandria, being her interpretation of the dreams of certain priests in the city of Rome which they saw there; the priests numbered one hundred. They all saw in the same night dreams which were alike in form and significance. They informed the king of Rome, who said, "we desire someone who can interpret this vision for us."[93]

These eastern versions, which also extend into the twelfth century, appear to have emerged from the surviving Coptic community in Egypt and, together with the Old French texts, represent the last examples of the use of the Late Roman prophetic form in the High Middle Ages. The continuity is remarkable testimony to the value of the Tiburtine format for social and political commentary throughout these centuries.

Readers and Writers of Prophetic Texts in the Roman Empire

The vast diversity of traditions surveyed in this chapter is impossible to set in any one social context. The range of texts mirrors the range of interests across the span of literate society and its fringes in the Roman world. At one end, the corpus of oracular texts was influenced by technical works of philosophy, theology, and other literature. At the other end of the scale, traditions of oral storytelling could, and did, have a significant impact on the form of some texts, and are partially responsible for continued interest in some traditions.

One of the problems inherent in trying to say much more than this is that it is very difficult to define or describe the "literate society of the Roman empire and its fringes." According to one estimate, the number of fully functional literates, those capable of reading and writing a simple statement about themselves, rarely exceeded 10 percent of the population in any part of the empire outside Italy.[94] This estimate may be too low, but it does seem to be the case that the vast majority of people in the empire were not fully literate in either of the languages of government, Greek and Latin. This does not mean that they lacked the capacity to read and write their own languages. There is certainly evidence for continued writing in Phoenician, Aramaic, Hebrew, Demotic Egyptian, Coptic, and Syriac. We know less about writing in the languages of Celtic Europe, but here too we may assume that there continued to be some. Furthermore, there is a well-attested tendency in modern society for people who are literate in their native language to be illiterate in their second tongue and, further, for people who are multilingual to be illiterate in all the languages that they speak.[95] It is therefore misleading to measure cultural diffusion in terms of actual literacy in Greek and Latin. This is even more the case when even the lowest estimate of those literate in Greek and Latin is compared with a reasonable estimate of those who were literate before the advent of Hellenistic and then Roman administration. Literacy in Greek and Latin among even 10 percent of the population would be a tremendous increase over literacy in previous periods (where rates around one percent may be too high) and would imply that there might have been as many as six million people capable of writing Greek or Latin in the empire as a whole in the second century.[96] Such people clearly existed in sufficient numbers to influence the views of their fellows and, as was often the case, to control their behavior. Moreover, the association of the written word with Roman power seems to have convinced people that they needed to know the languages themselves. The use of inscribed tombstones in the Roman fashion throughout the empire, even in places where such commemoration had not been used before, is perhaps the most powerful illustration of this point.[97] The Roman empire was an empire of the written word. The emperors communicated with their subjects through a combination of the written word, visual art, buildings, and ceremonies. Their subjects may have responded vocally at first (when they did not do things like tear imperial edicts off walls), but their responses also found their way into writing in oracular form. As religious language provided the vocabulary for conceptualizing temporal power, so too it provided a natural format for authorizing responses to the actions of the powerful. To retain their authority they had to be written down. The use of ancient and revered prophetic figures or prophetic forms gave responses in the present instant authority as the wisdom of a respected member of cultured society.

A survey of oracles in the ancient world would be glaringly incomplete without the figure of the "oracle monger," the *chresmologos*.[98] The *chresmologos* did not claim authority as a prophet for himself (as far as we know this seems to have been an overwhelmingly male profession): his claim to importance rested upon his credibility as an accurate purveyor of ancient wisdom. As denizens of the streets or aristocratic waiting-rooms, they are rarely named or described in the sources. But their presence may be divined behind statements to the effect that "oracles everywhere predict his power over the world" (*FGrH* 80 fr. 36.50) or that the Roman people were disturbed by a prediction of the end of the city (Dio 57.18). Their presence may also be detected behind acts of government such as Augustus' gathering of 2,000 books of prophecy that he had burned in the Forum as improper (Suet. *Aug.* 31).[99] We may safely assume that he did not plunder the libraries of senators and equestrians to find them, but rather that he had some *chresmologoi* rounded up so that he could seize their books. So too in A.D. 19, when Tiberius ordered an investigation of "all the books that contained any prophecies," for public inspection, we may assume that he was concerned to find people whose recitations were stirring up crowds in the streets, and that these people were not members of the governing class (Dio 57.18.5). We cannot know where Caninius Gallus got the sibylline book that he had placed in the collection at Rome in A.D. 32 (Tac. *Ann.* 6.12), but it is more than likely that he received it from someone whom he considered a reputable dealer in prophetic wisdom. This is not to say that members of the high aristocracy could not buy such books for themselves: Pausanias clearly knew people who could provide him with the prophetic books that he read. These are not the sort of things that would have been found in city libraries. The various Greek prophetic texts that have been discovered on papyri show that books of this sort were kept in private hands, for personal study and, no doubt discussion. We may also be certain that the possessors of these books rarely or never wrote these prophecies themselves. They bought them, and, like the *chresmologoi* who sold them, they communicated their contents to others. The process of transmission is therefore neither purely "literary," nor is it "oral"; it was the ubiquitous *chresmologos* who spread the wisdom of the inspired sages throughout ancient society. In the next two chapters, these people will appear time and again on the fringes of aristocratic society.

The notional authors of prophetic books were respected cultural figures. This is why, for example, sibylline shrines could be important tourist attractions, and sibylline books that were not part of the official collection at Rome were thought to be good things for Christians to cite in order to impress theological antagonists.[100] The Sibyl was thought by Ammianus to be remarkable, her works were studied by Pausanias, cited as authoritative by the author of a commentary on Alcaeus, and discussed with approval by Plutarch.[101] Aelius Aristides and Dio Chrysostom also cited her with respect as a prophet whose words were to treated with honor.[102] Ancient prophets had a respected place in the world of the local aristocrats of the Greek east. The readers and authors were plainly people of some standing in their communities. The quality of the Greek, in both prose and verse, does not suggest that people like Pausanias would sit down to write such things themselves; they were more likely to have been composed by the sort of local dignitary who would take him on his tour of a famous site.

Oracular books were a feature of the literate environment of the Roman empire. They provided material for discussion, comfort, and information both for members of the highest aristocracy and for the humble inhabitants of the cities and countryside. Their importance stems from the fact that they provided a format for the communication of difficult, interesting, and, at times, dangerous ideas in such a way that people who lived in a world where the constant intervention of divine powers was taken as a fact of life could relate to them. They provided a constant reminder to people in all walks of life that the gods or God cared about them, their present circumstances, and their future.

[3]

Prophecy and the Informed Public

> Therefore, let us praise god, but next let us descend to
> those who have received their scepters from him. We
> began with kings, and the practice we had with them
> also accustomed us to giving panegyrics and singing
> reverent hymns to the almighty, so we must first begin
> our praise with god and use it as training and then ex-
> ercise the training through god; the purpose is to have
> in us the exercise of reverence for god as well as praise
> for kings. We must also render them compensation for
> spreading before us the prosperity that comes of such
> great peace. A king's virtue—indeed his name alone—
> is the arbiter of peace. For a king is so called from the
> light step with which he sets his foot even upon the
> highest authority, because he achieves dominion over
> the discourse that brings peace, and because he was
> born to outdo barbarian kingship inasmuch as his name
> is the token of peace. (*CH* 18.15–16 trans. Copen-
> haver)

THIS PANEGYRIC, possibly datable to the beginning of the fourth
century A.D., which is found at the end of a tractate in the collection
of wisdom known as the *Corpus Hermeticum,* is impressive evidence
for the all-pervasive nature of imperial propaganda in the Roman
empire. For centuries, Rome's subjects had been told that their
safety resided with the emperor, and for centuries they had responded, in public, with soothing echoes of the imperial message.

The power of the Roman government, and claims to that power, were projected by a variety of media. The Roman emperor was not simply "what the emperor did"; he was an image in the eyes of his subjects. This image remained extraordinarily consistent throughout the centuries between Augustus and Constantine. The fact that it did so is remarkable testimony to Augustus' success in forging an idiom for the expression of power; it is also testimony to his ability to exploit the wide range of media available in a complex society to broadcast his vision. But not even Augustus could ensure that it would always be taken the way that he meant it to be.

Oracular Responses to History

Faced with a mass of visual and verbal information about their rulers, the inhabitants of the Roman empire turned to the gods and the sages of the past to provide an interpretative framework for it all. The gods and sages were implicitly concerned with power, and their words could distill complex matters into more readily comprehensible forms. Their words could situate contemporary events in broader patterns of human history and divine intention. These words could either validate or undermine the message of public discourse.[1]

A number of different schemes could be used in order to determine the importance of any event. Some of these depended upon numbers that were thought, for one reason or another, to be significant, in that they indicated the number of years that would pass between one great moment and another. The issue may be illustrated by the problem that arose when the consul Norbanus, who had always been devoted to the trumpet, played his instrument at dawn on the first of January A.D. 19, and a statue of Janus fell down. The connection between these events is somewhat obscure, but Cassius Dio noted that they were obviously linked with the death of Germanicus. He went on to observe that people were disturbed by an oracle reputed to be sibylline that ran "when thrice three hundred revolving years have run their course, civil war and the folly of Sybaris will destroy the Romans," despite the fact that they bore no obvious relation to the duration of Rome. Tiberius was then at great pains to prove that these lines were a fake, but it would appear that his efforts were not thoroughly convincing (Dio 57.18.3–5). For, after the great fire at Rome in 64, the same lines were once again on people's lips, and when Nero reported that these lines were not in the official collection, another sibylline verse began to circulate. It ran, "Last of the sons of Aeneas, a mother-slayer will rule," and Dio observed that it proved true even if it could not be established whether it was truly an inspired remark of ancient days or one that the people were divinely inspired by contemporary events to utter.[2] The continued interest in these lines may be a reflection of general interest in the number 900, displayed by a contemporary as a reasonable length of time for Rome's existence. A scholiast on line 564 of the first book of Lucan's poem on the civil war identifies a "fearful prophecy of the Cumaean prophet that was spread abroad amongst the people" as a sibylline oracle predicting the end of Rome after 900 years, and, two generations later, Juvenal mentions nine ages of iron that will give way to a golden age (13.28–30).[3]

The interest in this prophecy may have been enhanced by its evident connection with a scheme that divided world history into ten *saecula*. A *saeculum* was defined as the span of the longest human life in a generation, or defined by the life span of the last person to die who had been present at the foundation of a city, or, more simply, defined as a generation.[4] There was some feeling that the world would end after ten of them. This scheme was kept very much in the minds of the Roman people by the celebration of a festival to commemorate the change of a *saeculum*, the *ludi saeculares*, and it is interesting that the consul of A.D. 19 should have sparked speculation along these lines by blowing a trumpet. In 88 B.C. the senate had consulted the haruspices about the beginning of a *saeculum* when it was alleged that a trumpet blast had been heard from heaven.[5] It was remembered as presaging the horrendously destructive wars of the Sullan age. In A.D. 61 it was rumored that another blast had been heard in the hills around Capua, just after Nero had ordered the murder of his mother (Tac. *Ann.* 14.10.3). The fact that people thought of the *saeculum* is also testimony to an unwillingness to trust official reckonings of such events. Such an unwillingness may subsequently have been enhanced when Claudius celebrated *ludi saeculares* in 48, revealing that there was a good deal of uncertainty about the proper count in the highest quarters despite Augustus' celebration of the games in 17 B.C. The problem was compounded by Domitian in 88, Septimius Severus' celebration of the *ludi* in 204, and Philip the Arab's problematic celebration of the games in 248. The response to such events in the provinces is perhaps best illustrated by a passage from the Babylonian Talmud observing that "they observe yet another festival in Rome which occurs every seventy years," which is to say every generation, a Jewish understanding of the nature of the *saeculum*.[6]

The use of allegedly significant numbers was a widespread and complex phenomenon. They could be used prospectively, as was the case with the prophecy of weeks in Daniel, the fascination with the number seven manifested by the author of Revelation, or numbers in the Tiburtine Sibyl.[7] Numerical prophecies could also be used as a tool to contextualize contemporary events. This appears to have been a concern of the Egyptian readers of the *Oracle of the Potter,* when they speculated on the identity of the kings of two and fifty-five years (pages 194–199 below). It is also what seems to have been the intention of the author of some lines in the current *Thirteenth Sibylline Oracle,* when he contemplated Philip the Arab's celebration of the millennium in 248:

> so shall the Persians be very far from victory at that time, as long as the dear nurse of the Italians situated in the plain by the renowned stream of the Nile shall bear the portion of the harvest to seven-hilled Rome. The limit for this has been set. For your name contains in numbers the expanse of time allotted to you, Rome, and for that number of years will the great godlike city of the Macedonian king willingly provide you with grain.

An author writing in 248 would have known that Rome had not yet ruled Egypt for the number of years in the name of Rome (948), and thus that the millennium did not spell the imminent collapse of Rome.[8] Another author, whose words are preserved in the current *Twelfth Sibylline Oracle,* introduced a prediction of dis-

6. A list of emperors from Augustus to the first year of Decius (A.D. 249) giving the total number of years as 268 (instead of 280). It omits six emperors and is an excellent example of the difficulty that people had in knowing just how long the empire had been in existence (*P. Oxy.* 35; photo courtesy of the University Museum, University of Pennsylvania).

aster following upon the death of Commodus in 192 with the words:

> My heart weeps, my heart weeps within me, from the time when the first king, proud Rome, established noble law among earthbound mortals . . . until the death of the nineteenth king, twice two hundred, twice twenty, twice two to which six months are added will fill out the time of years.[9]

This count gives 52 or 51 B.C. (depending upon when news of Commodus' death on December 31 would have been known) as the beginning of the empire, suggesting that the author may have been more concerned with producing an impressive-sounding number (the Greek *dis hekaton dis eikosi dis duo* has a nice ring to it) than with actually counting the years, and, possibly, that he was conscious of the fact that something less than 250 years had actually passed. The Christian apologist Theophilus seems to have used a similar impressionistic count when he stated that 225 years had passed between Caesar and Lucius Verus in 165 (*Ad Aut.* 3.27). These numbers acted as symbols, "forms within which to organize everyday reality," and, as such, they allowed people to come "into contact with essential dimensions of transcendent reality," revealing what was truly important.[10]

The interest in the number 900 in first-century A.D. Rome suggests that careful count of the number of years from the foundation of the city (a point that was open to dispute anyway) was not of great importance to the readers of prophetic texts, readers who might anyway place greater faith in prophetic computations than in those of scholars. Thus it is not surprising to find similar lack of concern with texts that seem to have been first circulated in the Greek east. This is perhaps best illustrated by some lines in the current *Eighth Sibylline Oracle* where a prophecy concerning the end of Rome is connected with the emperor Hadrian:[11]

When the sixth generation of Latin kings will complete its last life and leave its scepter, another king of this race will reign, who will rule over the entire earth, and hold power over the scepter; and he will rule well in accordance with the command of the great god; the children and the generation of the children of this man will be safe from violation according to the prophecy of the cyclic time of years.

When there will have been fifteen kings of Egypt, then, when the phoenix of the fifth span of years will have come . . . there will arise a race of destructive people, a race without laws, the race of the Hebrews. Then Ares will plunder Ares, and he will destroy the insolent boast of the Romans, for at that time the luxuriant rule of the Romans will be destroyed, ancient queen over conquered cities. The plain of fertile Rome will no longer be victorious when rising to power from Asia, together with Ares, he comes. He will arise, arranging all these things in the city from top to bottom. You will fill out three times three hundreds and forty and eight cycling years when an evil, violent fate will come upon you, filling out your name. (*Orac. Sib.* 8.131–150)

One prophecy, that concerning the "sixth generation of Latin kings," is plainly concerned with the Flavians: Nero was the sixth Caesar (counting from Julius Caesar again), and it would appear that it was written before the death of Vespasian, since it mentions his children without saying that they actually reigned. The next line shifts abruptly to the time of either Hadrian (the fifteenth emperor, starting with Caesar and including Galba, Otho and Vitellius, the three short-lived emperors of A.D. 69 who are included in counts of emperors that appear in the *Fifth* and *Twelfth Sibylline Oracles*) or Commodus (if the emperors of 69 are forgotten, as, for instance, they were in Revelation).[12] In order to make his point more clearly, the author has correlated the span of time with periods of the phoenix, the bird who rose from the ashes every 540 years. It is now impossible to know when this author thought the first phoenix had flown, but is of some interest that, if the author was using the date awarded for Rome's foundation by the third-century Greek historian Timaeus, 814 B.C., the 948th year of Rome would fall during the Bar Kokhba revolt in Palestine, while the Varronian date, 753, would give A.D. 195, when Septimius Severus was in the east.

The agent of destruction in the year 948 is a king from the east. It is conventional to identify this figure with the returning Nero (about whom more anon), but this is not a necessary assumption. The idea that Rome would be overwhelmed by such a ruler had been commonplace since the Hellenistic period. Some of the oracles collected by Phlegon refer to this character, and a good deal was made of such prophecies in the year 69, when Vespasian exploited popular expectation of "a king from the east" in his bid for power from his base in Judaea.

Another number that attracted some attention was 365 (quite

possibly because it was the number of days in a Julian year).[13] Thus in the 390s a very interesting story came into vogue to the effect that Peter had ensured through sorcery that Christ would be worshipped for this span of time (Aug. *Civ. Dei* 18.53–54). Traditional believers may have learned from Christians by this time that Christ was thought to have been crucified in A.D. 29, and have been intrigued by the possibility that the great event would occur in 394. The authority for this statement was an oracle, and it is not without interest (and possibly, coincidence) that the overtly anti–Theodosian usurper, Eugenius, appeared on the scene in precisely that year. The choice of this number may even have been influenced by Christian belief or, at least, beliefs current on the fringes of Christianity. A bishop of Brescia named Filastrius, who compiled a list of no fewer than 156 heresies in the 380s, noted one whose devotees thought that the world would end 365 years after the incarnation.[14] Another line, that there were 365 angelic powers ruled by Abrasax (whose own name rather conveniently added up to the same number), had been promoted by the Basilidean gnostics in the second century.[15] The number may not have been without relevance before this in a pagan context: Livy has Camillus observe that the Gauls destroyed Rome precisely 365 years after its foundation (5.54.5).

Significant eras were often used in connection with significant numbers to time the coming of spectacular events. One of the most popular was a scheme of ten ages. It could be connected with *saecula,* the complexities of which have already been noticed, or completely independently, as in the *First, Second,* and *Fourth Sibylline Oracles.* A second scheme is that of the four kingdoms, which appears to have developed on the basis of the tale of the ages of gold, silver, bronze, and iron in Hesiod (pages 186–189 below) and to have enjoyed widespread popularity.

Perhaps the most famous use of this scheme appears in the biblical book of Daniel. This book was widely read in the imperial period by both Christians and Jews who sought to relate it to the imperial period (ultimately attracting considerable criticism from the philosopher Porphyry, whose interest is a sign of the book's importance). The techniques that these readers employed in their reading and updating of their interpretations are of considerable importance in a broader context as an example of the way any text might be handled, even though there are obviously some points in their interpretations that were not necessarily of interest to people who were neither Christians nor Jews. Among these points would be the belief in what may be conveniently referred to as the sabbatical millennium. According to this doctrine, the world would last for 6,000 years because God had created the earth in six days, and a day in the eye of God was 1,000 years of human time. This view was important to some exegetical efforts, and seems to have had the coincidental effect of encouraging a particularly Christian scheme (or schemes, as there were two in circulation by the early fourth century) of measuring time in years from the Creation.

Josephus, who tried to put Jewish history in the best possible light for outsiders, clearly thought very highly of the book of Daniel. In his view, Daniel was important because "he not only was wont to prophesy future things, as did other prophets, but he also fixed the time at which they would come to pass," and he foretold an ultimately happy future (*AJ* 10.267–268). But he also had a few things to say that might prove embarrassing, especially if one adopted, as Josephus clearly did, the view that the empire of iron must be Rome: if the actions of the prophetic object resembled those of a contemporary person or institution, it must represent that person. Thus, as the statue of four metals in Daniel 2 is destroyed by a stone, Josephus contents himself with the statement that "Daniel also revealed to the king the meaning of the stone, but I have not thought it proper to relate this, since I am expected to write of what is past and done and not of what is to be" (*AJ* 10.210). It would never do for a man who was closely connected with the Flavian house to go on about the destruction of the empire even though he seems to have firmly believed that Daniel must be right about it.

On the Christian side, the bishop Hippolytus of Rome, writing on Daniel in the early third century as part of an extensive literary program aimed at ridiculing views that he thought harmful, provides the most important exposition of the text that has survived from that time. He appears to have been a more sophisticated reader than most, and his exegesis is significant both for the amount of its detail and for its clear desire to reconcile the teachings of Daniel with Christian theory. He too is explicit about the meaning of the kingdom of iron, and goes to great trouble assigning periods of time for various of the kingdoms (this was important to him because he wanted to make it as clear as possible that the end of the world and the return of Christ were some time off). Thus he writes that the statue in chapter 2 contained the form of "the empire of the world." At the time of Daniel, he says, "the Babylonians ruled: they are the head of gold of the statue, after them the Persians were masters for 245 years"; next were the Greeks for 300 years; and, finally, "the Romans succeeded them, that is to say, the legs of iron of the statue, because they are strong as iron; then come the digits of the feet, which indicate future democracies, which separate themselves from one another like the ten toes of the statue, composed of iron mixed with clay" (*In Dan.* 2.12).[16] This remarkable view is picked up in Hippolytus' discussion of Daniel's vision of the four beasts (Dan. 7) where he writes that "after the Greek empire, no other will be raised up except that which possesses the domination in our own day and is solidly established: this is a fact evident to all. It has teeth of iron, because it kills and tears to pieces the entire world by its own force, just like the iron. *It destroys those who resist with its feet,* because there remains no empire after it except for the ten horns that grow on it . . ." (*In Dan.* 4.5). He goes on to say that these ten horns correspond to the ten toes on the beast of chapter 2 representing chaos to follow upon the dissolution of empire, which, as he points out, "is not one nation, but an assemblage of all languages and all the races of man; it is a levy of recruits with a view to war" (*In Dan.* 4.8). In the late fourth century Jerome felt no such compunction when he wrote that "its feet and toes are partially of iron, and partially of clay, which is manifestly proved true in this age, for in the beginning there was nothing stronger and harder than the Roman empire, just as in the end there will be nothing weaker, since in civil wars and wars against foreign nations we are dependent upon the aid of other barbarian nations" (*In Dan.* 1.45).

Hippolytus seems to have been interested in arguing that the end was not about to come, and that it would not come while the Roman empire endured, an interesting perspective for one whose lifetime coincided with the beginning of a period of extraordinary chaos; and it is one that he backed up with numbers. He thought that 6,000 years had been allotted to the span of human history, and that 5,500 had passed before the birth of Christ, "and, since the Persians dominated and ruled for 230 years, and after them the Greeks, because they are more notable, ruled for another 300 years, it is therefore necessary that the fourth beast, which is stronger and grander than all those preceding it, have a dominion of 500 years" (*In Dan.* 4.24). He seems to have been moved to this view by the conduct of various contemporaries who had made fools of themselves by setting out to encounter the returning Christ (*In Dan.* 4.18–19).[17]

Hippolytus' interpretations and numerology stop well short of identifying any specific individuals with features of the beast; and it obviously had to, since Hippolytus' point was that the year 6000 was some way off. Others were not so restrained, which is perhaps not surprising since the prophecies of Daniel were written with precisely that end in mind (the ten toes and ten horns that Hippolytus was so interested in were nine Seleucid rulers and one Ptolemy). In this regard, perhaps the most fascinating reading of the text appears in the Genesis Rabbah, where the author (commenting on Gen. 27:40) observes that the sentiment of "From the hand of my brother, who comes against me with the strength of Esau," is "in line with this verse"; "I considered the horns, and behold, there came up among them another horn, a little one, before which three of the first horns were plucked up by the roots" (Dan. 7:8). He justifies this position on the grounds that Daniel is predicting the careers of Odaenathus of Palmyra, the usurpers Macrianus and Quietus, and the brigand Cyriades in the 250s and 260s, in "the wicked realm, which imposes taxes on all the nations of the world."[18] The tendency to identify contemporary figures with well-known prophecies is also illustrated by another mid-third century text, the *Thirteenth Sibylline Oracle,* where the author identifies Cyriades, who evidently played a highly visible role in the Persian capture of Antioch in 252, with the returning Nero.[19] Similarly, Constantine explained that Arius the heretic was the figure whom the Sibyl had predicted as the ruin of Libya (Gelasius *HE* 3.19), and a Christian named Lucan identified Decius as the forerunner of the Antichrist (Cyp. *Ep.* 22.1). Caracalla was immensely pleased to be identified as a beast in an oracular text that was fabricated during his trip to the east (and persisted in mentioning it even after the author identified it as a fake), while a very curious passage in the *Twelfth Sibylline Oracle* ascribes the death of the usurper Avidius Cassius in 175 to another beast, by which the author presumably intended to indicate Marcus Aurelius.[20] This use of prophetic texts is well attested in all ages, but its significance here is that it reveals the way in which people could interpret contemporary history in terms of what, to us, was a murky world of evolving myth connected with various members of the imperial household.

Long-lost members of famous families have an important place in Roman politics from at least the end of the second century B.C., when the revolutionary tribune Saturninus produced a gentleman named L. Equitius, claiming that he was a previously unrecognized son of Gaius Gracchus. In the aftermath of Caesar's murder, the Roman people were fascinated by a "new Marius" until Antony disposed of him.[21] In the reign of Tiberius, a slave named Clemens aroused considerable popular interest when he posed as the recently murdered Agrippa Postumus, and, later, a young man claiming to be Drusus Caesar caused something of a stir in the east before he was arrested and killed.[22] Immediately after the death of Nero, two "false Neros" were apprehended in the east, and a third caused a stir in Roman relations with Parthia during the 80s. In the reign of Elagabalus, a false Alexander toured the Danubian provinces.[23] All these characters represent a tendency to reject or rewrite official versions of imperial history, as well as the place of the imperial household in popular imagination.

This tendency is evident in lines dealing with the reign of Trebonianus Gallus in the *Thirteenth Sibylline Oracle*. It was rumored that Gallus had betrayed Decius to his death in battle against the Goths in 251, and his relations with Decius' surviving son were extremely difficult to understand. At first this son, Hostilianus, reigned as co-emperor with Gallus, while Gallus' own son, Volusianus, was Caesar. This arrangement lasted for a couple of months in the summer of 251. Hostilianus then disappears from the historical record (he is said to have died of the plague). The author of the relevant lines in the *Thirteenth Sibylline Oracle* seems to have been unable to understand this, and simply equips Gallus with a "bastard son," who he says killed him. This author lived in Syria and clearly did not think much of Gallus, in whose reign the Persians ravaged his homeland; his readers seem to have been satisfied.[24]

It is time now to return to the center of power and look in more detail at the ways in which the image of power was communicated to the authors of these texts.

The Emperor's Message

There were essentially two categories of imperial communication: official ad hoc public pronouncements and institutional observances. Public announcement of imperial activity took two forms: verbal and visual. Verbal information was conveyed through the prescripts to edicts and laws, the imperial titulature, and messages for publication through the local imperial authorities. Such documents would have been displayed first in public places where the emperor was resident, as was a ruling on local councillors that Caracalla (211–217) posted on the stoa of Babylon in Egypt (*P. Oxy.* 1406.10–12), the persecution edict of 303 posted outside the imperial palace at Nicomedia, and Julian's discourse on the state of his beard at the Tetrapylon of Antioch.[25] Copies would then be sent to various officials who would in turn post them in the chief cities of their provinces and any other important places.[26] Any city or individual could then copy it or record it in any way that they might wish.[27] The arrival of such a decree seems to have been regarded as an event of much solemnity and some interest. When imperial decrees arrived they were read out, while local inhabitants listened in silence, their heads uncovered. In the Tannaitic commentary on Deuteronomy a rabbi commenting on Deut. 6:5, "which I command thee this day," notes: "they should not be in your eyes like some antiquated edict to which no one pays any attention but like a new edict which everyone runs to read."[28] This text is of particular interest because the setting is a rural area where the languages of government were not those of the natives. But, as the archive of a woman named Babatha, whose papers in Nabataean, Aramaic, and Greek span the period 94–132, shows, the facility to deal with government in its own language was a necessary feature of life, and access to imperial decrees was readily available even beyond the immediate area of Hellenized or Latinate communities.[29]

News traveled by edict with varying efficiency. The persecution edict of 303 moved very quickly. It was posted in Nicomedia on February 24, reached Palestine in March, and Christians in North Africa were being executed on the basis of it by June 5.[30] On the other hand, an edict of Caracalla that was posted at Rome in July 212 was not available in Egypt until February of the next year, and it took nine and a half months for an edict promulgated by Gallienus (253–268) at Naples in 257 to reach Alexandria.[31] These cases, however, all seem to be exceptional. A careful study of the speed with which news of the death of an emperor reached Egypt reveals a mean delay of 57 days if the emperor had died in Italy, and 101 days if he had died outside of Italy (news evidently would travel first to Rome and then be transmitted to the provinces).[32] In all cases the news would travel faster in summer than in winter, and it would travel faster to places that were more closely linked to the capital by the system of imperial supply for Rome. In general terms it might take 30 days for news to travel from Rome to Egypt in the summer, and 80 days in the winter. Off this track, it might be possible for news from Rome to reach a city such as Stratonicea in Asia Minor in 75 days in the summer.[33] Depending on the time of year, therefore, there might ordinarily be a time lag of anywhere between two and four months (six months at the outside) between the time an emperor issued an edict and the time he could expect it to be known to most of the inhabitants of his empire.

Edicts told their readers things about the emperor that he or his advisers thought people should know (for present purposes, the question of how much of a role the emperor personally had in drafting such documents is irrelevant). By the beginning of the second century these would tend to include the emperor's name, his most noteworthy accomplishments, perhaps something about what he believed was important, and what he had been doing recently. The expansion of imperial titulature with the emperor Trajan may be a result of the fact that an emperor who had had extensive provincial service before coming to the throne was more acutely conscious than his predecessors of the propagandistic possibilities inherent in nomenclature, and it was soon widely recognized that the selection of names and titles was a key to understanding what the emperor wanted his subjects to know about him.

Thus, for instance, anyone who had been in communication with Septimius Severus (193–211) would learn that the emperor was an active defender of civilization from a very distinguished family (rather than that he was a usurper descended from the North African aristocracy). Documents emanating from his court were headed Imperator Caesar L. Septimius Severus Pius Pertinax Augustus (a list of however many barbarian nations he claimed to have destroyed by the date of the communication) son of the divine Marcus Antoninus Pius Germanicus Sarmaticus, brother of the divine Commodus, grandson of the divine Antoninus Pius, great-grandson of the divine Hadrian, lineal descendant of the divine Trajan and of the divine Nerva.[34] The fabricated family connection was clearly very important: thus a dedication was set up at Rome to Nerva as Septimius' "ancestor" (*ILS* 418), and Marcus was referred to as "our parent" and Commodus as "brother imperator" in correspondence (*ILS* 423; compare *CJ* 12.35.4).[35] Severus' belief in the importance of titulature is perhaps best illustrated by the observation that the emperor ceased emphasizing the titles that he took from his eastern campaigns when he was concerned about relations with Parthia.[36] Cassius Dio thought that Macrinus (217–218) must have suffered a disaster in his campaign against the Persians when he did not take the title Parthicus, a statement that underlines the significance of Severus' conduct in this regard (Dio 79.27.3). A century later, Constantine (306–337) adopted Claudius Gothicus (268–270) as an ancestor after the death of his father-in-law Maximian under dubious circumstances,[37] and the rationale provided for the revelation of this link appears to be similar to that in Severus' case. Claudius was one of the few third-century emperors about whom nothing bad seems to have been alleged. The absence of a negative tradition made it easier to present him as the man who could be described as the first to restore the pristine order of the Roman empire, a direct challenge to the claims that Diocletian and his colleagues had been making about themselves.[38] As a descendent of the great Claudius, Constantine was welcomed by the gods of his fathers when he entered the palace, and no longer owed his place to his connection with the regime of his immediate predecessors.[39]

The reader of the *constitutio Antoniniana,* the edict that granted Roman citizenship to most of the free inhabitants of the empire in 212, would have discovered that Caracalla had been preserved from some peril by the gods.[40] An inhabitant of the empire who happened to see the decree of Severus Alexander (222–235) on the practice of sending gold crowns to the emperor upon the anniversary of his accession would most likely have been pleased to learn that Alexander was remitting arrears in payment. To Alexander, it was also undoubtedly important, given the horrendous reputation of his predecessor, that he have the opportunity to advertise his claim that he was not like him. Thus the edict explains that, "wherefore I have formed this design, not wanting in precedents, among which I wanted to follow the example of Trajan and Marcus, my own ancestors and emperors who have made themselves specially worthy of admiration, whose policy in other matters also I am resolved to emulate . . ." (*P. Fay.* 20).[41]

The reader of Diocletian's price edict of 301 could get a potted history of the whole reign or, at least, the details that the *imperator* C. Valerius Diocletianus Pius Fortunate Invincible Augustus, *pontifex maximus,* who had defeated the Germans six times, the Sarmatians four times, the Persians twice, and the Britains, Carpi, Armenians, Medes and Adiabenians once each thought important (*Price Edict* 1). The titulature itself is a fair history of the imperial wars, and the reader could then learn (without much surprise) that the emperor had fought successfully, was grateful to the gods, that he wanted the state to run well, and hoped that the gods who had aided the empire against various barbarian peoples would surround the peace that he had established for eternity with the necessary defense of justice. It was only when the reader had got through all this that it would become evident that the emperor was outraged that people were charging such high prices that his soldiers could not live on their wages (*Price Edict* 5–8). The reader of the edict against the Manichaeans would have learned that the emperor had heard that they had emerged as a new and unexpected monstrosity from the land of the Persian enemy, while the reader of his edict on the level of taxation in Egypt would have learned that the emperor was desperately interested in justice.[42]

The rhetoric of imperial edicts was carefully constructed to create an appropriate imperial image, and the number of edicts that we know of that were directed to the population of the empire as a whole is a very small proportion of the total attested corpus of imperial communication. The vast bulk of an emperor's correspondence with his subjects took the form of responses to question or appeals.[43] In most cases, therefore, the emperor could craft his statement to fit a particular audience. The emperor Constantine appears to have been a master of this technique, and his conduct provides a good introduction to the next varieties of imperial ideological statement, the speech and the letter. In the year 313, Constantine let it be known that he had been inspired by a very powerful divinity indeed.[44] Two years later a triumphal arch was completed at Rome on which the inscription ran, "To the *imperator* Caesar Flavius Constantine, Greatest, Pius, Fortunate Augustus, the Roman senate and people dedicate this arch decorated with his victories because, by the prompting of a divinity, by the magnitude of his mind, with his army, he avenged the state on the tyrant and all his faction at one moment by a just victory" (*ILS* 694). Constantine knew by this time that this divinity was the Christian God, but he seems not to have stressed the point in a general decree. Christians, who heard a great deal from Constantine, knew this, but his subjects who were not directly affected by his Christianity may never have been very clear as to just where his sympathies lay. The best testimony to the confusion resulting from Constantine's ability to manipulate the obfuscatory language of imperial exposition is provided by a letter from Constantine to the people of Umbria acceding to their request for independence from Tuscany in the last year of his life. The letter began, "The *imperator* Caesar Flavius Constantine, Greatest, Germanicus, Sarmaticus, Gothicus, Invincible, Triumphant Augustus and Flavius Constantine and Flavius Constantius and Flavius Constans. We embrace all things that protect human society in the deliberation of our watchful company."[45] One of the things that the people of Umbria were interested in doing to celebrate their new freedom was to set up a temple in honor of Constantine's family, and he was clearly not interested in telling them that he was a Christian, a fact that does not seem to have penetrated their consciousness to any degree. This view may be confirmed by a remarkable passage in Fimicus Maternus' book on astrology, written at about the same time as the appeal from the Umbrians, which also suggests that Constantine's image in the west had not changed much since the 320s (*Math.* 1.10.13–14). Nor would it on this occasion, since he was most interested in telling them of his military glory and general probity while recommending that they not let any "vile practice" defile their new temple. By "vile practice" he meant sacrifice, and this could be reconciled with the antipathy to animal sacrifice current in some polytheistic circles.[46] In the east, however, when writing to Christians or ordering the closure of a temple where he had learned that rites of which he particularly disapproved were celebrated (he seems to have had a strong aversion to temple prostitution and oracles), he appeared in quite a different light.[47]

The publication of imperial speeches in the senate and of senatorial decrees emanating from the emperor's own hand had a very long history. Tacitus suggests that the daily record of events at Rome was circulated throughout the provinces to let people know what was happening in Rome, and communities or individuals could extract from it things that interested them.[48] This practice may explain why we know something of the content of Augustus' funeral elegy upon his deceased friend Agrippa from a papyrus, the speech that Claudius gave on the subject of admitting Gauls to the senate from a bronze tablet found at Lyons, and a debate in the senate over the price of gladiators.[49] Sometimes, of course, the senate or emperor might order the publication of select decrees of importance. This happened with what is perhaps the most astonishing epigraphic discovery in this century, Tiberius' final disposition of the case against Gnaeus Calpurnius Piso on a charge of treason in A.D. 20, known from bronze tablets that have recently come to light in Spain.[50] As with another group of tablets found at the town of Siara in southern Spain, providing details of the funeral honors for Tiberius' deceased nephew Germanicus, this document offers provincials a detailed exposition of the ideology of the regime.[51] Both were published throughout the empire on the express orders of the senate at the prompting of Tiberius.[52]

Letters to the empire at large could also be a useful way of announcing imperial triumphs. Ammianus Marcellinus writes with some annoyance that in the wake of his nephew Julian's victory over the Alemanni at Strasbourg in 357, the emperor Constantius claimed the success for himself and dispatched one of those edicts in which, carried away by the eloquence of his flatterers, he told lies about many things. He often claimed, according to Ammianus, to have defeated foreign nations and raised up foreign kings when he was nowhere in their area. If one of his generals won a battle over the Persians while he was in Italy, he would send missives "to the ruin of the provinces" describing the way that he had fought in the front rank and omitting to mention the general anywhere. The imperial records office was full of documents in which he praised himself to the skies (16.12.67–70). In other words, Constantius did for himself what the author of a third-century handbook on rhetoric urged a good orator to do in an oration on any emperor: "you will have opportunity here to link up a passage on wisdom, saying that he himself was the planner, the commander, the discoverer of the moment for battle, a marvelous counselor, champion, general and orator" (Men. Rhet. 2.374.21–25 trans. Russell and Wilson). To judge from the extant examples of such letters preserved in the corpus of the writings of Julian (several justifying his revolt against Constantius in 361), these letters could be quite long.

The surviving evidence suggests, however, that these letters made less of an impression than did specific responses from the emperor. As noted above, these constitute the vast bulk of our information about the activity of the Roman emperor. The reason for this is not simply that the composition of such responses was the primary activity of the emperor, or even his primary concern. Rather it is that his responses to appeals from cities of the empire were far more relevant to his subjects than any of his other compositions—so much so that it is easy to be misled as to their true significance: most letters to the emperor from communities that have survived on stone or papyrus are themselves responses to imperial decisions, appealing matters of imperial intervention in local affairs, asking for a change in the way that the emperor or his predecessors had decided a local dispute, or for an exemption from standard practice. The enormous number of imperial responses that have been preserved in the extant collections of Roman legal documents are similarly stripped of their immediate context so as to preserve observations that jurists found significant.[53] On the other hand, while this evidence may not define the action of the imperial office, it did help define the way in which the office of the emperor was perceived by the inhabitants of the empire. For the emperor, attention to the desires of his subjects was simply one part of a job that seems to have been concerned primarily with ensuring the safety of the frontiers, the stability of the state's revenues, the security of the capital city, and the general moral climate of his realm.[54] In responding to appeals from his subjects he could right wrongs and, in doing so, give them some information about the way he thought the world should work. For his subjects, these responses helped to define their place within the empire as a whole, and it is interesting that they seem to have come to form the basis of what are essentially local histories that center upon a city's connection to the ruling power.

The most striking examples of this activity, which can be traced back to the emergence of the great kingdoms after the death of Alexander the Great, are walls containing copies of letters from kings, emperors, and other people that reflect upon the standing of a community.[55] The typical "history wall" was inscribed on part of a centrally located public monument. At Priene in Asia Minor (one of the earliest of these walls), this was the left anta to the temple of

Athena Polias and a portion of the adjacent sidewall of the ante-chamber leading into the temple itself.[56] At Magnesia on the Meander, the stoa in front of the temple of Artemis Leucophryene was used for display of the documents connected with the initiation of a "crowned" festival in honor of the goddess, recognition of the temple's right of asylum, the message delivered by the city's ambassadors, and favorable responses from various kings and cities in the late third to early second centuries B.C.[57] A stone inscribed in the second century A.D. from the area of the temple of Apollo at the same city that contains part of a letter from the Persian king Darius I (522–486 B.C.) was plainly part of a history inscribed on the wall of that temple as well.[58]

The practice of inscribing civic history in this way continued well into the period of Roman domination. At Aphrodisias in Caria, the wall by the left entrance into the theater was inscribed with letters from the Roman senate and emperors remarking on the city's privileges in the reign of Septimius Severus (193–211); while the shrine of the emperors at Cyrene was evidently the location for a large stele containing letters from the emperors Hadrian (117–138) and Antoninus Pius (138–161) remarking on the city's superiority over its neighbors.[59] In the reign of Marcus Aurelius, the city of Coronea in Boeotia elaborately inscribed on the wall of a building eleven letters containing favorable responses to it (and unfavorable responses to its neighbors) from Marcus, Antoninus Pius, and Hadrian: this was local history with a real point to it.[60] Perhaps the most remarkable of all of these walls dates from the third century A.D. It is the wall of the temple of Zeus at Baetocaece on the crest of the Jebel Ansariyeh in modern Lebanon, upon which was displayed a dossier of letters from Hellenistic kings that proclaimed its privileges, below a favorable response from the emperor Valerian (253–260) asserting that the ancient benefits that the temple had obtained from these kings must be maintained in the face of a challenge from an "adversary."[61]

Collections of documents inscribed on "history walls" are different from ordinary inscribed civic decrees and letters from potentates in that they were assembled over a period to form a coherent group: they were not ad hoc inscriptions reflecting

7. The history wall at Aphrodisias. The whole of the wall of the *skene* building by the left entrance into the theater is inscribed with letters from emperors to the city. The collection provides a history of the city's positive dealings with Rome (photo courtesy of Dr. R. R. R. Smith).

immediate public concerns. Also, unlike civic decrees and important letters, they were not necessarily verbatim transcripts of the original. Several of the texts on the wall from Cyrene, for instance, contain the phrases "chief points from the letter of the divine Hadrian" and "chief points of the lord Antoninus" (the heading in the former case reveals that the inscription was carved after the death of Hadrian, who would have been referred to as "the lord" if the text had been carved in his lifetime).[62] The letters in the Aphrodisias collection are notorious for the omission of the proper titulature of Roman emperors; it was their sentiments that mattered.

These histories were created by a decision of a civic body to advertise a specific claim that the city wanted to make. They were not the only medium for the expression of such ideas, as we shall see shortly, but they were clearly very useful when it came to making a point to visiting representatives of the ruling power, and as sources for other appeals. This said, the emperor was not the only person who could help instruct the provincials on the best way to view the emperor. The creative role of imperial officials and others who might be anxious to please should not be underestimated. It was Paullus Fabius Maximus who, after lavish praise of Augustus, suggested that the provincial assembly of Asia should henceforth begin the new year on September 23 in commemoration of the emperor's birthday and his benefactions to the human race (E&J 98). In the reign of Tiberius, a governor of Asia wrote to a community in Pisidia, "it is the most unjust thing of all for me to tighten up by my own edict that which the Augusti, one the greatest of gods, the other the greatest of emperors, have taken the utmost care to prevent, namely that no one should make use of carts without payment."[63] In A.D. 31, P. Vitrasius Naso, governor of Crete and Cyrenaica, appears to have been the chief source of information for the people of Gortyn when he saw to the inscription of a large stone (in Latin) to commemorate Tiberius' preservation from a "dangerous conspiracy" (E&J 52). In his edict as prefect of Egypt in A.D. 69 Tiberius Julius Alexander advertised the evils of the old regime and the advantages of the new one that he had helped create (McCrum and Woodhead 328). The imperial freedman Helikon reminded the people of Ephesus of the evident and obvious providence of the emperor Septimius Severus and the hideous conspiracy from which he had just been saved.[64] In the reign of Constantine, Aurelius Victorinus, the prefect in charge of the supply of food for Rome, had a stone erected at Ostia to let the people know that Constantine was the restorer of public liberty, the defender of the city of Rome, and responsible for the safety of all mortals (ILS 687). In 362 the praetorian prefect Saturninus Secundus informed Ancyra that the emperor Julian was the lord of the whole world, that he had come in one year from the British ocean to the Tigris, laying open the road through barbarian states, slaughtering those barbarians who opposed him (*ILS* 754). It was an egregious lie, but it gave the people of Ancyra information that would help them deal with the new ruler.

Even when direct official participation is not specifically attested, it may be suspected that it often lay behind acts or the form of acts commemorating the emperor, especially those that conveyed information about something that was not of local significance— even if this act was only the erection of a statue. Herodian notes that public statues of Severus were a source of information about portents that preceded his assumption of the imperial dignity.[65] Governors must have been the source of this extraordinary knowledge. This may also have been the case with a series of statues erected at Ephesus in honor of Gordian III and his wife in the 240s, for the Greek inscriptions manifestly translate a Latin text.[66] The same process may explain the description of Julian as a man who ruled in accordance with the dictates of his philosophy and every virtue, taking the whole universe into his care, that was inscribed by the people of Iasus in Asia. Mention of Julian's philosophic interests is otherwise attested (as far as I know) on only two other monuments, one at Pergamon, the other at Ephesus, for which the governor of Asia, Dulcitius was responsible.[67]

Edicts and the like were not ordinarily very detailed, and people might even have regarded their contents as somewhat commonplace. Moreover, they might soon be forgotten, and, as the evidence of the publication of imperial letter on "history walls" suggests, people seem not to have been interested in including material that was not directly relevant to their lives. The emperors therefore turned to other media to help reinforce their message more vividly. Paintings, for instance, were very useful, and they seem usually to have come with short captions to help people understand the significance of their message. Herodian tells of pictures that Septimius Severus sent to Rome illustrating his Persian wars, and may have used them as a source for his history of those events.[68] He likewise reports some pictures that Maximinus Thrax (235–238) sent to the city depicting his wars on the Rhine, and seems also to have used them as a source.[69] His account suggests that these pictures presented a highly stylized narrative of events. One seems to have shown the emperor crossing a bridge; another, the burning of German villages; a third, barbarians hiding in the woods and skirmishing with Roman troops led by their emperor; the fourth, a battle in a swamp. These scenes recall typical scenes on, for instance, the column of Marcus Aurelius, where river-crossing scenes represent the departure of the Roman army into the land of the barbarians; scenes of village burning, the vengeance of the state; fearful barbarians, the power of Rome; and battle scenes prominently displayed off to one side, his direct responsibility for the triumphs of Rome.

The influence of such pictures may also be detected at various points in the extant Greek verse collections of sibylline oracles. Thus, in the *Fifth* and *Twelfth Sibylline Oracles,* it is said that Thrace, Sicily, and Memphis will crouch before Augustus.[70] The language suggests the image of a defeated nation prostrate before the emperor that is so common on reliefs or in statue groups connected with the dynasty. The Sebasteion at Aphrodisias, with its panels depicting the subjugation of Britain by Claudius, of Armenia by Nero, and of several nations by Augustus, is a case in point.[71] A contemporary work of art is also likely to have been the source for the account of the Rain Miracle of Marcus Aurelius in the *Twelfth Sibylline Oracle.* The text reads, "then he will destroy the whole country of the Germans, when the great sign of god will appear from heaven and he will save the exhausted bronze-clad men because of the piety of the king; for the heavenly god will give ear to him and he will shower down timely rain in answer to his prayers" (12.195–200). Like the life of Marcus in the *Historia Augusta,* it emphasizes the role of Marcus' prayers in obtaining the miracle. The attribution of the miracle to a great god is also in line with the presentation of the event on Marcus' column and the tacit admission by Tertullian that the miracle was due to the beneficence of "the god of gods," Jupiter. It is free of contamination from the later accounts that variously attribute the storm to the Egyptian magician Arnouphis, Julianus the Theurgist, or Christian prayers.[72]

Variations on the norm could also be significant, and were not

8. Claudius and Britannia from the Sebasteion at Aphrodisias. Idealized representations such as this reflect local adaptations of imperial propaganda, emphasizing the role of the emperor as conqueror and divinity. Representations of the emperor in heroic nudity would be out of keeping with the aristocratic image of the emperor at Rome and thus reveal how flexible the media and interpretation of imperial propaganda could be (photo courtesy of Dr. R. R. R. Smith).

always a success: centuries of repetition had accustomed the people of the empire to certain images of government, and efforts at too-rapid change or excessive personalization were noticed. Eunapius remarks with horror on an event in the hippodrome at Constantinople when an official named Perses decided to emphasize the importance of the Christian god to the house of Theodosius with pictures that showed a hand coming down out of the clouds and the inscription "The hand of God chases away the barbarians." A critic complained that he should have depicted the courage of the emperor, the strength of the soldiers, and the course of the war (Eun. fr. 68 Blockley). The picture that Elagabalus sent to Rome to accustom the senate to his attire as high priest of the god Elagabal seems to have been a propagandistic disaster, and it is interesting that he is presented in normal dress on his coins (Herod. 5.5.6–7). No one could have expected Rome's enemies to be in a position to sneer, as ultimately they were. The fifth-century historian Priscus tells that Attila, then ensconced in the imperial palace at Milan, "saw in a painting the Roman emperors sitting upon golden thrones and Scythians lying dead before their feet . . . [and] sought out a painter and ordered him to paint Attila upon a throne and the Roman emperors heaving sacks upon their shoulders and pouring out gold before his feet" (fr. 22 Blockley).[73]

Coins could spread the image of imperial glory more broadly, if less precisely, than works of art. The portraits on imperial coinage clearly represented the claim to power, and displayed the image with which the emperor could be comfortable.[74] Suetonius says that both Augustus and Nero took a personal interest in the designs on their coins (*Aug.* 94.12; *Nero* 25.2). Dio makes it clear that emperors could be interested in removing coins from circulation because they had portraits of deceased predecessors on them.[75] He also tells the story of a person who was tried for treason because he took a coin of Caracalla into a brothel (Dio 77.16.5). In 324 the emperor Licinius assumed that Constantine's use of money stamped with his own image to pay troops who had pursued barbarians into his own territory represented a claim to his throne (Pet. Patr. Exc. Vat. 187), and one of the first things that the usurper Procopius did in 365 was to send emissaries around with coins having his image upon them (Amm. Marc. 26.7.11).

As imperial coins were taken to be representations of the emperor's power, it was also natural that people should think that abnormalities appearing on those coins reflected the particular interests of an emperor. No one might be very excited about a reverse that represented a cornucopia, defeated barbarians, or a new building project: these represented activities that every emperor was

9. The coin on the upper left was minted in the last years of the reign of Constantius II (337–361); the coin on the upper right is typical of the emperor Julian (361–363). Julian distinguishes himself from Constantius by a beard and by the nature of the reverse (lower left). He seems to have intended the bull to symbolize his devotion to traditional cult, and people did connect it with his interest in sacrifice. The reverse on Constantius' coin (lower right), depicting a Roman victorious over a barbarian, is a much more typical design (*RIC* 8, 166 n. 348; *RIC* 8, 229; photos courtesy of the American Numismatic Society).

supposed to be interested in. But people were clearly struck (and in no very positive way if they were Christians) when the emperor Julian minted coins with a representation of a sacrificial bull on the reverse, and Eusebius says that Constantine authorized a coin that showed him in prayer.[76] It is unfortunate that we do not have any more explicit account of, for instance, reaction to the obvious iconographic break between the coins of Constantine and those of Diocletian's generation, or the astonishing series of gold coins minted in the reign of Decius that commemorate the deified emperors of the past. It is also somewhat hard to know just how impressive any one coin type may have been since, as yet, we have no very good way of tracing the circulation of imperial coinage.[77]

Paintings and coins were probably the most pervasive form of imperial self-advertisement, but they were by no means the only forms available. The construction of permanent architectural memorials to one's own success had become a feature of Roman political life in the republic; the adornment of private houses with permanent trophies of victory and the construction of religious edifices and public buildings are all amply attested by the time of Julius Caesar. With Augustus, senatorial self-representation in this way was eliminated, and the capital became increasingly crowded with imperial commemorative buildings.[78] But such structures were not limited to Rome, even under Augustus. A permanent memorial was erected to Drusus Caesar on the Rhine after his death in 9 B.C., and after the death of Germanicus in A.D. 19 the senate, acting in consultation with Tiberius, saw to the erection of three triumphal arches, one in Rome, another near the memorial to Drusus on the Rhine, and the third on Mount Amanus in Syria. Ideologically these arches symbolized the service of Germanicus from one end of the empire to the other, and with their sculptured representations of conquered peoples, commemorative inscriptions, and images of the imperial family, they show that the empire as a whole had already become a stage for the display of imperial victory.[79]

By the time of Augustus, building projects of other sorts had long been recognized as a worthy task for prominent persons. In the republic such projects in the city had been the province of successful members of the aristocracy, but during his long reign they became the exclusive province of the *princeps*. This was not the case in the provinces, where a bridge, aqueduct, library, Nymphaeum, theater, or stoa might be an appropriate form of self-commemoration for a local worthy. But these projects were too significant to be left solely in the hands of such people, and Pliny's correspondence from Bithynia suggests that governors were on the lookout for major projects that would increase the dignity of the emperor. Thus Pliny suggests that a canal linking the lake by Nicomedia with the sea would be appropriate to Trajan's eternal renown, giving him a chance to surpass rulers of distant ages (*Ep.* 10.41).[80] The ideology behind such gifts receives what may be its clearest expression in the preface to the early Augustan architect

Vitruvius' handbook on architecture: "I observed that you cared not only about the common life of all men, and the constitution of the state, but also about the provision of suitable public buildings so that the state was made greater by you not only through new provinces, but also because the majesty of the empire had the eminent authority of its public buildings" (*De arch.* pref. 1.2). Often such projects were funded simply by remission of tribute, or attributed to the emperor's beneficence simply because he had permitted them to be undertaken, but at other times—the Olympeion at Athens is a spectacular example—they were completed as a result of the express intervention of the emperor himself.[81] It was important that the centers of power look the part, and that the emperor be seen aiding the advance of civilization. Emperors who came from the provinces could also feel it necessary to exalt their hometowns above their neighbors; Philip the Arab, who constructed a major city at his birthplace in the province of Arabia, is perhaps the most interesting case.[82] Such projects were significant both in economic terms, insofar as they redistributed tax money back through provincial communities, and in ideological terms, insofar as they planted memorials to imperial munificence and triumph throughout the empire.

From the time of Augustus on, the emperors also sought to inform their subjects by involving them in the commemoration of great events in history. The ever-changing festival calendar of the Roman state and its provincial equivalents offered the most effective way of doing this. From the reign of Augustus, there is ample evidence from Lyons and Cologne of the use of cult to bind local dignitaries into the imperial system through commemoration of the imperial family, and of the commemoration of the imperial house in communities throughout Italy. Thus at Pisa in A.D. 2 the public records office was called the Augustaeum, and it was there on September 20 that members of the town council met to oversee the inscription of a decree listing the annual celebrations that were to be instituted for the memory of Augustus' grandson, Lucius Caesar, at an altar in the forum. Two years later, despite chaos in the local elections, the decurions of Pisa met on April 2 to decide how to respond to news that "Gaius Caesar, son of Augustus, the father of the country, guardian of the Roman empire and leader of the whole world, the grandson of the divine Caesar, waging war with success after his consulship beyond the most borders of the Roman people, and doing well with regard to the state, having conquered and received the surrender of the greatest and most warlike nations, having received a wound on behalf of the state, was stolen away by the cruel fates as a result of that accident" (E&J 69). In A.D. 19 we now know that the people of Italy and of the citizen colonies and municipalities throughout the empire were commanded by the senate to join in annual remembrance of Germanicus, the nephew and adopted son of Tiberius, who had died in Syria.[83] Both in life and in death, the genius of Augustus received cult throughout Italy, while in the east and throughout the empire he was worshipped as a god, thus setting the fashion for future rulers.

The imperial cult evolved out of the commemoration of benefactors in the Greek world, and from the time of Augustus through the fourth century it became the single most important institution for communication between the emperor and his subjects because it provided a ready way to introduce the emperor into a civic context.[84] Over time the imperial cult became ever more important, and civic storehouses of imperial images came to resemble museums of imperial history. By the third century, the creation of these images came to be a direct concern of the imperial government (up to this time the art market seems to have sufficed as a source of information for local artisans).[85] Wax images (in one case we even know of a portrait) were dispatched to the cities of the empire from wherever the emperor happened to be proclaimed, and their arrival was treated as an actual imperial visit.[86] The announcement of a new emperor's accession was the occasion for a lengthy public celebration. Thus, when Pertinax replaced the murdered Commodus in 193, the people of Alexandria in Egypt were told: "All of you, making sacrifice and praying for the well-being of the invincible emperor and his whole house, are to wear crowns for fifteen days, starting today."[87] At the time of Hadrian's accession in 117, ten days of celebration were ordered, and one papyrus preserves part of an account of a public display in which an actor playing the God Apollo said that he had come to the people to announce the new emperor after having escorted his predecessor to heaven in a chariot drawn by white horses.[88]

Accession ceremonies, as well as the periodic celebration of the cult, provided fora for spreading news of the emperor's accomplishments. Hymnodoi and Sebastologoi who celebrated the emperor with hymns and rhetorical encomia are attested throughout the Greek east, and the images of the emperor would be paraded through the streets so that people could know what he looked like.[89] The whole performance was, of course, highly stylized, and, to judge from Menander Rhetor's handbook on the way to compose speeches for all occasions, a consistent image of power was more important than accurate discourse on the facts of the reign. This situation was very much in keeping with the sort of material that could be obtained from the emperors themselves.

In addition to processions, sacrifices, and speeches, public executions were a standard part of the commemorative fare. The destruction of local criminals not only reminded the people of the superior power of the imperial government but also provided an occasion for the resolution of local disputes that would draw the inhabitants of the empire into a symbolic union with their masters.[90] The emperor might even provide prisoners taken on recent campaigns, whose deaths could allow people to participate in his efforts to protect them.[91]

Games could also serve to advertise imperial policy and to commemorate great events. Thus Augustus reenacted the battle of Salamis at Rome before Gaius set out for the eastern frontier in 2 B.C.; Claudius, to celebrate his return from Britain in 43, staged a reenactment of a battle there, to which, it seems, he summoned governors from their provinces; and the transportation of a captured British chieftain to the capital in 50 (where another military demonstration was staged) was evidently done with such broad advertisement that people came from all over to see it.[92] Septimius Severus ordered the annual celebration of his victories by the army, and gave great games at Rome to commemorate them. At least two cities in the Greek east, Aphrodisias and Aezani, seem to have taken Severus' action as an indication that a request to do the same would not go unheeded. They were correct.[93] In 242 Gordian III founded games of Athena Promachos at Rome before setting out on campaign against the Persians, and all along his route the cities of the Greek world held games that could be connected with his chosen theme: the historic confrontation between the civilized world and the barbarian east.[94] It was an impressive example of the capacity of the central government to inform (or misinform) its subjects through the exploitation of local media for communication or amusement, and people actually came to believe that the teenage emperor was leading the army in person.[95] The emperor Hadrian expressed a very clear interest in ancient culture (symbolized above all by his completion of the temple of Olympian Zeus at Athens and the creation of the Pan-Hellenic League), and a number of games founded during his reign appear to have reflected local responses to his intellectual, rather than his bellicose, interests.[96] Thus the artistic contest founded at Oenoanda in Lycia by Gaius Julius Demosthenes, as well as "mystic contests" at Ancyra and Side, while the Mouseia at Thespiae in Greece were renamed so that they could incorporate Hadrian's nomenclature.[97]

Local festivals, which allowed the people of the empire—or at least those who lived in proximity to cities—to participate in the emperor's victories and interests, may have been the most effective means of spreading the information that emperors and their advisers thought that people should have. People could enjoy themselves, they could see their foes humiliated before their eyes, and they could be reminded of basic facts about the emperor and his family and how their own experiences were connected with the formative moments of classical culture. But it all cost a great deal of money, and, as was often the case with building projects, the burden tended to fall upon the local governing class. Some benefit could accrue to those responsible: they could earn the goodwill of their neighbors, demonstrate their own capacities as gentlemen, wear special clothes, and, possibly, impress representatives of the central power. But these events could also be occasions for fiscal malfeasance, and might well threaten the finances of the cities and individuals that sponsored them. And they were events concerned with the images rather than the realities of the emperor's power.

Analyzing the Emperors' Messages

If a person living in one part of the empire wanted to learn precise details about events somewhere else through media that were not provided by the imperial government, that person was faced with a very difficult task indeed. Even the emperor had trouble learning of things that occurred in the remoter regions of his domain (Amm. Marc. 31.4.3). This issue, which is central to appreciation of the content of oracular texts, is best observed through the progressive disintegration of contemporary historical writing after Augustus. This disintegration is a feature of the increasing separation of the highly literate classes of imperial society from the management of imperial affairs as the primary business of government became ever more the task of defending the empire from its enemies. War, of course, was a perfectly respectable theme for history. But the stories of the empire's wars seem no longer to have been the subject of *commentarii* by those who would have known best what happened. The satirist Lucian gives a fair sample of the historiographic explosion that occurred in the wake of Lucius Verus' Parthian war of 161–165, and one of the most notable features of his survey is that, with the exception of the pedestrian work of a minor officer, none of it was the work of a participant.[98] Although it would be wrong to suppose that Lucian was even remotely interested in giving a full survey of the work that began to appear, we have no reason to doubt his word that there was never an authoritative study of the campaign by a senior officer. The most extensive fragment of a work on this war, Fronto's history, which may have been informed by Lucius himself, was never finished. The extant portion suggests that it more closely resembled a rhetorical encomium, setting forth the official version of the events, than a modern equivalent of Tacitus' *Histories*.[99] There was a similar outpouring after Julian's invasion of Persia in 363, some of it preserved through Libanius' eighteenth oration. But in this case too, the people who were most qualified to speak about what happened kept their silence. It was only when the doctor Oribasius, who was by Julian's side throughout the campaign, made his notes available to the sophist

Eunapius that it was possible even for a participant like Ammianus to gain an overview of the emperor's strategy.[100]

On one level, imperial history rapidly became whatever the emperor said it was, its contents determined by whatever he decided to tell people through his public pronouncements or personal reminiscence of events that authors had witnessed some of it for themselves. On another level, it became a matter for gossip and innuendo. In a notorious passage of his *Annals,* Tacitus explains why people should not believe that Tiberius poisoned his own son. This section is ordinarily taken as a prime example of Tacitus' notable ability to blacken the reputation of the emperor through nasty insinuation. Tiberius did not kill his son, as any well-informed person must know: people only thought that he did because he and his evil genius, Sejanus, were felt to be capable of any crime. On one level this view of Tacitus' technique is no doubt correct. But the concluding sentence of this section indicates that his purpose was more profound; it offers crucial insight into his perception of how people acted at all levels of power and of the crucially important lessons offered by history to his contemporaries: "The reason I described and refuted this rumor is so that I might refute all false rumors with a clear example and appeal to those into whose hands our care has come that they not cling to tales that are incredible, widely told, and avidly heard, although truth has been corrupted into fantasy" (*Ann.* 4.11.3). In his view rumor all too easily became reality because too few could be bothered to discover the truth. Truth was not easy to come by.

Tacitus appears to have been highly conscious of the fact that the official record rarely told the whole truth. The recent and remarkable discovery of several tablets bearing an account of the final disposition of the case against Gnaeus Calpurnius Piso in A.D. 20 is a case in point. Plancina, the wife of Piso, was deeply implicated in her husband's crimes, but in the final description of Piso's governorship of Syria, her role (evidently amply attested) is simply omitted.[101] If a person really wanted to know what happened, it was a good idea to talk to someone who had been there. No public record of the Roman state reported the fact that Tacitus claims to have heard from his elders: that Piso seemed to have a document in his hand that might incriminate Tiberius, and that Sejanus convinced him not to (*Ann.* 3.16.1). The story may or may not be true (Tiberius was emphatic on the point that it was not), but the important point is that the oral record was not necessarily less accurate than the written.

The historians of the empire did a lot of talking (and writing) to their friends and contemporaries. Tacitus asked Pliny how his uncle had died during the eruption of Vesuvius so that he could improve the story that he had. He then asked Pliny what he had been doing.[102] It was a less interesting tale, but Pliny was pleased to comply, and also offered to tell Tacitus about other things, including conversations between Verginius Rufus, his guardian and the man who had turned down the throne in 68, and another historian, Cluvius Rufus.[103] A good deal of what Ammianus Marcellinus seems to know about the emperor Constantius may be traced to a eunuch named Eutherius, a man "of prodigious memory" whom the historian met at Rome.[104] Other sections of his history read like the *res gestae* of Ammianus rather than of the empire as a whole (a point that gives his history its special charm), and, as noted above, Eunapius came to history through his friend Oribasius. This feature of historical writing is even more plain in the histories written by Dio and Herodian about the period after the death of Marcus Aurelius.

Cassius Dio was quite frank about the way he set about composing the history of his own time.[105] Without claiming that he could produce an ideal product, or even necessarily the truth, he wrote that he would follow the stories that he found in official communications and correct them in light of hearsay, reading, and the evidence of his own eyes so that his work would represent an independent judgment on what had transpired (53.19.6). He was aware that "a great number of things began to happen in secret and to arise from hidden causes, and if anything was by chance made public, it was not believed, because it could not be proved" (53.19.3). All things were said and done at the behest of those in power, and thus "much that never happened is babbled about, and much that did is ignored" (53.19.4). Moreover, because the empire was so large, no one except the participants in events could have accurate information about them, and many never knew that they took place (53.19). This statement stands in evident contrast to another in the history where he says, "I will describe the events of my own lifetime in detail, and I will describe them in more detail than those of preceding times because I was present at them, and because I know of no other person who is able to put a more accurate account of them in writing than I am" (72.18.4). The stress here, however, is on his capacity as compared to that of others, and it stops well short of any claim to the recovery of the truth. The stress on personal involvement is also revealing, for the quality of the narrative depends precisely upon where Dio was when something happened. It seems true that he did not know many people who were better informed than he was; but then he doesn't really seem to have known the right sort of people very well.

On two occasions Dio reveals that he does not know basic facts about the emperor.[106] Given the fact that Dio was a senator (and that one of the more interesting features of his history is the personal information that he provides about his important contemporaries) this suggests a great deal about the level of ignorance that might be current at even quite respectable levels of society outside of Rome. It is also the sort of ignorance that is perhaps best illustrated by Dio's story of cities that melted down their statues of Severus' powerful guard prefect, Plautianus, when a rumor spread that he had fallen from power. The rumor was false, and a lot of people died, including a provincial governor whom Dio knew personally, and whose prosecution seems to have been quite an event (Dio 75.16.2). This was clearly an extreme case (and possibly something of an overstatement prompted by the trial), but throughout his account of the reigns of Severus, Caracalla, and Macrinus, Dio was clearly pushed to find people who could tell him what was going on. Thus, his account of Plautianus' actual fall from power in 205 is simply a record of the report that Severus sent to the senate, followed by a record of his reasons for disbelieving it, reasons stemming both from his feelings about Caracalla and from common sense.[107] It is interesting that he also says that no one knew that Plautianus had castrated a hundred Roman citizens of noble birth until after he was dead (75.14.4). Since Dio clearly did not like

Plautianus, it appears that he was willing to believe this, even though it bears all the marks of being a posthumous slander put about to justify the murder.

Simply because he was a senator, Dio had access to a good deal of information about events that took place in the senate house, and because he lived in Rome and Capua for much of his life, he could also provide a good deal of information about events and characters that he might have noticed or met. It is notable that all but one of the portents presaging the death of Caracalla that he lists were reported precisely in the area around the twin poles of his Italian existence. So too all that he can tell his readers about an alleged conspiracy against Severus is that one of the alleged conspirators was bald, that he was uncovered by Severus in the senate house, and that everyone checked the top of his head when emperor made this announcement (76.8.4). He was also in a position to provide his readers with a special view of the spectacle that Commodus made of himself in the Coliseum when he waved the head of an ostrich at the senate during the games of 192 (72.21.1–2).

When Dio was out of Rome, he had to depend on information from others about events in the senate. He knew who the important people were who were killed during the reign of Elagabalus, partly because he was in Pergamon and was able to collect firsthand information about some of the executions, and partly, it may be surmised, because he talked to people after returning to Rome.[108] He knew the details of Macrinus' death because the former emperor was arrested near his home city of Nicaea (79.39). But for most of what happened at Rome, he was clearly at a loss for serious information, and, as has already been seen, he was prone to believe the worst of people he did not like. Thus, despite the circumstantial detail that Dio provides, it is somewhat difficult to believe that Aurelius Zoticus became the chief official connected to the imperial bedroom because he had the largest penis in the empire, and that he lost his job when he lost his capacity to penetrate the emperor on their wedding night (allegedly because of the love potion his enemies had given him) (80.16.1–6).[109] Dio's account of the reign as a whole is a guide to the sort of thing that he talked about with his friends: senatorial deaths and imperial eccentricities.

When Herodian's history is read beside that of Dio, it is sometimes difficult to believe that the two men were writing about the
same world. The difference in social standing and age between
Herodian and Dio may explain some of this. Herodian's description
of Commodus' games suggests that he read about them or heard
about them, rather than that he had attended them in person over
forty years before he wrote (he seems to have been a bit younger
than Dio). He also appears to have been some sort of civil servant
and certainly not a member of the senate. Thus it is interesting that
whereas, unlike Dio, he has none of the details about senators killed
by Elagabalus, he does know a good deal more about that emperor's
public display. He was able to get proper information about the
imperial family, and he knew about the picture that Elagabalus had
sent to Rome (he seems to have seen it). He knew what the god
Elagabal looked like, and he could describe his worship and both
of his marriages: one to Minerva, and a second, when the first one
did not work out, to Dea Caelestis of Carthage.[110] On the other
hand, he never mentions Zoticus. It is a lapse that can be compared
to the learning not only of Dio, but also of the much better informed person who provided the information employed by the
author of the *Historia Augusta*. This writer, probably Marius
Maximus, knew about Zoticus' wealth, his tenure in office, and
certain other exploits.[111] Marius had been prefect of the city under
Macrinus, and the quality of his information may again illustrate
the variation in the quality of gossip from circle to circle, as well
as the quantity of information that was available at different levels
of society. Unlike Dio and Marius, Herodian did not have access
to much news about senatorial gatherings or the inner workings of
palace politics, and was restricted to reporting what he could learn
in other quarters. The survival of his work suggests that his audience
did not find this a great drawback.

Location and social and political status appear to have been the
most significant limiting factors for the composition of history.
They dictated interests as well as the ability to discover facts. As
Dio observed, the Roman world was without a ruler for two days
after the death of Caracalla, and no one save those in the camp
knew it (79.11.4). As we have seen, it was usually a matter of some

months before news of a new emperor reached the provinces. Dio also implies that educated people routinely disbelieved whatever they were told by the central government, even when they had no evidence to hand (53.19.4).

Imperial History in the Sibylline Oracles

The emperors defined the history of the Roman world. Their images and monuments filled the public space of their cities, their words were heard in silent awe by their subjects or read with interest; their names provided the framework for the measurement of time. They were the arbiters of fashion, they were the last court of appeal for the downtrodden, they were the leaders of the civilized world. Or so it might appear to those who viewed the emperors solely as the sum of their most widely advertised and visible tasks. Dio and Herodian, however, plainly did not take this view; and neither did the recipients of the barrage of news that Dio and Herodian attempted, with their various successes and failures, to penetrate.

There was another side to the emperor. This was the power that lay behind the governor who traveled from city to city dispensing a brutal justice for all to watch, the power supported by the ubiquitous tax gatherer or the local centurion. The inhabitants of the Roman world may not have been well informed, but there is no reason to believe that the emperors ruled a population of morons either. The emperors' subjects had their own paradigms to help them determine the broader significance of the deeds that were reported to them, paradigms that did not depend on their masters, and sources of information that were beyond the control of their masters. In the first section of this chapter I discussed the ways in which prophetic texts were exploited to provide alternative chronologies to imperial history and were connected with various fantasies about the imperial house. The Sibylline Oracles offer further insight into the way this happened, and it will become immediately clear that the outlook of these authors, historians of a sort in their own right, is closer to that of a Dio or Herodian than has often been realized.

There are five *Sibylline Oracles* that provide descriptions of imperial history. The form of these prophecies is "dynastic," in that they provide clear identifications of Roman rulers, and some interpretation of their deeds. The form evolved in the Greek world with the emergence of Hellenistic kingship as a natural response to chronological schemes based upon royal reigns.[112] Such lists are notionally the work of a Sibyl who was thought to have lived in a very early period of human history, and their purpose appears to have been twofold. One was to provide a selection of prophecies that a reader could recognize as being substantially true so that the reader might be inclined to believe whatever other information the author was seeking to purvey. The second was to provide a temporal framework for predictions about the future.

The accuracy of oracular lists of rulers could vary a great deal for reasons connected with composition and authorial learning. The *Twelfth* and *Thirteenth Sibylline Oracles* seem to be little changed from texts that originally circulated in the mid third century A.D.; the *Fifth* and *Eighth* oracles contain a bizarre amalgam of material from a variety of dates. The *Fourteenth Oracle* offers completely incomprehensible "dynastic" list of rulers in the first 283 lines to introduce a detailed description of the Arab conquest of Egypt in the final 63 lines.

The only control on the content of the oracles was the learning of the reading public, and this varied greatly depending on geographic proximity to the location of events, and the chronological relationship of the compilers of the extant texts to the material they included. As they now stand, all the extant texts are collections of earlier oracles that were written at various places and took something like their present form at roughly the time of the last event that they predict. Thus, a passage that appears to be internally consistent and deals with the emperor Claudius was probably written early in the reign of Nero if it includes the emperor's death. There is no reason to think, however, that it would have been written in the same place, or by the same person who composed a passage about Nero that follows it in one of the extant oracles. Nor is there any reason to assume that the two texts were necessarily circulated together before the compilation in which they presently stand.

When the compiler of one of the extant texts—for example, the person who assembled the current *Twelfth* and *Thirteenth Oracles*—was well informed, the final product is reasonably comprehensible. When the compiler was less capable, the result is horrendous. The passage from the *Eighth Oracle* that was discussed in the first section of the chapter is one illustration of the problem, and a few instances from the current *Fourteenth Oracle* will offer further illustration. In line 21 two rulers are introduced both of whom have names beginning with *mu* (the number 40 in the alphabetic Greek numbering system that was routinely employed in prophecy); such a pair corresponds with Maximian Galerius and Maximinus Daia between 305 and 311. In lines 52–57 a person is introduced in the following terms: "and then another great-hearted Ares will rule the arrogant Romans, appearing from Assyria of the first number and establish all things through war; at the same time he will show his rule to the soldiers and establish law; then, quickly, bronze Ares will destroy him, destroyed by soldiers' plots." The reference here can only be to Antoninus Caracalla, born of a Syrian (and thus Assyrian in the language of these texts) mother, who was murdered at the behest of his praetorian prefect in 217, although in this text he is succeeded not by Macrinus, but rather by a group of three. At line 105 the compiler introduced two rulers, one of the number 300, the second (who will succeed the first) of the number 3. This sequence indicates rulers whose names begin with the Greek letters *tau* (300) and *gamma* (3), a pair identifiable only as Tiberius and Gaius, as there was no other time prior to the Arab conquest when the Roman world was ruled in succession by men whose names began with these letters.[113] Moreover, the second ruler in this pair is represented as committing murders in the capital and as being hostile to the senate, not a bad description of Caligula as things go (*Orac. Sib.* 14.107–115). They are succeeded by a king with no name at line 116, and by another whose name also begins with *tau* at line 126, in this case an emperor who wages war in the east, a situation that corresponds well with the reign of Trajan. The name of the next ruler, at line 137, begins with *lambda* (the number 30); he is said to be like a beast and to be active along the Danube. This might be the fourth-century emperor Licinius.[114] In lines 199–200 a man appears in Egypt who will call himself Dionysus. If this is a Roman at all, it is very probably Marcus Antonius the triumvir.[115] The detail in each of these cases suggests original authors who were more familiar with the history of Rome than the one who included these various passages in his poem with no sense as to who the people described in them might be: to him they are symbols.

The ubiquitous character of the oracles lends them their particular value as historical evidence.[116] This is especially true as there is no reason to assume that oracles were composed by people who were actively opposed to the imperial regime. There is no way now to know what prompted an author to write, or what prophecy was originally connected with the bits of verse that were included in the present compilations. As their purpose could simply have been to date and lend authenticity to some remark of purely local interest, they are not a priori the work of people who were contemplating the end of the Roman empire. For this reason they should be taken as a fair reflection of the way that the inhabitants of the Greek world interpreted the messages that they were receiving from the imperial government.

On the whole, the picture of the emperor is quite simple. Most of the time the emperor is seen killing people, usually, but not exclusively, barbarians. Thus, at the beginning of the *Twelfth Sibylline Oracle* Augustus is portrayed as the man who will take power and hold it through "man-destroying war, and then establish law and pass power on to a successor" (12.19–23). He is portrayed in much the same way in the *Fifth Oracle,* and the connection with war and Caesar is stressed in some lines in the *Fourteenth (Orac. Sib.* 5.14–20; 14.185–188). Some of this description looks as if it was based upon representations of the emperor, and the stress on victory, law, and the family is very much in line with the image projected by Augustus throughout the empire. In the *Fifth Sibylline Oracle,* Tiberius is presented as a man who will subdue the Medes and Babylonians (5.21–23), while the *Twelfth Oracle* includes the Germans and a variety of other eastern peoples (12.39–44). Although this might, at first glance, appear a somewhat odd way to present the reign of a person whose unwillingness to undertake foreign adventures led the historian Tacitus to suggest that some might find his reign boring (*Ann.* 4.32.2), it does correspond in a rather interesting way to the vision of Tiberian policy that was presented to the public in the empirewide commemoration of the deceased Germanicus in 19. Claudius too appears as a great conqueror (although here mention is made only of campaigns in Thrace rather than the conquest of Britain), and Caligula is remembered as a mass murderer.[117] Nero is an altogether different character, perhaps fittingly so given the place that he occupied in popular imagination. Vespasian and Trajan tend to be remembered for military exploits, especially in Judaea, although one text also stresses the former's role as the founder of a new dynasty.[118] Domitian is described in one place as a powerful warrior who will bring peace (*Orac. Sib.* 12.124–46). An account of Marcus stresses his military success (and the Rain Miracle), while one of Caracalla in the *Twelfth* stresses destruction.[119] Given this sort of picture, it is not surprising that the god Ares is routinely identified with the emperor.[120]

When the emperor is not fighting, he tends to be collecting money. Caligula is described as a person who will gather immense sums from all over the earth (*Orac. Sib.* 12.50–52); Hadrian is described as a person who will take everything from his subjects (*Orac. Sib.* 8.5–53); while Nero and Caracalla are said to have killed wealthy men for cash (*Orac. Sib.* 12.78–81, 266). Marcus Aurelius comes across in one text as sitting upon the collected wealth of nations *Orac. Sib.* 8.69–70). The emperor as a distributor of largess makes less of an impression. Only Hadrian is said to provide benefits to all the cities (*Orac. Sib.* 12.166–168), while decoration of Rome is credited to Marcus Aurelius and an unidentified ruler in the *Fourteenth Oracle* (*Orac. Sib.* 12.191–193; 14.209–213).

In many cases there is little to distinguish one emperor from the other. With the exception of Augustus and Nero, it cannot be said that there is any consistent portrayal of any emperor who is mentioned in more than one text except at the banal level that has been outlined in the last few paragraphs. This homogeneity probably reflects the view of their subjects. Augustus seems to have occupied a special position in popular memory as the bringer of peace to the Mediterranean world. Nero, who so captured the imagination of his subjects that he was believed to be alive decades after his death and was the one emperor who became an eschatological figure of significance, is portrayed with exceptional detail. He will wrestle in matches and drive chariots, he will found games in which he will participate with song and cithera, try to dig a canal through the isthmus of Corinth, and make himself a god.[121] This picture, which appears in both the *Twelfth* and *Fifth Sibylline Oracles* is very similar to that upon which the false Neros played. It may be doubted if any of them looked very much like him (the one described by Tacitus doesn't seem to have borne more than the most cursory resemblance), any more than we may think that Clemens was identical with Agrippa Postumus or the false Drusus with the real one. But they could act like him, so long as lyre playing and song were all that was required.[122] Other personal peculiarities that drew some notice were Hadrian's interests in magi and Antinoos, Elagabalus' religious mania, and Commodus' blond hair, gladiatorial performances, and obsession with Hercules.[123] These observations are paralleled in a horoscope that mentions "Antoninus the queer" and in the *Acts of Isidorus,* which notes the influence of court women on Claudius.[124]

Aside from the fascination with imperial eccentricity, one of the most interesting features of the extant oracles is the wide variation in the quality of the information that they purvey. It is plain that the authors of the various passages that have survived were trying to give the gist of what they thought was important or memorable about a ruler in the eyes of their potential readers. Thus one author thought that the most important thing about Vespasian was that he founded a new dynasty, another that he killed Jews, and that one author should think of Antinoos when writing of Hadrian while other should produce panegyric.[125] This is all the more striking because it often appears that the authors of the lines that we have are adapting the same material.[126] In the case of Hadrian; one wrote, "He will participate in all the mysteries of magic shrines, he will show forth a child as a god, he will undo all that is owed reverence"; while another simply wrote, "He will set all the rites of the magic shrines to rights." The author of the former lines also accused Hadrian of plundering the earth, while the author of the latter praised his beneficence. In these cases, at least, some signs of contemporary debate that was reduced to oracular format has survived. In other cases, there is but a single perspective, but even when this is all that has survived, it is usually enough to reveal something about the author's place in the world.

Claudius regarded the conquest of Britain as one of his greatest achievements. Yet the author of the lines on Claudius in the current *Twelfth Oracle* records instead campaigns on the Danube that were conducted by Claudius' marshals in 46 and 49, as well as an eclipse that was particularly relevant to the Pannonians. It is fairly clear therefore that this person lived somewhere in the vicinity of the Danube and was not particularly interested in Claudius' Britannic adventures. The author whose characterization of Domitian has come down in the same text seems to have known little or nothing of the disasters on the Rhenish and Danubian frontiers that filled his reign; nor does the author who commented on Vespasian's activity in Palestine seem to have known about Civilis' revolt (*Orac. Sib.* 12.124–144, 99–109).

The account of the civil wars that followed on the death of Commodus opens with a bit of numerology (see page 102) and then moves on to Pertinax with the words "Eighty [the letter *pi* for Pertinax] will make clear the number of years, his name and the grievous age that he bears" (*Orac. Sib.* 12.238–239). It is then said that he will rule for only a short time, and that his reign will be filled with warfare. It would therefore appear that all this author knew was the emperor's name and the fact that he was old (but not how old, since he was actually sixty-six), and these two pieces of information could have been gleaned from a portrait (and the speedy arrival of that of his successor). The compiler of the *Twelfth Oracle* did not have much better material on the reign of Pertinax's successor, Didius Julianus. He is said to have been the cause of many griefs before falling to powerful Ares (12.245–249). This information is not relevant to anything in Didius' sixty-two-day reign, and, like the description of Pertinax, it seems to depend more upon assumptions about the way in which emperors conducted themselves than upon anything else.

The treatment of Pescennius Niger is a different matter entirely.

In this case an author says that he will come from the east and go as far west as Thrace; from there he will flee to Bithynia, and thence to the Cilician plain. Finally, he will fall to "soul-destroying Ares" in the Assyrian plain. This is an accurate tale of his military adventures, and it compares more than favorably with many other such accounts. It is certainly better informed, for instance, than the lines concerning Gordian III's Persian war in the *Thirteenth Sibylline Oracle,* which reflect no knowledge of Gordian's defeat at the hands of Sapor I in Mesopotamia during the winter of 244, and allude to the (incorrect) rumor that he was murdered by Philip the Arab. They are also rather better than the accounts of Decius and Gallus in the same text, which also appear to refer to the incorrect tale that Decius fell through Gallus' treason in 251. They are of the same order of information as the tale of the great Persian invasion of Syria in 252 that occupies thirty-four lines in the *Thirteenth Oracle,* an event that clearly meant far more to the author than anything that happened with Decius and Gallus in their struggle with the Goths.[127] In light of the quality of the information about Pescennius Niger, it is all the more striking that the compiler of the *Twelfth Oracle* does not seem to have been aware that Severus had been in command in the Balkans when he rebelled against Julianus, and that he had absolutely no information regarding Severus' other rival for power, Clodius Albinus. Striking, that is, but perhaps not surprising. The variation in the quality of information here, as in the *Thirteenth Oracle,* reflects the way in which information traveled and was interpreted. It also reflects that fact that events that took place in one part of the empire were not always of great interest in another. This picture is complicated only slightly by two other interests that the authors of the extant texts manifest: prodigy and imperial assassination.

Prodigies reflected the view that the gods were taking of contemporary events, and were thus of obvious interest to people interested in the matrix of human and divine power in the Mediterranean world. The Rain Miracle connected with Marcus Aurelius was well known because the emperor had seen to its broad advertisement throughout his realm, and it provided a model for a similar claim to divine aid for Severus, as well, possibly, as the story that bread fell from heaven to save the army of the emperor Probus in Gaul during the 270s.[128] It is a little less clear how the sudden dark cloud that enveloped Rome just before the death of Commodus impinged upon the consciousness of the oracular author who recorded it, but the civil wars that followed it, if not Severus himself, who had published throughout the empire the signs connected with his rise to power, may have done something to perpetuate its memory.[129] The same cannot be said of the rain of blood that is placed in the reign of Caligula in the *Twelfth Oracle*, or the furious rain that seems to have been dated to the reign of Tiberius in the *Fourteenth*,[130] or the eclipse and terrible hailstorm placed in the reign of Claudius, again in the *Twelfth Oracle*. Given the scant space devoted to any ruler in the oracles that have survived, the sheer amount of space given over to the description of such events is interesting in and of itself, as well as the fact that such descriptions are quite different from the generic statements that there will be a spate of natural disasters elsewhere.[131]

Another thing that tended to be discussed was the way that emperors died. It is often the case that men are said to have been murdered were not, or not in the way described. Tiberius, allegedly smothered on his deathbed, is said to have fallen victim to burning steel;[132] Vespasian, to have perished through the rage of his army; and Titus, to have been slain with bronze on the plain of Rome (*Orac. Sib.* 12.115–116, 121–123). Nerva too is said to have been killed (*Orac. Sib.* 12.145–146), and the stories about the deaths of Gordian III and Decius in the *Thirteenth Oracle* are not based on reliable traditions.

In all these cases, as in those discussed at the beginning of this chapter, there is no reason to think that the interpretation of history was intended to be subversive. These texts are post eventum rather than prospective; they seek to analyze rather than to influence events. They do permit us, however, to observe the ways in which prophetic texts were used to deconstruct the endless communications sent by the central authority to its subjects. They provided a history that people could trust. This point was not lost on the masters of the world.

[4]

Prophecy and Personal Power
in the Roman Empire

I gather that Marcus Lepidus was a serious and wise
man in those years, for he turned many things proposed
by the savage adulation of others to the better, and he
did not do so in an ostentatious, disagreeable fashion,
as he flourished with equal authority and goodwill in
the eyes of Tiberius. From this I am compelled to
wonder if the favor of monarchs to some, the dislike to
others, is set by fate or lot at birth, or if something
should be left to our own counsels in walking a path
free from peril and ambition between abrupt contu-
macy and disagreeable obsequium. (*Ann.* 4.20)

THE LINK THAT Tacitus perceived binding notions of predestination and fate with autocracy was a powerful one;[1] and it is no
surprise that, when advertising their own claims, emperors tended
to favor fatalistic interpretations. The monarch had been chosen by
the gods, his lot set at conception or birth, and there was nothing
that anyone could do about it. Hence the collection and public
advertisement of signs relating to the future greatness of rulers and
great men to justify their position.

Midway through his long reign, in 12 B.C., the emperor Augustus commissioned a great project on the Campus Martius that
would come to fruition in the sixty-third year of his life, the "grand
climacteric," a point that he looked to with anticipation and some
dread.[2] This project, including a *horologium* (sundial) that employed

10. A coin from Lyons depicting Augustus on the obverse and Capricorn, the sign under which Augustus was conceived, on the reverse. Suetonius says that Augustus was responsible for this advertisement of his horoscope (*RIC*² Lyons 49–50 no. 124; photo courtesy of the American Numismatic Society).

an obelisk brought from Egypt, served to commemorate the position of the stars at his conception and birth, showing an imperial horoscope to all Romans.[3] Well before this, Augustus had made his horoscope public. Suetonius observes that he was responsible for coins with Capricorn, the sign of his conception; and coins from the province of Asia suggest that the horoscope was published in 27 B.C., when Augustus' position at the head of the state was redefined.[4] This event marks a high point in the personalization of prognostication by members of the Roman aristocracy that seems to have begun as the Roman state began to dominate the Mediterranean. It was a tendency that was for some time in conflict with the oligarchic principle of communal control over divine communication that was a feature of the government of the republic.

The Republican Background

P. Scipio Africanus was the finest general of his generation, and one of its most tiresome politicians. His great victories over the Carthaginians in Spain were not without rumor of aspiration to kingship (even though he specifically turned down the title of king when it was offered to him by the Spaniards), and he inspired his troops for the daring assault on New Carthage in 208 B.C. with the tale of a dream of Neptune. He may also have been the first beneficiary of an oracle to the effect that Scipios were destined to be victorious in Africa, a text that was still in circulation when Caesar proved it false at the battle of Thapsus in 46 B.C.[5] When challenged by his political rivals for fiscal malfeasance in the 180s, Scipio interrupted the trial by observing that it fell on the anniversary of his decisive victory over Hannibal at Zama in 202, and led a crowd that had assembled in the Forum to the temple of Capitoline Jupiter to offer thanks for his existence. There is some reason to think that he may have been the recipient of cult honors.[6] Scipio Aemilianus, the adoptive grandson of Scipio Africanus, may have benefited from the same oracle. Precisely two hundred years after Scipio's capture of Numantia, an oracle turned up in Italy, allegedly given by a Spanish prophetic woman, predicting that the Roman world would be ruled by a man from Spain (page 172 below).

All previous republican self-advertisement pales by comparison with that of L. Cornelius Sulla, the source for much interesting information about himself. He is said to have been identified as the future "greatest man in the world" by a "Chaldean" while he was praetor in the east (Plut. *Sulla* 5). It is firmly attested that Sulla noted in his memoirs that Trophonius had predicted his second victory over the armies of Mithridates just after his first triumph in the field in 87. Shortly after receiving this news, Sulla received another oracle from the same place announcing the outcome of events at Rome (Plut. *Sulla* 17). Before the decisive battle against the younger Marius at Praeneste, Sulla had a dream in which the elder Marius told his son to beware the coming day. In his account of the battle, Plutarch notes that the god fulfilled the words that Sulla had heard in his dream (*Sulla* 28). This detail was likewise probably found in the memoirs. This work, in twenty-two books, which Sulla completed two days before his death, ended with the observation that the "Chaldeans" had foretold that he would die at the height of his powers. His further connection with the divine was advertised in his very name and those of his children. L. Cornelius Sulla Felix is the Latin version of the name Epaphroditus, which Sulla says he took on the advice of an oracle; his daughter was named Fausta, and his son Faustus.[7]

In many ways Sulla was Rome's first *princeps,* and he seems to have enhanced the aristocratic tendency to claim firsthand advice from the gods in public image making. Gaius Marius is no doubt the source of the tale that his seven consulships were presaged by his childhood discovery of seven eagles (no doubt a fact that became known only when the seventh consulship had been achieved), and Cicero was not above manufacturing a few visions for himself to fill out the poem that he wrote on his travails. They were appropriate to an epic hero.[8] Quintus Sertorius campaigned in Spain with a prophetic doe by his side, and it appears that Catiline's colleague Cornelius Cethegus appealed to a sibylline oracle predicting that three Cornelii would hold supreme power at Rome in 63 B.C. Another Cornelius, Cornelius Lentulus, appears to have been talking about the same text in the weeks leading up to the civil war that broke out in 49 B.C. (Caes. *B.C.* 1.4.2).[9] Julius Caesar had a great deal to say about his own divine connections. This was precisely the sort of personal connection with the divine that the senate's ruling oligarchy had established strong institutional safeguards to discourage. These safeguards began to fail along with the political order.

The Roman republican aristocracy was loath to admit that any of its members could be in direct, personal communication with a god. The Roman people, on the other hand, seem to have been deeply fascinated by this possibility. Thus there was a constant tension between the claims of individuals and the claims of the state. In the eyes of the senate, and later of the emperors, only prophets and prophecies that had been duly investigated and determined to be reliable by experts could be admitted into public life. No emperor was any more pleased to learn that one of his politically significant subjects was in direct communication with a higher plane than the republican senate had been to discover that one of its members was closer to the gods than others. The system of dealing with divine revelation was therefore set up to control access; it was not, and could not be, completely successful: the subject was just too interesting.

In the early republic there were two *collegia* to oversee divine communication, the augurs and the *quindecimviri sacris faciundis*. The augurs were concerned with revelations that could be obtained through the observation of natural phenomena. The *quindecimviri* were concerned with *prodigia* and divine advice as to how to respond to them. Since they sought this information through consultation of the *libri sibyllini,* which were written in Greek, they were, by extension, concerned with "foreign rites." In the middle republic a third form of divination became popular at Rome. This was *haruspicium,* an Etruscan form of divination based upon the detailed examination of the internal organs of sacrificial animals and natural phenomena.

The *quindecimviri* acted when the senate received a report of a prodigy that it thought was genuine, and were charged with the authentication of new oracles (the Romans were aware that there might be more sibylline oracles than were in their collection). In the first century B.C. one test of legitimacy was the presence of acrostics in the texts, but there may have been others: it is hard to believe that the board would admit a prophecy that Rome would be destroyed just because it contained an acrostic. In general terms the Roman collection seems to have been concerned primarily with oracles that concerned prodigies (although there are some exceptions), and it may well be that this was what the *quindecimviri* were also looking for. It is also notable that the final decision did not rest with them, for the board then reported its findings to the senate when it had assembled its collection.[10]

Another investigation of oracular texts was carried out by Augustus, acting in his capacity as a *quindecimvir.*[11] Great as the authority of Augustus may have been in this matter, his purification of Roman prophetic books did not put an end to the process of selection. Tacitus reports that the tribune Quintilianus complained in the senate in A.D. 32 when the *quindecimvir* Caninius Gallus had wrongfully caused a book to be included among the sibylline oracles, and that the senate wrote to the emperor Tiberius asking his advice as to the way it should handle the situation. Tiberius responded, "moderately criticizing the tribune on the grounds that he was ignorant of ancient custom because of his youth. He rebuked Gallus because he, a man experienced in religious lore and ceremonies, had brought the matter before a badly attended meeting of the senate, on dubious authority, without the approval of the *collegium* and not, as was customary, after the oracle had been read and evaluated by the magistrates" (Tac. *Ann.* 6.12.1–2).

It is likely that a fair amount of time was spent discussing precisely these issues, for it was as essential to the emperor as it had been for the republican senate to control the record of "authentic" divinely inspired prophecy. This is why Augustus had burned 2,000 prophetic books in the Forum that were deemed "false," and it is why he had moved the books from the Capitoline to the temple of Apollo on the Palatine (Suet. *Aug.* 31). The temple was located next to his house, and Apollo was credited with special interest in the welfare of Augustus himself.[12] Interestingly, it was also in the time of Augustus that the notion that the Sibyl had been inspired by contact with Apollo seems to have become popular.[13]

As has already been amply demonstrated, there was reason for the state to try to control the material that offered its subjects alternative paradigms to its own view of history, or inspired public distress. The state could do no more than take occasional exemplary action in this regard, and could exert no real control over the books that were in circulation; it could merely seek to question their authority. Given that there was a clear distinction in Roman thought between private religion and the official cults of the state, it is perhaps not to be wondered that the state took action only against these books, as it took action, against forms of private worship only when they seemed to threaten the political order. Individuals were left to make their own arrangements so long as they did not clash with those of the community as a whole. So too, in the realm of prophetic books, given general interest in the subject, there was ordinarily no reason to bother.

The augurs, the second group connected with oversight of the state's relations with the gods, were not directly concerned with the future. Rather, they were concerned with establishing the view of the gods about the propriety of actions as they were being taken. Although the art itself was plainly not a purely Latin phenomenon, it came to be regarded as the characteristically Roman form of interpreting communications from the gods, or, more specifically, communications from the god Jupiter.[14] The art consisted primarily

11. A coin of Sulla depicting the instruments of an augur: the augur's staff *(lituus)* and a jug, symbolizing the act of sacrifice *(RRC* 359; photo courtesy of the American Numismatic Society).

of interpreting the actions of birds that were thought to be Jupiter's messengers, and the ability to determine when a natural phenomenon such as a clap of thunder affected the outcome of a ceremony. Errors in the interpretation of divine signs, *vitia,* were offensive to the gods and could lead to disaster if they were not corrected.

The consular elections of 163 B.C. offer an interesting example of the role of an augur in uncovering *vitium,* and into the weaknesses of augury as a system of divination. The consul Tiberius Sempronius Gracchus, who happened to be an augur, was overseeing the election when the first *rogator,* an official charged with reporting the votes of the centuries to the magistrate in charge of the election, dropped dead. Gracchus consulted the *haruspices,* who were coming to be a significant factor in the interpretation of signs, and they told him that he should not be holding the election. Gracchus took this as a suggestion that he was in error and was outraged. "Is that so?" he said, "Am I not in order, I who as consul opened the election, and as augur took the auspices? Do you Etruscan barbarians control the law of the auspices of the Roman people, and are you in charge of the elections?" (Cic. *De nat. deorum* 2.11) He therefore continued the election, and two consuls were duly elected and took office in January.

A few months after they had taken office, the new consuls had gone out to command their armies in the provinces when the senate suddenly received a letter from Gracchus, who was then holding a command in Sardinia. Gracchus explained that when he had been reading the books of the augurs, he had suddenly realized that he had been wrong to continue holding the election because, although he had taken the auspices when he had left the city before the election, he had forgotten to take the auspices again when he had returned to the city to conduct a meeting of the senate, and thus had not properly taken the auspices before the election. It was necessary to take the auspices whenever a magistrate undertook a public act. The senate decided that there was indeed an error in the election of the consuls and compelled them to resign.[15]

The art of taking the auspices, *auspicium,* was not solely the province of the augurs. All Roman magistrates were expected to take the auspices whenever they undertook any public business. Since they would not necessarily be augurs, it was expected that they would be able to interpret basic signs. These signs were of two sorts, "requested" *(imperativa)* and "offered" *(oblativa).* Requested signs were granted as a result of actions by the person taking the auspices, "offered" signs were portentous events that occurred while the magistrate was taking the auspices or engaged in public business. The observation of the eating habits of the sacred chickens was an effort to obtain a "requested" sign, a sudden clap of thunder, hailstorm, or other natural phenomenon could be an "offered" sign. It was up to the magistrate to decide if something that could be interpreted as an "offered" sign was in fact significant. The only time that a magistrate had no choice in the matter was when an augur was present to instruct him.[16] A sign of either variety was good for only one day.[17]

Aside from their participation at sacrifices, augurs oversaw the conferral upon magistrates of the ability to take the auspices, the designation of sacred areas, and the interpretation of signs that were brought to their attention. In cases of the inauguration of a magistrate or a sacred area, a single augur could be empowered to administer the ceremony. In cases in which questions about the auspices were raised, the *collegium* as a whole had to speak. Thus, in the case of the dying *rogator* at the consular election of 163 B.C., Sempronius Gracchus had to write to the senate when he realized that he had made a mistake; the senate then referred the matter to the *collegium*, and acted only when the *collegium* agreed that there had been a *vitium*. It was then up to the senate to decide what to do; in this instance it decided that the consuls who had been elected had to be removed from office even though they were already well into their year of office.

To help them decide the answers to questions, the augurs had books containing records of past results, appropriate prayers, and the tricks of their trade. These books were not regarded as books of prophecy, but rather as instructional manuals. Similarly, books by individual augurs on their trade were no more than technical treatises: they might interest other augurs and even other members of the Roman aristocracy, but they could not be used as guides to the future.[18] As a result, although augural divination could serve to defuse potentially explosive political events either by bringing them to an end (if an augur perceived a problem at any point in an election, for example, he could stop it) or by diffusing the blame for a disaster by revealing problems in the state's relations with the gods, it was not an effective device for mediating change. By the beginning of the second century, the augurs had serious competition in interpreting divine will.

Haruspicium offered prediction of the future and description of the present state of human and divine relations. We do not know when the *haruspices* began to be recognized as accurate diviners who were worthy of Rome's attention, but it is clear that by the time of the Hannibalic war even the senate thought that their advice should be sought. Thus the consul Fabius Maximus consulted them when numerous prodigies were reported while he was on campaign in 215 B.C., and the senate ordered sacrifices in accord with their *responsa* in 213 B.C. (when Fabius was again consul).[19] The loss of ten books of Livy's history, covering the later fourth and the bulk of the third century, makes it impossible to know when consultation of the *haruspices* actually became common at Rome, but it is possible that the practice began after the final conquest of Etruria in the early third century B.C.

The *haruspices* could be consulted about the innards of sacrificial animals *(exta)*, lightning *(fulgura)*, and prodigies. Their prognostic

12. An Etruscan bronze mirror depicting the legendary haruspex Tages reading a liver. He is holding the liver in his left hand, and his left foot is on a stone (Vat. MEG 12240; photo courtesy of Monumenti Musei e Gallerie Pontificie).

ability depended upon books that seem to have recorded what had happened in cases involving similar signs. Before consulting the books, it was necessary to make as careful an observation as possible of the phenomena that were to provide the clues to the future. In the case of a prediction on the basis of *exta,* a *haruspex* had to be present at the slaughter of the animal.[20] When the animal was killed, he took the liver in his left hand while standing with his right foot on the ground and his left foot on a stone, and read it clockwise. In dealing with lightning, the *haruspex* would try to determine which part of the heavens the lightning had come from. For predictive purposes the sky was divided into sixteen regions, and the significance of a lightning bolt depended upon which sixteenth of the heavens it appeared in and what, if anything, it hit. The interpretation of portents appears to have been based primarily upon the ability to assess an event in light of precedent. Thus, in our last sighting of the *haruspices* on campaign (with Julian in A.D. 363), they appear with their books of "portents in time of war" after the emperor had been brought a dead lion to tell him that the sign prohibited an invasion (Amm. Marc. 23.5.10). Julian, advised by philosophers who seem have convinced him that they could alter the prescriptions of fate, ignored the warning. He died in battle while trying to withdraw from Persia a few weeks later.[21] There is plenty of evidence for *haruspices* in a private context later, or for the use of the word, for it is often difficult to tell if the term is being used in a technical sense or as a generic word for diviner (see pages 178–180).

Haruspical responses could be quite long and complex, as is evident from one of 56 B.C. that can be reconstructed from Cicero's speech *Concerning the Response of the Haruspices* suggesting that it referred to the actions of his political enemies (rather than of himself as they had proposed). The response opens with a description of the prodigy and continues with a number of general suggestions about what this prodigy signifies about the state of Roman affairs. The opening words were: "Whereas in the Ager Latiniensis a loud noise and a clashing has been heard, expiations are due to Jupiter, Saturn, Neptune, Tellus, and the heavenly gods" (Cic. *De res. har.* 20). The report of the prodigy was followed by a number of remarks on just what was wrong with Rome, including "games carelessly celebrated and profaned," "envoys slain in violation of earthly and heavenly law," "good faith and oaths neglected," "ancient and secret sacrifices carelessly performed and profaned," "dissensions among the *optimates*," "occult designs" on the republic, the continuing accrual of "honor to the worser sort and the rejected," and, at the very end, a warning to take care "lest the constitution of the republic be changed" (Cic. *De res. har.* 34, 36, 37, 53, 55, 56, 60).

The construction of new *responsa* for each new event sets the discipline of the *haruspices* apart from that of the *quindecimviri*, who had to be content with the oracles that they found. The difference in the information that could be obtained from an augur and a *haruspex* is brought out very well in Livy's account of a consultation that took place in 213 B.C. involving the consul Tiberius Sempronius Gracchus (the grandfather of the consul in 163 B.C.). Livy reports that when the sacrificial victim was killed two snakes came out of nowhere and began to eat the liver. The *haruspices* advised another sacrifice (it was standard practice to repeat a sacrifice once something had gone wrong to make sure that a bad sign was really being given). When it was performed again, the same thing happened. The *haruspices* then told Gracchus that he should beware "hidden men and veiled plots" (Livy 25.16.2–4). He failed to heed their advice and was killed. An augur would simply have said that the sacrifice had to be performed again, or that the consul should do nothing until he could get a sacrifice to come out correctly since it was clear that the gods were displeased about something. This is the same sort of difference that we have already seen in the two responses to the death of the *rogator* at the consular election of 163 B.C. As an augur, Gracchus insisted that only augural precedent was relevant and, as he thought that he had properly observed the signs, the death of the *rogator* could have no meaning. To the *haruspices,* the death was obviously a *prodigium* indicating that something was wrong. This congruity could be taken, as Cicero takes it in his account of the incident, as a sign that both forms of divination were correct. But elsewhere Cicero, who had much to say in favor of augury after he became an augur, is scathing about *haruspicium.* Like a number of Romans of his class, he sneered at *haruspices* as foreigners, and there may have been more to his objections than that.

The *haruspices* had no official standing in the Roman state until the emperor Claudius created a specific *ordo* of sixty-one *haruspices* in A.D. 47. They spoke either when the senate decided that it needed to consult them (which would mean that neither the *quindecimviri* nor the augurs could provide the needed information on some point) or when an individual asked them. Indeed, the rise of *haruspices* as personal advisers to Roman aristocrats appears to parallel the decline of aristocratic government at Rome in the late republic. Great individuals like Sulla and Caesar had personal *haruspices*.[22] Julius Caesar also seems to have taken a particularly dim view of Etruscan senators who claimed expertise in *haruspicium* and served the cause of his political enemies.[23] Cicero, when expressing his true thoughts on the subject, seems to have disliked the *haruspices* for very similar reasons: their wisdom was too often at the ready disposal of his adversaries.[24] All of this mattered because people felt that the gods could intervene in human affairs whenever they felt like it, and because these communications were more detailed and less susceptible to collegiate interpretation by members of the Roman aristocracy. It is also interesting that they were not formally integrated into the state system of divine interpretation until the reign of Claudius, who was personally fascinated with Etruscan antiquity. His excuse for doing so was to preserve a discipline that was being lost. This may not be surprising: with the emergence of the monarchy, prognostication that bore on political events was dangerous if it was not to be banal, and the members of the class from which the important *haruspices* of the republic emerged, the upper class of the cities of Etruria, could find other, safer things to do until their learning could be used by the emperor.

Court Politics

At the same time that personal *haruspices* began to appear in the trains of great Romans, other diviners began to be visible and to acquire increasing political significance. The emperor Tiberius was devoted to astrology, and he is rumored to have conducted a rather unpleasant search to find himself a suitable personal guide to the stars. It is said that when he was on Rhodes, Tiberius took various astrologers out behind his house to an area overlooking some cliffs, and if he suspected that they were frauds, he had them thrown off. Finally Tiberius brought a man named Thrasyllus to this spot, and when Thrasyllus told him that he would be emperor he asked him some basic questions about himself: did he know the hour at which he, Thrasyllus, had been conceived, the year, and the day? When asked these questions, Thrasyllus cast his own horoscope and then said that he realized that he himself was in great danger. Thereupon

Tiberius knew he had an accurate prognosticator, and kept Thrasyllus by his side throughout his life.[25]

Thrasyllus was no common street-corner astrologer, any more than were Herennius Figulus, personal *haruspex* to Gaius Gracchus, Postumius, who filled the same role with Sulla; and Vestricius Spurinna, Caesar's *haruspex*.[26] Skill in interpreting divine communication offered the well-born provincial an avenue to high favor at Rome, and Thrasyllus appears to have been related by marriage to the royal house of Commagene.[27] It took more than a knowledge of the stars to survive dinner with Tiberius. Thrasyllus appears to have written on Plato, and his grand-daughter seems to have married the praetorian prefect Sutorius Macro. His son, Tiberius Claudius Balbillus, was prefect of Egypt in 55, and flourished with equal favor under both Nero and Vespasian. A descendant, the poet Balbilla, appears in the retinue of Hadrian when he visited Egypt.[28]

Thrasyllus and Balbillus were men of no small influence. Thrasyllus seems to have been important in the propaganda campaign unleashed by Tiberius before his return to Rome in A.D. 4, he was dining with Augustus a few days before his death, and it is alleged that one of his horoscopes sped Tiberius to his grave by convincing him that what proved to be a terminal illness was mild and hence not worth consulting a doctor about.[29] Another of his predictions that attracted public notice was that Caligula had as much chance of becoming emperor as he did of riding over the gulf of Baiae on horses. Caligula subsequently built a bridge across the bay and drove across in a chariot, at which point his courtiers let it be known that he was fulfilling the prediction (Suet. *Gaius* 19.3). This was not the only time that astrology and the succession were linked in these years. Tiberius supposedly predicted, on the basis of a horoscope that he cast himself, that Servius Sulpicius Galba would become emperor,[30] and he finally resorted to prognostic technique to chose between Caligula and his own grandson Gemellus for the succession. In this case, when the augury that he had rigged to work in favor of Gemellus came out on Caligula's behalf, "he saw himself utterly shorn of confirming his own choice of a successor to his imperial office since the power from on high had not been vouchsafed him" (Jos. *AJ* 18.214 Loeb trans.).

If things had worked out in Gemellus' favor as he wished, this incident might have been used by Tiberius to bring Gemellus to public recognition in a way that might have recalled Tiberius' earlier reliance upon signs of divine favor as he maneuvered for power in the last decade of Augustus' life. As Thrasyllus' prophecy was used to explain Caligula's behavior, so members of the court could make private personal contact with the divine well known in the upper echelons of society, and Tiberius' reputation as an astrologer could only have helped. In the case of Thrasyllus' prediction about Caligula, we are told precisely that this prediction was communicated by the emperor's intimates. A similar process may be divined behind the report that the favor of the Roman people was inflamed on Nero's behalf by reports of prodigies. There were two versions (at least). One had Nero protected by two serpents, the other, Nero's, reduced the number to one (Tac. *Ann.* 11.11.3). Augustus is said to have "put the story about" that he had put his left boot on the wrong foot on the day that a mutiny in the army almost ruined him (Plin. *NH* 2.25). It is fair to assume that he did this through his friends. Such storytelling may also lie behind the account of Titus' visit to the oracle of Aphrodite on Paphos where a private consultation soon became public knowledge (Tac. *Hist.* 2.3–4). It is firmly attested that Julian told his friends that he saw the genius of the Roman people on the night that he was proclaimed in Paris, and that he saw her again (complete with cornucopia) leaving his tent on the night before he died (Amm. Marc. 20.5.10; 25.2.3).

In Quintus Cicero's handbook on electioneering, advice is given to the prospective political candidate that he ought to be kind to his slaves and freedmen because they talk to members of the lower orders in the Forum (*Comm. pet.* 17). An aristocratic Roman household contained people of all sorts, enabling direct communication throughout society. It is also significant that such communication was directed toward people who might be in some sort of physical proximity to the court. Chatter of this sort accompanied the emperor and prospective emperors wherever they happened to be.

Communication between the palace and the upper echelons of Roman society through the medium of prognostication did not end with the Julio-Claudians. Signs of the use of court astrology in politics appear to be preserved in the corpus of the astrologer Vettius Valens, which contains a horoscope that may be connected with Licinius Sura explaining his preference for boys,[31] a horoscope for Hadrian's putative successor Pedanius Secundus explaining the latter's death, and a horoscope for Hadrian himself, all cast by Antigonus of Nicaea. The second of these cannot have been made public until 137, when Pedanius was executed, and it looks as if it was part of an effort to convince people that this deeply unpopular act should not be blamed on Hadrian but rather on the stars.[32]

The war of opinion over the murders committed at the end of his life was not the only one in which Hadrian deployed the gods. Trajan never named a successor during his lifetime, or, at least, not before he lay on his deathbed in 117. Hadrian, who appeared to have been marked out for this role when young, seems to have been eclipsed in the last decade of Trajan's life by various of his generals. Perhaps this is not a surprising development, since Trajan spent much of his life in the field and may not have found the company of the young man as congenial as that of his fellow officers. Hadrian's accession, while the internal crisis that had wrecked Trajan's Parthian expedition raged, was marked by the murder of four of these senior officers and, it would appear, by a certain amount of communication about divine favor that had been manifested at earlier stages. According to a tradition that was of some importance in the fourth century, Hadrian consulted an oracle at the Castalian spring at Daphne near Antioch about his prospects. He dipped a laurel leaf in the spring and found his fate written upon it, and then blocked up the spring so that no one else could do so. The future might be fixed, but it was not always a good idea to let people know what it would be.[33] Hadrian's consultation of the Castalian oracle could have occurred only in the immediate context of the Parthian war, perhaps in its very last stages (it is difficult to imagine that Trajan, who clearly did not plan on dying when he did, would have taken kindly to such actions by a member of his house). But this is less significant than the public relations ploy of closing the shrine: no clearer statement that the gods had spoken concerning him could be made to those surrounding him.

It is almost certainly in the same context that a response that could be interpreted as indicating an imperial future from consultation of Vergil became known, and a man named Apollonius the Syrian (a Platonic philosopher) revealed that an oracle at Nicephorium had predicted the same thing. In Apollonius we can see once again the role of a court favorite in "leaking" prophetic information to the world (*HA V. Hadr.* 2.8–9).

Every emperor about whom any detailed information has survived advertised some sort of divine favor, and it was not just court favorites who spread it abroad. The panegyric was the ideal way to let the emperor's followers know what was important, and it is therefore not surprising that the younger Pliny equipped Trajan with an oracular indication of future greatness, in the extensive panegyric that he worked up on the basis of one that he delivered to mark his consulship in 100.[34] In a passage ostensibly designed to remind the emperor of facts of his life, and in fact to remind the mass of his auditors, he recalled:

> Their [the gods'] choice of you, Caesar Augustus, and their divine favor were made manifest at the very moment of your setting out to join your army by an omen without precedent. The names of all your predecessors were revealed to those who sought the oracles either by a gush of blood from the victims or a flight of birds on the left; but in your case as you mounted the Capitol, following due precedent, the citizens gathered there for other reasons hailed you with a shout as if you were already emperor; for when the doors of the temple opened for your entry, the entire crowd gathered at the threshold cried *Imperator!* At the time it was thought that they were addressing Jupiter, but events have proved that the title was intended for you, and the omen was thus interpreted by all. (*Pan.* 5.3–4 Loeb trans.)

Two centuries later, the panegyrics delivered before the emperor Constantine revealed all sorts of secrets about that monarch and his dealings with the god, suggesting a complicated pattern by which information passed from the inner sanctum of imperial power to speakers drawn from the upper echelons of Gallic society, whose words could be expected to publicize the message of the moment. Thus, the panegyrist from Autun who delivered a speech in honor of Constantine was a former imperial servant who had sons in the imperial service, one of them evidently a reasonably well placed lawyer in the imperial financial service, an *advocatus fisci*. He was therefore an appropriate person not only to reveal the secret of Constantine's descent from Claudius to the world, but also to describe an encounter between the emperor and Apollo after the death of Maximian.[35] He further observed that Constantine was the person to whom the "divine songs" of the prophets referred when they mentioned a person destined for dominion over the whole world.[36] The orator of 313 who noted that Constantine had "a secret connection with the divine mind" that ruled the world when he invaded Italy the year before, was also experienced in speaking before the emperor, and knew that this was the line for the year.[37] This was all that people outside the Christian church needed to know about the remarkable personal experiences that led to one of the most profoundly important religious decisions in the history of Europe: Constantine's adoption of Christianity. Eight years later, an experienced orator from Bordeaux named Nazarius was given a different story about the divine inspiration for the march, two miraculous riders sent by the divine Constantius, riders who had been seen and heard by people around the emperor as well.[38] The scene is also set in close proximity to the emperor, a reflection of the process by which such news was spread outward from the inner circle. A different, explicitly Christian story was revealed to Eusebius by Constantine himself sometime later.[39]

Just over a century before Constantine began his ascent to power, Septimius Severus, the first emperor since Vespasian who actually had to fight for the throne, seems to have bolstered his claim by publication of the signs of divine favor well beyond the circle of court favorites. It is alleged that Severus received the first glimmerings of future greatness from an astrologer who cast a horoscope for him. When the astrologer perceived its significance, he asked Severus for his "own nativity, and not that of another man." When Severus assured him that he had given accurate information, the

astrologer "revealed to him all the things that later came to pass."
The story is not unlike one told about the emperor Augustus in 44
B.C.; the resemblance is probably no accident.[40] Likewise, Severus
is the most probable source for the tale that he selected Julia Domna
as his second wife because he discovered that her horoscope indicated that she would marry a monarch (*HA V. Sev.* 3.9). Herodian
reports that Severus described the dreams, oracles, and signs that
encouraged him to take the throne both in his autobiography and
in his public dedications of statues (2.9.4). One sign of the reaction
to this sort of direct imperial indication of taste is Cassius Dio's first
historical work, an account of the portents that inspired Severus to
take the throne.[41] In later years this taste was graphically illustrated:
Severus had a picture of the stars painted on the ceiling of the
palace. On public display there was a version that was accurate in
all respects save for the actual position of the stars at the moment
of his birth, so that people would not know exactly when he would
die. The fully accurate version was depicted in his private apart-
ments (Dio 76.11.1).

Dio tends to reflect the interest and attitudes of his class. Unlike
Tacitus, who may have been a somewhat anomalous intellect, he
was not one to question the role of fate. He is explicit about the
dream that encouraged him to continue his historiographic enterprises after he had received a warm response to his work on dreams
from Severus (72.23.3–5), and his history reveals a firm belief in
the reality of divine intervention. It was convenient, and perhaps
more personally satisfying than frustrating, to know that the gods
controlled the events of his lifetime that were beyond his own
control.[42]

It was not always sufficient, of course, to depend upon others,
and not everyone was interested in the stars. But there were other
possibilities, and these enabled the emperor to send more complicated messages than those connected simply with the fact of his
power. In the spring of 361, the railing that restrained the excited
spectators in the first row of the circus at Antioch broke opposite
the emperor Constantius. A number of people were injured, and
a man named Amphilochus died. Just the day before, this
Amphilochus had presumed to take a place in a group of high court

officials who went out to meet the emperor as he returned from a campaign on the eastern frontiers. Other officials in the group had protested his presence on the grounds that he had fomented discord between the emperor and his brother Constans, who had been murdered in the west during a revolt more than a decade earlier. When the cry that Amphilochus should be executed for treason had gone up, Constantius had calmed the crowd by observing that, although he thought Amphilochus guilty, he could not kill a man who had not been openly convicted of a crime. But when Amphilochus died in this accident, Constantius is said to have rejoiced that he had demonstrated a knowledge of future events (Amm. Marc. 21.6.2–3).

The source of our knowledge for this event, Ammianus Marcellinus, was not present in Antioch during 361, and is thus recording an imperial response that must have been given some publicity at the time. This is particularly interesting since Constantius, a devout Christian, was thus using a symbolic method to communicate the idea that he was a man of special quality, a notion that had much currency among the pagan aristocracy both of his own time and of earlier centuries. This quality was illustrated by his knowledge of things that were about to happen. The incident itself was of political significance because civil war was then brewing between Constantius and his nephew Julian, who had presumed to assert a claim to the rank of Augustus during the previous spring. Constantius was thus using this accident to remind people that he was precisely the sort of emperor that they wanted.

Claims to personal prophetic power were important features of personal image making on both sides of the religious divide between polytheists and Christians. Prophetic power is obviously connected to claims about the receipt of actual divine revelation, but different accounts of it do not mention a specific divinity. Rather they suggest that waking contact with divine forces was a sign of superior moral quality. One theory of such presentiment is propounded by Apollonius of Tyana in the speech that Philostratus invented for the sage to deliver at his trial (also invented) before Domitian. Here Apollonius explains that he is able to perceive the future because his vegetarian diet has protected his senses with an imperceptible clear air, so that there should not be any foul matter around them, and it enables me to see, as if in the gleam of a mirror, all that happens and will happen; for the wise man does not await the exhalation of the earth, or the corruption of the atmosphere, lest evil should flow in from on high, but he knows all of these things while they are on the doorstep after the gods perceive them, but more rapidly than average people; for gods perceive the future, mortals the present and the wise man sees what is approaching. (8.7.9)

The point Philostratus made here is crucial to the distinction that he wanted to draw between Apollonius and magicians, and, although there might not have been general agreement on the cause of this ability, there was little dispute about the phenomenon in question. The ability to perceive what was hidden to others was the mark of the superior individual.

The Neoplatonic philosopher Porphyry wanted to convince his readers that his master, Plotinus, was a completely extraordinary person with a superior soul. He even seems to have believed that this quality had saved his own life. Plotinus, he says, had perceived that he was contemplating suicide, and came up to him while he was staying inside to tell him that the desire to do away with himself was the result not of a rational desire, but rather of a bilious disposition. Nor was he the only one to experience the effects of his master's enhanced perspicacity. He noted that Plotinus was in the habit of predicting how the young men around him would turn out: in the case of one named Polemon, he correctly divined that he would be subject to the cravings of the flesh and not live long. On another occasion, when a valuable necklace was stolen, he assembled the slaves of his household and pointed to one of them with the words "This is the thief." The slave denied the charge but, after a flogging, confessed and returned the stolen object (*V. Plot.* 11). What makes this record of elementary physiological observation so significant is that it falls in the section of the biography that is concerned with the special power of the Plotinian soul, illustrating the essential doctrinal point that knowledge comes naturally to the sage. Porphyry had just quoted Plotinus on this point with specific reference to divination.

A similar desire to outfit heroes with special perception appears in another Neoplatonic work, Eunapius' *Lives of the Philosophers*. Here, for example, after recording that Iamblichus denied the story (told by his slaves) that when he prayed he was suffused with a golden hue and floated ten feet in the air, Eunapius, as proof of the philosopher's excellence, tells a story about Iamblichus' ability to tell that a funeral procession had just passed along the road by which he too was traveling. In doing so he makes it clear that he has heard the story from Chrysanthius of Sardis, who had heard it from his own teacher, Aedesius, one of Iamblichus' leading pupils (Eun. *VP* 458).

A compatriot of Ammianus, the rhetor Libanius, provides some of the best evidence for the importance of prophecy in defining a person's standing. In his letters he repeatedly congratulates himself for various demonstrations of his own *mantike,* and various compatriots for theirs. It is clear from the context of these statements that he uses the word with the same implication that it had in earlier Greek: the ability to divine the future in an extraordinary way; Libanius even compares various acts of foresight with the prognostication of the legendary seers Amphiareus and Bakis. In his autobiography, completed in 392, he writes that his great-grandfather had not only an acquaintance with Latin, but also the power of *mantike,* and thereby that he foresaw that his sons would be executed; Libanius credits his own *mantike* for his survival during Valens' horrific campaign against magic, carried out at Antioch in 372 (*Or.* 1.3, 119).

Centuries earlier, the historian Josephus had saved his own life by breaking into a prophetic fit before the general Vespasian— telling him that he would become emperor—and Cassius Dio believed that the emperor Caracalla had predicted his own death on several occasions (78.8). The elder Pliny tells the story of an equestrian named Corfidius who appeared to have died. While his brother was preparing the funeral, Corfidius came back to life and ordered his servants to prepare for the brother's funeral instead, and told them where his brother had buried some gold. The servants went in search of the gold, and after they had found it they returned home to find that Corfidius' brother had indeed just died. Pliny goes on to say that life is full of such prophecies, even though they are not worth collecting because, more often than not, they are false (*NH* 7.177). This story was true, however, because he had it on the authority of the great antiquarian Terentius Varro, who was in Capua when it happened. To Pliny this was a true case in which a soul had wandered far from the body, an instance that might confirm similar stories that were told in literature about Aristeas of Proconnesus and Hermotimus of Clazomenae (*NH* 7.174–175).

All these are cases in which the individual seems to have acted without the direct intervention of a divinity. There are numerous other instances in which people mention dreams, oracles, and other portents that revealed secrets that would otherwise have been hidden. The elder Pliny himself wrote history upon the instructions of a ghost, that of Caesar Drusus, who appeared to him in a dream instructing him to record Drusus' deeds so that they would not be forgotten (Plin. *Ep.* 3.5.4). This is significant because Pliny told people about it and because his nephew the younger Pliny thought that it was worth recording when he was asked for a summary of his famous uncle's work. The younger Pliny records that he had a dream that revealed that he was in peril of his life at the hands of the emperor Domitian just before that emperor succumbed to a conspiracy in 96, and the historian Appian reports that his life was saved by a prophetic bird while he was fleeing from rebellious Jews in Egypt during the great revolt of 117.[43] Cassius Dio says that his account of the death of Caracalla was given to him by Septimius Severus in a dream (which may explain why he does not seem to have tried to ferret out the truth in any great detail), while both Pliny and Tacitus evince interest in the story that an obscure equestrian named Curtius Rufus saw a divinity in North Africa who predicted a great future for him.[44]

Prophetic events of this sort were not simply the domain of professionals or philosophers. They were an important part of life, and they revealed the interest that the gods took in the fortunes of the rich and famous. They were not the only way in which a famous person could make contact with the gods, but the ability to claim a direct connection with a divinity was clearly important and worth talking about. It might also be useful to claim divine advice from more public sources before embarking on serious enterprises.

Emperors were not averse to being seen consulting oracles or to making public reference to other forms of divination. Augustus is said to have made some sort of vow with respect to the Megalesian games in A.D. 7, "because some woman had cut some letters on her arm and practiced some sort of divination" (Dio 55.31.2). It is reported that he did so not because he believed that she was really possessed by a divine spirit, but, "inasmuch as the populace was terribly wrought up over both the wars and the famine (which had now set in once more), he, too, affected to believe the common report and proceeded to do anything that would make the crowd more cheerful" (Dio 55.31.3 Loeb trans.). We have a record on stone commemorating contact between Trajan and the shrine at Didyma (possibly in connection with an oracle that predicted his future greatness), and we know that Germanicus stopped at Claros on his way east in A.D. 18.[45] The response that Germanicus received was not encouraging, however, and that may indicate that his trip was fraught with political complications, perhaps inspired by his uncle, Tiberius, who, as we have already seen, was a past master of religious manipulation. Trajan also seems to have consulted the shrine of Zeus Belus, near Apamea, just before setting out on campaign against the Persians.[46] Hadrian took an open interest in Delphi, and so, evidently, did Julian, whose emergence as Augustus, according to Libanius, brought the oracles back to life.

Such consultations can often be associated with moments of political tension. As he went on campaign against the Danubian tribes in the 160s, Marcus Aurelius seems not to have had qualms about making a public display (throwing lions into the Danube) on the basis of an oracle of Glycon that Alexander of Abonuteichos sent him; and Vespasian had a response concerning Veleda inscribed on stone (page 16 above). Zenobia of Palmyra engaged in a very public consultation of Sarpedonion at Seleucia in Cilicia and at the shrine of Aphrodite at Aphraca before going to war with Aurelian in 272.[47] The record that she received responses portending disaster no doubt reflects an effort to appease Aurelian. Thirty years later, Diocletian used the oracle of Didyma in an effort to fire up public opinion in the months before the promulgation of his first persecution edict in 303. Maximin Daia may have been oracle-hunting at Stratonicaea in 312, and was much interested in a new oracle that opened at Antioch at exactly the same time.[48] Indeed, the petition from the city of Antioch to Maximin that is preserved in Eusebius' *Ecclesiastical History* appears to have been influenced by the oracular statue of Zeus Philios that Theotecnus of Antioch activated at this time.[49] This statue seems to have been similar to other oracular statues in the area, making it all the more effective because the technique had a good track record.[50]

Such public activity could reach a wider audience than palace intimates, and no doubt it was intended to do so. Messages from these shrines would be likely to carry more weight because the shrines would seem less likely to be under the direct control of the emperor, and they tended to be at the center of independent nexus of communication with cities that were their regular clients. In at least one case it appears that a shrine that had a well-advertised connection with the house of Severus made a speedy effort to distance itself from that house as soon as Caracalla was murdered. Zeus Belus near Apamea is said to have pointed Severus, while still a private citizen, to a passage of Homer that could be interpreted as a sign that he would rule. Dio recalls that when Severus consulted it again, after his accession, the oracle pointed him to a passage of Euripides' *Phoenissae*: "Your house will perish utterly in blood" (78.8.6). It is difficult to believe that Severus revealed this to anyone, and rather easier to believe that this response was revealed by the oracle itself immediately after Macrinus became emperor in 217. A year later this oracle seems to have distanced itself from Macrinus by publicizing an oracle, again from Homer, suggesting that he would soon fall victim to a younger rival (Dio 78.40.4). The record of Trajan's consultation of this oracle, which included prediction of his demise, is probably of the same sort. So too might be the record that the Apis bull refused to take food when Germanicus consulted it (Pliny *NH* 8.185).

"Nothing inspired them so much as the burning of the Capitol. The city had once been captured by the Gauls, but the empire had remained while the seat of Jupiter was whole: a sign of heavenly anger had been given by the fatal fire, and the Druids sang with their vain superstition that this portended the possession of all human affairs for the transalpine races" (Tac. *Hist.* 4.54.2).[51] The revolt of Bar Kokhba in Palestine during the reign of Hadrian may offer another example of prophetic subversion, for the rabbi Achiva seems to have made quite an impression by anointing Simon ben Kosiba as the Messiah, and Simon himself appears to have tried to play the role with various demonstrations of supernatural power.[52] Apocalyptic visions may also have played a part in the Jewish revolt of 116–117, and were a feature of the revolt in 65.[53] At the same time that the Druids uttered their words in A.D. 69, the German prophetess Veleda seems to have played a significant role in inspiring the tribes north of the Rhine against Rome. Native Egyptian traditions may also have been invoked by the leaders of the revolt of the Bucoli in Egypt during the reign of Marcus Aurelius (Dio 71.4).

Prophecy and prodigy could help provide an ideological foundation for open rebellion against Rome, and they could play a role in fomenting civil unrest. Members of the Athenian aristocracy seem to have arranged for a statue of Athena on the Acropolis to turn from east to west and spit blood between 21 and 19 B.C. to upset a visit by Augustus.[54] Similarly, priests at Pergamon in 48 B.C. seem to have tried to subvert Pompey's control of the east even before Pharsalus by arranging for a mysterious sound to emanate from the temple of Dionysus. Strange noises that may also be connected with local opposition were heard at Olympia when Caligula ordered the statue of Olympian Zeus moved to Rome in A.D. 40.[55] In another context, the sudden fireballs that disrupted Julian's effort to rebuild the temple at Jerusalem may be seen as Christian efforts to prevent Julian from proving that Christ's words about the destruction of the temple could be false.[56] On the other side of the religious divide, Dionysius of Alexandria attributes an anti-

Christian pogrom in Alexandria during 248 to the actions of a local prophet, and several Christian writers note that natural disasters were interpreted as signs of divine disfavor indicating a need to remove Christians from a community.[57]

In the republic and empire, the determination as to whether some event was in fact a significant prodigy at Rome or relevant to Roman territory was left to the senate, which would decide if the *quindecimviri* should take account of it. Floods of the Tiber in A.D. 15, for instance, led to calls for a consultation, which Tiberius refused to permit (Tac. *Ann.* 1.76.1). The existence of this procedure is an indication of concern, rather than that the Roman state was really able to calm popular unrest connected with such events. In 53 B.C., for instance, Tiber floods prompted the belief that the *impiety* of Gabinius—who had restored Ptolemy Auletes to the Egyptian throne in the previous year, contravening the command of a sibylline oracle that had been found in the official collection—had upset the relationship between human and divine (Dio 39.61.3–4).

But floods and earthquakes were not the only events that could lead to trouble. As has already been noted, various more mundane events could be taken as signs that the gods were upset. This sort of event was much easier to fabricate if someone was inclined to cause trouble for the regime (as the prophetic woman in A.D. 7 may indeed have been trying to do). It is therefore not surprising to find it recorded, in the context of other prodigies reported in the context of Varus' disaster in A.D. 9, that a statue of Victory in Germany that had faced toward the enemy was turned around so that it faced Italy (Dio 56.24.4).

In A.D. 68, just as Galba was declaring himself in Spain against Nero, an ancient ring was found at a town that Galba had chosen as his headquarters. It contained a precious stone engraved with a Victory and a trophy. At the same time it was reported that a ship from Alexandria loaded with arms arrived at Dertosa with no one on board, "removing all doubt that the war was just and holy and undertaken with the approval of the gods" (Suet. *Galba* 10.4 Loeb trans.). Galba also seems to have found a prophetic young woman to utter some verses to the effect that a ruler of the world would come forth from Spain. A priest of Jupiter at Clunia in Italy found the very same verses, also uttered by an inspired girl two hundred years earlier, in the inner sanctum of the shrine (Suet. *Galba* 9.2). A few months earlier, at Rome the doors of the Mausoleum were said to have flown open of their own accord, and a voice was heard summoning Nero by name. At about the same time, the *lares* that had been adorned fell to the ground during the preparations for a sacrifice, and the keys to the temple of Capitoline Jupiter could not be found for some time (Suet. *Nero* 46.2). Tacitus notes that Nero was driven from the throne by messengers and rumors more than by arms (*Hist.* 189.2).

Vespasian seems to have been a master of the arts of religious subversion. Prophecies were spread throughout the east about the coming of a new monarch from that region, and his eldest son, Titus, made a public visit to Paphos to obtain a similar prediction.[58] Vespasian even healed the sick at Alexandria. But these events may have been less striking to the Roman audience than the sudden turning of a statue of Julius Caesar on the Tiber Island so that it faced east rather than west. Tacitus places this happening in the context of Otho's moves against Vitellius, but Suetonius secures a somewhat earlier date for the event: the day that Galba was riding to the elections that would give him his second consulship. Vespasian had plainly been involved in the conspiracy that brought Nero down, and Titus was heading west at the end of 68, seemingly so that he could be adopted by Galba. The revolt of Vitellius in the north forced Galba to look elsewhere for an heir, but this turn of events should not mean that the rumor that accompanied Titus' journey was a fantasy. The statue's sudden change of direction may have been a subtle reminder to the emperor arranged by Vespasian's friends at Rome.[59]

In the context of imperial politics such as those described in the last few paragraphs, the agents of prophetic disruption were almost certainly to be found among the personal friends of aspiring emperors, and in cases in which civic protests against Rome may be divined behind readily explicable (in human terms) signs of heavenly anger, members of the local aristocracy may have been involved.[60] But this is not always the case. Some of the prophetic problems attested at Rome can be connected not with highly placed political rivals of the emperors, but rather with general popular unease, prophetic commentaries on the general state of affairs. It was precisely this kind of activity that most imperial edicts before Constantine attempting to suppress prophetic activity seem to have been designed to halt. Even after Constantine and his sons put an end to activities at the principal prophetic shrines of the ancient world, and issued edict after edict against private divination, members of the upper classes seem to have had ready access to divine practitioners, and it may well be doubted that the personal adviser on the divine to any member of the imperial aristocracy was personally affected by imperial edicts unless the advisee had done something to attract imperial ire.[61]

In A.D. 11 Augustus issued an edict forbidding the consultation of prophets alone or concerning a death. The terms of the edict indicate that Augustus did not consider it practical to ban prophetic consultation altogether; rather, he wanted to restrict consultation about politically sensitive subjects. As reported, it appears that the terms of the edict assumed that people would not bring their friends along to ask questions about the fate of the empire or of the emperor (the death that no doubt most interested Augustus) (Dio 56.25.5). The trial of Libo Drusus in A.D. 16 led to more significant action. This was a *senatus consultum* that banned *mathematici* (astrologers), "Chaldeans," *arioli* (diviners) and "others who do similar things" from the city. Citizens found engaging in this arts were interdicted from fire and water (exiled from the city), and legal action against foreigners was provided for. According to Tacitus the edict led directly to the execution of two practitioners, who presumably were directly connected with Libo.[62] Like Augustus' book-burning, and his ban in 11, this law seems to have been aimed at a specific situation rather than conceived as a permanent solution, and there were exceptions. There is no suggestion that Thrasyllus was incommoded in the least by this action, while both Dio and Suetonius record that Tiberius forgave astrologers who petitioned him and promised to give up their practice (Suet. *Tib.* 36; Dio 57.15.8). It seems that some members of the senate intervened to protect their friends. Dio asserts that "all citizens would have been acquitted even contrary to his wish, had not a certain tribune prevented it." This tribune seems to have vetoed a motion by Gnaeus Piso granting an amnesty to all diviners who apologized, and given Piso's close connection with the imperial house, the question arises as to whether Tiberius had tacitly approved this course of action (Dio 57.15.9). There were similar incidents. Suetonius records that Tiberius banned secret consultation with *haruspices,* which does not look as though it can be connected with the language of this law, and that he sought to shut down oracles in the vicinity of Rome, but stopped when he was terrified by the power of the Praenestine lots. When he had them sealed up in a box and brought to Rome, he could not find them until the box was returned to the temple (another example of priestly subversion, so it seems).[63] Such laws do not seem to have been intended to have permanent force. The targets were lower-class subversives or the friends of a particularly dim member of the senatorial order at moments when they seemed to be getting out of control.

The same pattern of conduct appears in the context of other "expulsions" from Rome throughout the history of the empire down to the time of Constantine. In 52, for example, a *senatus consultum* was passed banning astrologers from Italy after the trial of Vibia, the mother of the man who had tried to overthrow Claudius in 42 for having consulted "Chaldeans" about the death of the emperor. Tacitus calls the measure harsh and useless (Tac. *Ann.* 12.52; compare Dio 61.33). Nero was experiencing a great deal of difficulty on the prophetic front in the last year of his life, tried to expel "sorcerers and astrologers" in 68.[64] Vitellius did the same in 69, and on this occasion Suetonius preserves the detail that the edict ordered them to leave by October 1. The "Chaldeans" said that this was fine with them because Vitellius would no longer be emperor at that point (Suet. *Vit.* 14.4). They were off by a couple of months, but the incident is further evidence of the strength of Vespasian's prophetic "underground" in the capital.[65] Vespasian himself renewed the edict when he arrived in 70, although it is likely that the decree was intended as a symbolic statement about public order: he owed too much to too many to have wanted to enforce the edict with great severity.[66] In the case of Domitian, two expulsion edicts can be tied directly to moments of crisis: that of 89–90 in the context of the revolt of the Rhine legions, and that of 93–94, a year notable for the execution of a number of leading senators on charges of treason.[67]

The situation in Rome may serve as a paradigm for imperial action in the provinces. Here the evidence is less good, but it is suggestive that the one ban on divination that has survived on papyrus comes in the context of an imperial visit to Egypt. This is an edict of 198–199 issued by the prefect Q. Aemilius Saturninus, and as it provides the most extensive coherent example of such a ban, it is worth quoting in full:

> Encountering many who believed themselves to be deceived by the practices of divination, I quickly considered it necessary, in order that no danger should ensue upon their foolishness, clearly herein to enjoin all people to abstain from this hazardous inquisitiveness. Therefore let no man through oracles, that is, by means of written documents supposedly granted under divine influence, nor by the means of the parade of images or suchlike charlatanry, pretend to know things beyond human ken and profess (to know) the obscurity of things to come, neither let any man put himself at the disposal of those who inquire about this or answer in any way whatsoever. If any person is detected adhering to this profession, let him be persuaded that he will be handed over to the extreme penalty.
>
> Let each of you take care that a copy of this letter is displayed publicly in the district capitals and in every village in clear and easily legible handwriting on a whitened board, and let him continually make inquiry, and, if he finds any person behaving contrary to the prohibitions, let him send him in bonds to my court. Nor will you be free from risk, if I learn again of such persons being overlooked in the districts in your charge, but you will undergo the same punishment as those being protected. For each of those, even though he dares deeds contrary to the prohibitions, is only one, whereas he who does not everywhere suppress them has himself become the cause of risk to many.
>
> Year 7 of Imperatores Caesares Lucius Septimius Severus Pius Pertinax Arabicus Adiabenicus Parthicus Maximus and Marcus Aurelius Antoninus, Augusti.[68]

Elsewhere, in the works of Roman jurists, it is clear that Roman governors were advised to make certain that diviners did not cause trouble. Ulpian, writing in the third century, says that consultations were banned by all the emperors, and that death was the penalty for consultation about the emperor, while those who consulted about their own affairs received lesser punishments (*Mos. et Rom. legum coll.* 15.2). He goes on to comment that these people were punished because they often exercised their arts against "public order" and the *imperium* of the Roman people. Paulus, writing somewhat earlier, likewise expresses concern lest "by human credulity public habits be corrupted to hope of something else," and advises that it is best to stay away "from divination and their science, and their books" (*Sent.* 5.21). He adds a line reflecting concern for domestic tranquillity as well: "slaves who consult about the safety of their masters are afflicted with the supreme penalty, that is, the cross; and those consulted, if they gave a response, are either condemned to the mines or deported to an island." Cassius Dio offers what may be the best practical summary of the state's attitude when he has Maecenas advise Augustus that "soothsaying . . . is a necessary art, and you should appoint some men to be diviners and augurs, to whom those will resort who wish to consult them on any matter; but there ought to be no workers of magic at all. For such men, by speaking the truth sometimes, but generally falsehood, often encourage a great many to attempt revolutions" (52.36.3 Loeb trans.). The ample evidence for the consultation of oracles throughout the empire shows that strictures against divination were ignored except when they were connected with crimes or disturbances of the public order frowned on by the state. The evidence for religious unrest in the context of the persecution of Christians suggests that there were times when prophets who inspired riots were considered less offensive than their victims.

Concern for public order (and spasmodic enforcement) appear also to characterize imperial enactments on the subject in the fourth century. Diocletian, for instance, issued a rescript from Sirmium in 294 in which he observed that it was acceptable to practice the art of geometry in public, but that the "detestable *ars mathematica* is forbidden" (*CJ* 8.18.2). An unpopular mathematics teacher, charged because of the possible confusion between his craft and that of an astrologer, presumably lies somewhere in the background. The bulk of the pronouncements concerning prognostication that have survived (twelve in all) were issued from 319 to 409 by emperors from Constantine to Honorius and Theodosius II. From 317 to 320, in the wake of his first war with Licinius, Constantine issued three edicts, two given to the prefects of Rome, the other at Aquileia, banning private divination while expressly stating that seeking information from the gods publicly was permissible (*C. Th.* 9.16.1–3). Interestingly, a rescript of 320, again to the prefect of Rome, states that if lightning should strike the palace, it is permissible to consult the *haruspices*. The wording in this case is significant, for it shows that Constantine was still observing the traditional distinctions with some care in public some eight years after his vision of the cross. He wrote:

> if it is established that some part of our palace or other public building is struck by lightning, the custom will be retained of the old observation about what it means, inquiry will be made of the *haruspices,* and, the writings, being diligently collected, it will be referred to our wisdom. The free use of employing this consultation shall be granted to others, so long as they abstain from private sacrifices, which are specifically prohibited.   (*C. Th.* 16.10.1)

Despite the deprecating tone in the first two edicts about public divination, a tone no more contemptuous than that used by Aemilius Saturninus, there is nothing that might be considered particularly Christian about the emperor's actions.[69]

There are two edicts and a rescript of Constantius II on record that ban private consultations (*C. Th.* 9.16.4–6). The emperor's language in the edicts (both issued in 357) is sweeping, and it does look as if he really did mean to make all divination illegal. He says that no one should consult a *haruspex,* an astrologer, or a diviner, "the depraved doctrines of augurs and prophets will be silent, the inquisitiveness of all men for divination shall stop forever" (*C. Th.* 9.16.4) But Constantius seems to have been well aware that it would take more than imperial fiat to end an ancient practice, and that he might be ignored quite close to home. The rescript of 358 was sent to the praetorian prefect Flavius Bassus at Rome. Bassus seems to have made explicit inquiry as to how he ought to handle cases involving the consultation of magi by members of the imperial household.[70] We cannot know what caused Bassus to make his inquiry, but if he was concerned about strange activity in the court of Julian Caesar, events were to prove that he had reason to worry. After his proclamation in Paris, Julian gathered prophetic friends around him, and seems to have consulted them extensively in private before marching east against his uncle in 361.[71]

Valens and Valentinian issued an edict on the subject on September 9, 364, and there are three laws from 370–371, a period when divination of all sorts was the subject of serious inquiry. On December 12, 370, the emperors wrote to Modestus, the praetorian prefect, specifically on the subject of astrology: "the discussion of astrology will cease. If anyone, by day or night, either in public or private, is arrested engaging in the forbidden practice, a capital sentence will be imposed on both, for the crimes of learning forbidden things and teaching them are not dissimilar" (*C. Th.* 9.16.6). There had recently been scandals at Rome. In 368 a former deputy urban prefect named Chilo and his wife, Maxima, complained that they were threatened with poison, and three men were arrested. They included an organ builder named Sericus, a wrestler named Asbolius, and a person named Campensis, who is described as a *haruspex*.[72] Soon after a former proconsul of Africa named Hymetius was brought to trial for consulting a *haruspex* named Amantius. The evidence that convicted him is particularly interesting for the light that it casts on how a distinguished member of the senate would consult such a character. It included a letter in Hymetius' own handwriting "asking him that, by supplicating the divinity with a rite of solemn sacrifices he should make the emperors better disposed toward him" (Amm. Mar. 28.1.20). Hymetius was exiled, and Amantius, who had tried to protect his client under torture, was executed. Prosecutions of all sorts then began, spurred on by the prefect Maximinus, until Valentinian put a stop to them when a senatorial embassy came to him at Trier to complain. One of the laws stemming from this embassy includes tacit acknowledgment that the consultation of diviners was so basic a fact of life that it could not, in and of itself, be considered a crime. Here the Christian emperor explicitly states: "I judge that divination [*haruspicina*] has no connection with cases of magic, and I do not consider this or any other sort of divine practice [*religio*] that was allowed by our ancestors to be a crime. The laws given by me at the beginning of my reign, in which free opportunity was given to everyone to cultivate what he had in mind, are witnesses. We do not condemn divination [*haruspicina*], but forbid it to be practiced with harmful intent" (*C. Th.* 9.16.9). There is some interesting semantic quibbling here, for the edict of 364 had specified "nefarious prayers" and "dangerous sacrifices," whereas that of 370 had mentioned only astrology *(tractatus mathematicorum)*. A third law, this one addressed to the prefect of the city, again stresses that cases of magic in which he cannot reach a decision should be sent straight to the imperial court (*C. Th.* 9.16.10).

For Constantine and Valentinian, therefore, the issues seem to have been primarily ones of public order in the traditional sense. Constantius II, a devout Christian, appears to have construed the issue more broadly as one connected with pagan forms of divination—even though he gave a public demonstration of his personal prophetic power, which he no doubt considered a sign of his moral excellence, when he had to. Indeed, it might be hard to determine just how far confessional issues could be pressed in these areas. As has already been seen, much traditional prophetic literature found a place in the Christian corpus, and the forms were readily clothed in a new rhetoric. Augustine records conversations with a Christian court official named Firminus, who was a believer, and he does not seem to have been at all extraordinary (*Conf.* 7.6). There were differences of opinion, as always. Constantius may have been an extremist on one side, as was Augustine, while Firminus was an extremist on the other side. We do not know what Valentinian or Valens thought, but the law of 371 suggests that they were not dogmatic on the issue.

Private divination was too difficult to control, and this fact may explain why a distinction was drawn between it and oracular activity at traditional shrines. Constantine confiscated the wealth of temples very soon after his victory in 324, and ordered the violent closure of several oracular shrines in the east.[73] At some point before his death, he seems also to have issued an order banning sacrifice by his officials.[74] The more famous the shrine, the more likely it was to have been affected: traditional practices were well attested in the sixth century in the countryside, where they were harder to control.[75] But still, sites are easier to control than people, and Constantine's actions do seem to have spelled the beginning of the end of more than a millennium of divination at the sacred shrines of the east. The urban communities of the empire were now being directed to the church for doses of divine wisdom, or to holy people on their fringes who, speaking from pillars, caves, or monastic cells now fulfilled the old functions of the shrines of the gods.

The ambiguous status of private divination in the late fourth century is perhaps best illustrated by the course of the horrific treason trials at Antioch in 372. It all began when a man named Procopius denounced two corrupt treasury officials for trying to kill through magic the official in charge of revenues from imperial estates, Fortunatianus. The two officials handed over their technical assistants, a man named Palladius (said to be an expert in poisoning) and an astrologer named Heliodorus. Ammianus' story, for he is the most detailed reporter of these events, reveals the interplay between high officials and divine practitioners on the fringes of the court, the same pattern of association that had been evident for centuries. Palladius immediately said that he knew something far more important: that some members of the court had tried to ascertain the identity of Valens' successor by divination (Amm. Marc. 29.1.5–6).

Under torture, one of those accused by Palladius revealed the details of their consultation, as follows:

> My lords, in an unlucky moment we put together out of laurel twigs in the shape of the Delphic tripod the hapless little table before you. We consecrated it with cryptic spells and a long series of magical rites, and at last made it work. The way in which it did so, when we wished to consult it about hidden matters, was this. It was placed in the middle of a room thoroughly fumigated with spices from Arabia, and was covered with a round dish made from an alloy of various metals. The outer rim of the dish was cunningly engraved

with the twenty-four letters of the alphabet separated by accurately measured intervals. A man dressed in linen garments, wearing linen sandals, with a fillet around his head and green twigs from a lucky tree in his hand, officiated as priest. After uttering a set prayer to invoke the divine power which presides over prophecy, he took his place above the tripod as his knowledge of the proper ritual taught him, and set swinging a ring suspended by a very fine cotton thread, which had been consecrated by a mystic formula. The ring, moving in a long series of jumps over the marked spaces, came to rest on particular letters, which made up hexameters appropriate to the questions put and perfect in scansion and rhythm, like the lines produced at Delphi or by the oracle of the Branchidae. (Amm. Marc. 29.1.29–31 Penguin trans.)

The words of this consultant convey some of the fascination and excitement felt by these imperial bureaucrats in being able to equal the great oracles of the past. On the occasion of what proved to be the fatal consultation, they asked the table to reveal the name of the next emperor. It offered the Greek letters ΘΕΟΔ, leading them to think of an official named Theodorus, whom they notified of their discovery. The incident seemed all the more remarkable when Valens, falling victim to the Goths at Adrianople (thus fulfilling an oracle that came to light in 375), was succeeded by Theodosius. Although Ammianus regarded these practices as "detestable," the details that he provides here suggest that he was struck by the fact that they worked.[76] Even Theodosius himself may have been impressed.

[5]

Eastern Wisdom in
Roman Prophetic Books

East and West in Fact and Fiction

The Roman empire was not simply a political entity devoted to the preservation of its rulers. The result of Rome's unification of the Mediterranean world was to spread the culture of the Hellenized world of which Rome was a part throughout western Europe, North Africa, and the Middle East. From the first through third centuries it created an unprecedented cultural continuum extending from Britain to the Euphrates, from the Rhine to the Atlas Mountains. This culture created a remarkable unity of expression and idiom that enabled people to communicate with one another to a degree that they had never done before. Wisdom from all quarters, times, and cultures joined in a stream of information that could enrich the life of the Roman citizen. Thus it was that the opportunity to encounter the wisdom of other peoples, to see that even their sages were interested in the events of one's own life, became a powerful factor in Roman intellectual life.

When Rome stood as the undisputed ruler of the civilized world (as it was conceived in Roman terms), it was natural to expect that all divinely inspired people had something to say about it. This changed in the fourth century. The prophets who had been accepted before the end of the traumatic political events of those years could still be heard to speak, but new discoveries from abroad were now to be treated with suspicion: Rome no longer appeared to be the unchallenged ruler of the world, and the wisdom of barbarians needed to be treated with fresh caution. In the last two chapters the theme has been the use of prophecy for political comment and political action. In this chapter the theme is the reflection of another sort of power, cultural power, the impact first of cultural Hellenism and then of Christianity, upon the prophetic traditions of the east.

The sages of the east carried with them the image of antiquity and mysterious authority; they represented cultures that people knew were older than their own, that had always been fonts of knowledge; the barbarians of the north had some ideas, but they were nothing like as interesting as those to the east. The practice of alleging eastern precedents for Greco-Roman wisdom was anything but new in the Roman empire; it had been going on since the fifth century B.C., if not before. But Plato's statement that he had derived the story of Atlantis from Egyptian priests, and others' assertions that he had been instructed by the magi, were all parts of a fiction, and the process of disentangling truth from impression, eastern construct from western, is a very complicated one indeed. There is no simple way to describe what was happening. Much of what passed as "eastern wisdom" in the Roman empire was a fraud, but there are significant instances in which it was not. Since the process is intimately connected with the ongoing reformation of Mediterranean culture under the impact of political developments, much of the following analysis will take as its starting point the second or third century A.D., simply because texts of this time stand at the end of a period of relative political and cultural stability. In examining some of the texts from this period it will often be necessary to reflect on the evolution of these traditions over the centuries before Augustus in order to gain a perspective on why it was that the wisdom of the east was taking the form that it did.

The first problem that must be faced is that what appear upon first glance to be parallels between practices or ideas in the ancient near east and those in the Roman world, practices that might be regarded as evidence for actual eastern influences upon Greek thought, often turn out, upon closer inspection, to be no more than coincidental parallels. Sometimes they are "orientalized" in the west to give them more authority, and sometimes they are reflections of Greek ideas in a near eastern context: Greeks were notoriously unwilling to read other people's literature.[1] Under these circumstances, it is sometimes very hard to define just what is meant by "oriental," or "eastern influence." These issues are complicated by the Roman empire's extension to the Euphrates by the middle of the first century b.c., and to the Tigris by the beginning of the third, which severely disrupted the ancient cultural continuum that had extended for millennia from the Persian Gulf to the Mediterranean. Ever since Alexander the Great's conquest of the Persian empire at the end of the fourth century b.c., these regions had been bombarded with Greek culture as Greeks had gone from being the ubiquitous employees of eastern kings (a role they had filled for centuries) to rulers. Still, the peoples of the western end of the fertile crescent, the descendants of Hittites or Iranian settlers on the Anatolian plateau, did not suffer instant cultural amnesia.[2] Their traditions might increasingly have to be expressed through the idiom of Greek culture if they were to be able to communicate with their political masters, but these traditions did, in and of themselves, constitute a strand of indigenous eastern wisdom. The same is even more true of Egypt.

In the Roman empire, "eastern wisdom" was learning handed down from the days of the independent kingdoms of the near east, or devised by sages beyond the frontiers of the empire. The modern historian has to be content with the fact that all of the "eastern wisdom" that penetrated the mainstream consciousness of the Roman world did so through the medium of literature written in Greek. Some of it may indeed fulfill the ancient definition, but much of it does not. Much of it is western wisdom overlaid with a thin (often very thin) veneer of eastern coloring to lend it more authority. More interestingly, what passes for real eastern wisdom, in that it can be found in texts that were composed in the indigenous languages of the near east, is sometimes western wisdom that had been absorbed in the east and recycled (with some additions) to the culture where it was originally formulated.

The view that history can be described as a succession of kingdoms (initially four) followed by an eschatological catastrophe provides an example of how a prophetic scheme could flow across cultural and linguistic barriers, and how deceptive a strict dichotomy between east and west can be. As has already been seen, it provided an important format for the interpretation of history in the Roman empire. Our objective here is to see how it came to be current in that world. Adopting the Greek view that anything eastern must be older, there is a tendency to look first to Zoroastrianism, where this theme appears in a prophetic book known as the *Bahman Yasht,* known from manuscripts of the thirteenth century A.D.

The *Bahman Yasht* is an immensely complicated text that expanded through the centuries to take account of new developments in the history of the faithful until the arrival of the Turks. Since it begins with the assumption that the faithful will be defeated by a foreign enemy, and vindicated by various saviors, it is generally assumed that it was first conceived, and began to be passed on orally, in the years after Alexander's conquest.[3] The earliest phase, and thus the argument connecting it with the Hellenistic world, is based primarily on the opening of the text:

> As it is declared by the *Studgar Nask* that Zoroaster asked for immortality from Ahura Mazda, then Ahura Mazda displayed the omniscient wisdom to Zoroaster, and through it he beheld the root of a tree, on which there were four branches, one golden, one of silver, one of steel, and one of unmixed iron. Thereupon he reflected in this way, that this was seen in a dream, and when he arose from sleep, Zoroaster spoke thus: "Lord of the Spirits and Earthly Existences! It appears that I saw the root of a tree, on which were four branches." Ahura Mazda spoke to Zoroaster Spitama thus: "That root of a tree which thou sawest, and those four branches, are the four periods which will come . . ."[4]

The fourth substance in this vision, "unmixed iron," has parallels in other late Zoroastrian texts and is intended to convey the picture of iron ore before the metal was extracted. The metaphoric use of the substance stands for an age in which enemy forces contaminated the national and religious life of Iran.[5] The image seems then to have been misunderstood by the author of the biblical book of Daniel, where Nebuchadnezzar of Babylon sees a beast with feet of iron mixed with clay (Dan. 2:33–34). Daniel interpets it as if he were viewing a statue in which the clay core around which the iron should have been cast was instead mingled with the metal and observes that "as you saw the iron mixed with miry clay . . . they will not hold together, just as iron does not mix with clay" (Dan. 2.4:42–43). The reinterpretation of the image suggests a familiarity with the concept of representing a series of ages in terms of metals, but an imperfect understanding of the way in which the metals would be viewed in their native context.[6] Moreover, a recently published fragment from the Qumran caves shows that the image of the tree, which may be connected with Zoroastrian tree worship, also passed into Judaic lore (though not necessarily in the context of a vision of Daniel).[7]

The priority of the Zoroastrian scheme of four kingdoms to that in the book of Daniel is suggested not only by the Jewish handling of the symbolism, but also by the earlier observation of this scheme in circles that had no contact with the world of Daniel's author. This appears in a marginal gloss that found its way into the manuscript of Velleius Paterculus' short history of Rome, completed in A.D. 30. Here it is stated that Aemelius Sura wrote in his early second century B.C. work on the chronology of the Romans that "the Assyrians were the first of all races to hold world power, then the Medes, and then the Persians, then the Macedonians, then . . . the world power passed to the Roman people. Between this time and the beginning of the reign of King Ninus of the Assyrians, who was the first to hold world power, lies an interval of nineteen hundred and ninety-five years" (Vel. Pat. 1.6.6).[8] Uses of the pattern were not, however, always eschatological. Dionysius of Halicarnassus exploited the notion in the preface to his *Roman Antiquities* as a way of pointing out that Rome was superior to the four previous kingdoms, and another Augustan historian, Pompeius Trogus, adopted it to give structure to his universal history.[9] In the second century, Appian used it very much as Dionysius had, in the preface to his collected histories of Rome and of Rome's wars and civil wars.[10] A variant on the theme in the *Thirteenth Sibylline Oracle* describes the emperor Decius (249–251) as being "of the fourth race," suggesting either that his reign was the prelude to eschatological catastrophe, or that he was a fitting representative of the fourth Hesiodic race, the race of iron.[11]

Hesiod's description of the decline of humanity from the golden race through silver and bronze to iron (with a brief interruption for a race of heroes) in his *Works and Days* (106–201) is relevant to more than just the question of how a third century A.D. reader would have thought about the emperor Decius. Since the passage is unusual, the parallels outlined above have been pressed into service to "prove" that it reflects the influence of eastern thought.[12] Unfortunately, none of these parallels is earlier the book of Daniel or the Persian scheme that has been postulated as the model for Daniel's author on the basis of the *Bahman Yasht*. Indeed, the Persian scheme, which assumes a series of three heroes who will appear in each of the first three ages, does not seem to have been conceivable before the end of the fourth century: in the text the first of the three saviors is named Ushedar, a rendering of the name Oxyartes, who (although the name is a common one) may be identifiable with a Persian nobleman in the time of Alexander.[13] Moreover, the fact that the theory of four ages can be reconciled with the earlier Zoroastrian scheme of world history only with some difficulty further suggests that it was injected into Persian thought from a foreign source. This source is most likely the Greek tradition best known through Hesiod.[14]

The theory of four kingdoms therefore seems first to have been articulated in the form that was current in the Roman empire in Iran during the late fourth or early third century B.C., whence it came separately into Judaism, where it is clear that the author of Daniel was not conscious of a Zoroastrian background, and into the Greek world, where it was noticed by Aemilius Sura. The reception of this notion must have been much easier, since the Iranian development of the idea was inspired by Greek thought.

The tale of the four kingdoms stands as an illustration of the difficulty of tracing the flow of influence from east to west. This effort is made all the more problematic by the fact that complex systems of thought like Zoroastrianism were not static. As a religious system that has succeeded in propagating itself over the course of three millennia, Zoroastrianism has shown itself extremely adaptable.[15] The fluidity of the tradition makes it hard to know just what would have constituted Zoroastrianism at any given point in the past. It also makes it difficult to decide if the effort is even worthwhile before the third century A.D., when a group of powerful Zoroastrians led by the priest Kartir sought to systematize their faith and establish it at the intellectual center of the new Sassanid dynasty.[16]

The theory of the four kingdoms was but one feature of the constantly changing Zoroastrian view of the world that penetrated the popular consciousness of the west in bits and pieces. It was Zoroaster who first described the creation of the world in seven days, resurrection of the dead, final judgment, hell, the heavenly struggle between good and evil, and a specific eschatological scheme for history. These ideas, separated from their founder, had an important impact upon the development of post-exilic Judaism, and exercised some influence upon other intellectual trends in the Roman world.[17] But there is no evidence that, by the time of Augustus, anyone thought that they were Zoroastrian. By this time Persian survivals in the west seem to have been absorbed into the urban life of Greek cities, and people who actually had access to accounts of the inspired visions of Zoroaster seem to have disappeared. When a man like Plutarch wanted to provide an account of the thinking of Zoroaster in his work on Isis and Osiris, he turned to Theopompus, an author of the fourth century B.C. who provided a garbled account of Zoroastrian ideas on the basis of what seems to have been a confused (or, more probably, heretical) personal informant.[18] Other writers were less conscientious, and as a result Zoroaster entered the intellectual demimonde. Historians of philosophy like Diogenes Laertius tried to find a place for him among the founders of Greek philosophy; others simply made things up and attributed them to him. Pliny, for instance, describes him as the inventor of magic (a bad thing in his view) and records a variety of opinions about when he lived (*NH* 30.3–5). Apuleius, who argues that his activities were respectable, says that he was the son of a sage named Oromazus, a view that he derived from Plato (*Apol.* 26; Plat. *Alc.* 1.121E). The longest of the works contained in the Coptic library that began to emerge from Nag Hammadi in Upper Egypt during the late 1940s and early 1950 presents itself as "Zostrianos; words of truth of Zostrianos. God of Truth, Words of Zoroast[er]," and describes a series of visions that have nothing whatsoever to do with Zoroastrianism.[19] The situation is summed up by Porphyry, who says that he "wrote a considerable number of refutations of the book of Zoroaster, which I showed to be entirely spurious and modern, made up by the sectarians to convey the impression that the doctrines which they had chosen to hold in honor were those of the ancient Zoroaster" (*V. Plot.* 16.15 Loeb trans.).

As it was with an individual, so too it could be with an entire group. There was an ancient tradition that Plato had learned some philosophy from the "magi," and, by the second century, it is clear that educated Romans thought that the magi could be encountered in Babylon. Thus, in the first book of his life of Apollonius of Tyana, Philostratus brings the wandering sage to Babylon, where he discusses philosophy with the local magi. Babylon is described as a great city with massive fortifications and numerous great works of art. The description depends somewhat upon that written by Herodotus seven centuries earlier, and not at all upon any contemporary witness.[20] So too the notion that Babylon was the home of the magi is a fiction, although it seems to have been regarded as a fact in the intellectual world of the Roman second and third centuries, where the word *magus* seems to have meant no more than "eastern wise man" when it did not carry the more negative connotation of "magician."[21] Properly speaking, magi were priests of the Persian pantheon who espoused the beliefs of Zoroastrianism, and they had nothing at all to do with Mesopotamia.

The fate of Zoroaster, his doctrines, and his priests, as well as the fate of Mesopotamian wisdom in general at the hands of western intellectuals may usefully be compared with the career of one member of the Babylonian priestly caste who did try to make his culture comprehensible to the Greek world. This man, Berossus, also became a character of fiction.

The historical Berossus seems to have been a man named Belre'usu who was connected in some way with the cult of Marduk at Babylon. He also seems to have been familiar with the basic tenets of Greek historiography, and thus in the reign of Antiochus he composed a history, probably titled the *Babyloniaka,* to demonstrate the importance of Babylon in the history of the near east. In this history he plainly drew upon texts in his native language, and he seems to have tried to present this material in a way that conformed with the tastes of his rulers.[22] Despite his best efforts, and perhaps because his effort took place in a virtual cultural vacuum, the *Babyloniaka* was not an outstanding success: it seems to have attracted relatively little notice until the first century B.C., when the historian Alexander Polyhistor produced a condensed version of it. After that it seems to have been ignored save by the authors of other specialized tracts on Babylonian history, or by commentators in Greek on Hebrew scripture (all but one of the extant fragments come from either Josephus or Christian writers).[23] The lack of interest in what was certainly the best account of Babylonian history in Greek, based on authentic traditions, is most strikingly revealed by the fact that when Diodorus Siculus, the author of a universal history in the first century B.C., composed his account of the early history of the near east, he turned instead to the indigenous (and almost completely fictional) tradition of Greek historiography. Although (or perhaps because) his history was so little read, Berossus soon acquired a completely different reputation: as the father of astrology. Vitruvius, the author of a work on the theory of architecture in the first century A.D., wrote that Berossus was the first of the Chaldeans who were versed in astrology to come west, and that he settled on Cos (*FGrH* 680 T 5). A number of other western authors cite his alleged doctrines with approval, and the elder Pliny even records that there was a statue of him in the gymnasium at Athens with a golden tongue, erected "because of his divine predictions" (*FGrH* 680 T 6). The astrological doctrines associated with his name, however, are all Greek.[24] In another tradition he became the father of a Sibyl who was said to have lived in the very earliest period of human history.

The cases discussed in the last few pages all illustrate the problem inherent in assuming that something that offers a near eastern parallel to a practice or idea that was current in the Roman empire must have derived from the near east, even when a Greek or Roman said it did. Two third-century texts offer further insight into the problem. These are the *Perfect Discourse* attributed to Hermes Trismegistus, a text of ostensible Egyptian origin; and the *Chaldean Oracles,* which purport to offer new "Chaldean wisdom" to readers in the Roman west.

Hermes Trismegistus and Julianus the Chaldean

Hermes Trismegistus' vision of catastrophe in Egypt, originally written in Greek, is now known only from translations into Latin and Coptic.[25] Composed no later than the end of the third century, it draws the reader into a sort of divine tutorial between Hermes and his disciple Asclepius. Hermes begins by asking Ascelpius if he knows that "Egypt is the image of the sky, or to put it better, the place on earth where the gods project everything that is governed or put in motion in heaven, or to put it more truly, our land is the temple of the whole earth" (*Ascl.* 24). Since it befits the wise to know everything that will happen in the future, he goes on to predict when it will seem that the Egyptians have honored their gods in vain. The evil will begin when "the gods, quitting the earth, will gather again in the heavens, Egypt will be abandoned, and the land that was the seat of religion will be widowed, destitute of the presence of the gods" (*Ascl.* 24). Egypt will be taken over by foreigners who are not bound by its customs: "that region and land will be filled with foreigners who are not only neglectful of religion, but, what is worse, there will be a prohibition, as if established by prescribed penalty of law, against religion, piety, and divine cult; then that most sacred land, seat of shrines and temples, will be chock full of tombs and the dead" (*Ascl.* 24). Egypt's religion will be forgotten by its people: "O Egypt, Egypt, only stories of your religion will remain, and they will not be believed by your posterity; only words inscribed on stone narrating your pious deeds will survive when the Scythian, the Indian, and another such, a barbarian from outside, inhabits Egypt" (*Ascl.* 24). Finally, things will get so bad that nature itself will be in disorder: "when the earth will not stand fast, nor the sea be sailed, when the sky will not be filled with the course of the stars, and the course of the stars will not be in the sky," the "old age of the world will arrive" (*Ascl.* 25–26). When this happens the great god will destroy the earth with fire and water and resurrect its pristine beauty (*Ascl.* 26). The vision of the old age of the world, its cataclysmic destruction, and its regeneration had a long history in Greek thought. Plato described it, and some Stoics even debated the possibility of alternate destructions by fire and water.[26]

Contrary to what the divinity has to say here, Egypt's religion was, by this time, very much the product of oral transmission, and the records that were inscribed on stone had long since ceased to play any significant role in determining the observances of its people. But the fact of a visible record of Egypt's past was crucial to reinforcing the idea of continuity. When tourists like the Roman imperial prince Germanicus came to Egypt, they expected a recitation of the contents of royal hieroglyphic inscriptions on the temples, just as Herodotus had when he came to Egypt centuries earlier.[27] As had been the case with Herodotus, Germanicus did not receive anything like a reading of these texts, but rather a story that had been created to make the kings whose deeds were recorded there seem more magnificent. These versions formed popular, and then scholarly, impressions of the history and culture of Egypt.[28] They fused with the existing tradition of storytelling to create a powerful image of Egyptian history that could grow with the passing of time and form a new history, mingling the old with the new. Thus, beneath the Greek surface there are ideas and forms that have a very real Egyptian past.

The phrase "that most sacred land" (*Ascl.* 24) is a description of Egypt that can be traced back to Pharaonic times.[29] The Indians and the Scyths were characters of the Roman world who symbolically marked the edges of the empire and thus of civilized society.[30] But the idea that the ruin of Egyptian society was marked by foreign domination has a much longer history. The "Asiatic" appears as the enemy whose coming signifies the collapse of public order in literary products of the First Intermediate Period and Middle

Kingdom such as the *Instructions of King Merikare* and the *Prophecies of Neferti*. In the early Ptolemaic *Prophecy of the Lamb,* these outsiders had become Persians. A century later, in the *Oracle of the Potter,* these foreigners became "girdle-wearers" and "Typhonians." The reason for the use of the term "girdle-wearers" is obscure—it may have come into general circulation to describe outsiders as a result of being used to describe Gallic mercenaries who rebelled against Ptolemy II in Egypt in 278 B.C.[31] The reference to Typhonians, however, reflects an ideological evolution that had been going on in Egypt since the Old Kingdom.

Typhon was the Greek name for the Egyptian god Seth, who came to stand for all things opposed to Osiris, Isis, and their son, Horus. In Pharaonic times he became the god of the desert and of the Asiatics in opposition to Egypt and its people, and he became the god of thunder and storms as opposed to the sun, and of the earth as opposed to the sky, which was the domain of Horus.[32] The Ptolemies had absorbed this ideology so that the king, like the Pharaohs before him, could represent himself as following in the footsteps of Horus while implying that his enemies were servants of Seth (*OGIS* 90). This language was not simply the language of court propaganda; it was language that the Ptolemies themselves had derived from their subjects. For their Egyptian subjects, it provided a framework in which to explore right and wrong, good and evil. Thus it also appears in a prophetic text copied around the time of the great Jewish revolt (115–117) exhorting Egyptians to defend themselves against the Jews.[33]

The description of the enemies of Egypt as "Typhonians" and "girdle-wearers" represents a fusing of traditional Egyptian ideology with some Ptolemaic royal propaganda, and the further replacement of the characters in this scheme by "Indians" and "Scyths" was the continuation of the ancient topos in a new guise. On a grander scale, the whole of Hermes' revelation corresponds quite closely with the general pattern of Egyptian "chaos" narratives, which begin with the disintegration of the social order on earth, followed by disintegration in the natural order and the collapse of the state's borders. Ideally they end with the reestablishment of new kingship.[34]

Another interesting feature of the Egyptian material is the evidence that it provides for the way in which views of the world could pass from prophetic book to prophetic book, as authors included their own interpretations in the oracles that they copied out (often without paying scrupulous attention to the actual wording of the original). This is perhaps illustrated through comparison of two versions of the *Oracle of the Potter* (major differences resulting from variations in wording, declension, or conjugation are marked in italics):

Version 1 (*P. Oxy.* 2332.11–21)

when this happens there will be war and slaughter that will destroy brothers and wives. These things will happen when the great god Hephaistos wishes to return to his city, and the girdle-wearers, being Typhonians, will destroy themselves . . . evil will be done; he will pursue them on foot to the sea, where he will rage and kill many of them, as they are impious. The one will come from Syria who is hateful to all men and . . . the one will come from Ethiopia . . . he from the impious will settle in Egypt in the city, which will later be deserted . . . the two-year [king] is not ours . . . Ammon said well.[35]

Version 2 (*P. Graf* 29787.24–35)

when this happens there will be war and impious slaughter *of brothers and wives. Memphis will wish* to return to the city, and the girdle-wearers, being Typhonians, will destroy themselves . . . evil will be done; he will pursue them on foot to the sea, raging, and he will destroy many of them as they are impious *together with those who conspire with them.* The *king* will come from Syria, who is hateful to all men. The two-year (king) is not ours;[36] *the fifty-five-year king is ours, who will bring the evils to the Greeks, which the lamb announced to Bacharis, and fortune will leave this race.*

The reference to the prophecy of the lamb given to Bacharis [sic] in version 2 is an effort to reconcile a statement in the *Oracle of the Potter* with another prophecy, the so-called *Lamb of Boccharis.* In order to see what was going through the minds of these two compositors, it is worth looking at the history of both texts in a little more detail. The *Lamb of Boccharis* is set in the reign of the last king of the twenty-fourth dynasty (ca. 715 B.C.). In the case of the *Lamb*

13. *The Oracle of the Potter.* The end of column 1 and the top of column 2 are translated in the text as version 2. The writing is that of a good copyist (*P. Oxy.* 2332; photo courtesy of the Ashmolean Museum).

of Boccharis, the story opens with a priest named Psinyras reading to his expectant wife from a book of fate. The papyrus that preserves the document is badly broken at this point, but it appears that he feels that the children must be cast into the Nile to avoid their terrible fate. But when his wife gives birth, she cannot bring herself to destroy the children, one of whom, it seems, is more beautiful than the other. Psinyras despairs that he cannot save his children from their doom, and although the papyrus again at this point is too broken to read, it appears that he begins to instruct the children on the evils that the book portends. The textual situation (to say nothing of the situation of Egypt) worsens, and a whole column of the papyrus, in which it is clear that something significant has happened, is lost. When it becomes possible to see what is happening again, Psinyras is listening to a lamb predict a list of woes that will befall the cities of Egypt. The talking lamb concludes, in response to a question from Psinyras, with a further prediction of good after 900 years of disaster, when he (the lamb) will assume the crown and the Egyptians will go forth into Syria, take control of these provinces, and restore the gods. His prophecy finished, the lamb promptly expires. Psinyras reports the events to Boccharis, who orders that the body of the lamb be buried in a golden shrine like a god. Since the prophecy of a lamb in the reign of Boccharis is reported by the historian Manetho, himself a priest of Heliopolis who wrote an account of Egyptian history during the reign of Ptolemy I, it must date before the end of the period of Persian domination in Egypt.[37] When he reported it, Manetho, who would have known better than anyone that the period of 900 years in the prophecy had not passed, was plainly taking it as a prediction of future events (and as being recorded on good authority; otherwise he would not have bothered with it). The reader of the *Oracle of the Potter,* who commented on the relevance of the lamb's words to those of the Potter, was still taking it in this way when he included his comments in the version of the *Oracle of the Potter* that we now have. So too must Satabus, son of Heraius, when he copied out the extant version of the *Lamb of Boccharis* in A.D. 2.[38]

We know a bit less about the circumstances under which the *Oracle of the Potter* was written. It is preserved in at least two versions on three papyri, one of the second century A.D., and the other two of the third.[39] The one papyrus that preserves the opening story records that in the reign of Amenophis (Amenhotep) a potter went to an island dedicated to Ammon-Re (Helios in the Greek text) where there was a temple of Isis and Osiris, and began to make pots. The locals, angered by this sacrilege, took his pots from the kiln and broke them. When this happened, the potter fell into a prophetic fit, explaining that he was the agent of the god Hermes (here identified with Chnum, the god of potters). His auditors were astounded and brought him to the king, where he began to speak again. The king ordered scribes to come and write down "all that would befall Egypt in a sacred book" (P_1, lines 1–35). After telling of disasters to come, followed by the arrival of a redeemer for Egypt, the potter dropped dead. King Amenophis, saddened by what he had learned, had the potter "buried in Heliopolis and placed the book recording his prophecies in the sacred archives and generously revealed them to all men." A concluding statement records that this text is the "defense of the potter to king Amenophis, translated as faithfully as possible, about what will happen in Egypt" (version 2, lines 50–57).

One important feature of this "defense of the potter" is the mention of a "king of two years," and the fact that two later readers had turned to two different prophetic texts to try to understand the reference. The writer of version 1 (P_2) seems to have found something about a "king of two years" in something attributed to the god Ammon, while the author of version 2 (P_3) turned to *The Lamb of Boccharis*. But when did these writers do so? The consensus of modern opinion is that the redactor whose hand appears in version 1 (P_2) tried to associate the text with an oracle of Ammon that made reference to a king of two years in an effort to reconcile the situation predicted by the potter with events occurring in his own time (the revolt of Harsiesis in 129 B.C., by this argument). Another seems to have quoted the passage in the *Lamb of Boccharis* that reads "the one of two, who is not our [king]; the one of fifty-five is our king," in order to correct the first interpretation. Since Harsiesis' rebellion had lasted only two years, the second author may be commenting on Harsiesis' failure by pointing out that he cannot have been the savior of Egypt predicted in the oracles, and commenting also on the possibility that king Ptolemy Euergetes II, who may have been looked upon as that savior by some when he reached the fifty-fourth year of his reign in 116 B.C., was not the right one either.[40]

The presence of these interpretations in texts that were written several centuries later raises a question that is difficult to answer. At what point does a prophetic text become "fixed"? At some point readers of the *Oracle of the Potter* stopped including new material or interpretations, and they seem to have done so several centuries before the copies we have were written. When these copies were written down, the text had clearly become something quite different from what it was originally intended to be. It seems to have been written as some sort of nationalist propaganda directed against the Ptolemies, but as the text became fixed, and interpretation in terms of specific contemporary events ceased, it can only have been read as an account of the form that the end of time would take. It ceased to become a text with specific reference and became, instead, a sort of sacred guidebook. As the last interpolations may be dated to the penultimate decade of the second century B.C., it is possible that this change in style of reading occurred then. It would have been obvious at that point that these efforts were not going to work, but this difficulty does not seem to have led to the conclusion that the revelation itself was without value if only the events described could be interpreted correctly. The parallel with the history of Christianity, founded upon the notion of the imminent end of the world, and with fights such as those in which Hippolytus was engaged during the third century is not coincidental. There are two basic ways to treat a prophetic text that is viewed as "historical": it may be read either as a guide to the immediate future or as a general indication of a divine plan.[41]

IT IS OF GREAT significance that both the *Oracle of the Potter* and the *Lamb of Bocchoris* show that actual Egyptian prophecies were still being read in the imperial period.[42] Both texts are manifestly connected with the genre of Egyptian writing known as "instruction literature." By the time that the Eighteenth Dynasty reunited

Egypt, and brought an end to the period of chaos known to modern scholars as the First Intermediate Period, this genre had already evolved into a very fluid medium for the exchange of ideas, the exposition of ideology, and simple political propaganda. There were three basic forms that this sort of literature could take: the didactic speech of father to son, the admonitory prophetic speech or speeches delivered by sages or other people cast in the role of defenders of the public good, and the dialogue in which two speakers defended contrasting points of view. Prose tales, which also emerged as significant literary creations in the Eighteenth Dynasty, ranged in content from human encounters with the divine to that of the *Story of Sinuhe,* which describes the adventures of a wandering Egyptian in terms that appear to be based closely on actual human experience.[43]

The most important feature of prophetic didactic literature and the prophetic prose tale is that they give the reader an account of the time and place of the prophetic utterance. The earliest surviving example of this genre is a text known as the *Prophecies of Neferti,* and it provides a fully developed generic parallel for later texts. It is set in the court of King Snefru, the fourth king of the Fourth Dynasty, one the builders of the great pyramids. These architectural accomplishments seem to have left the members of the Eighteenth Dynasty with a severe case of pyramid envy, with the result that their time is pictured as leading to the chaos that would come to an end only with Amenemhet I, the first ruler of the Eighteenth Dynasty.[44]

The story begins when the king asks his advisers to bring him someone who will "speak to me some fine words, choice phrases at the hearing of which my majesty may be entertained." The advisers, who "were on their bellies before his majesty once more," suggest Neferti, the great lector-priest of Bastet, and the king orders him to be brought forward. Neferti duly appears, and "as he deplored what had happened in the land, [he] evoked the state of the East, with Asiatics roaming in their strength, frightening those about to harvest and seizing cattle from the plough," with a long tale of woe that will only end when "a king will come from the south, Ameny, the justified, by name."[45] As the extant text breaks off there appears to be a section explaining how this story came to be written down, opening with the words "it has come to its end successfully by the scribe . . .'"

Framing episodes were also a feature of the Egyptian prophetic texts that survive from the Roman empire, and, as they did in classical Egyptian texts, they serve to date the prophetic event to a moment in the distant past, and to confer the ostensible stamp of Pharaonic approval upon the contents. We have already seen how the framing stories in the *Oracle of the Potter,* like the *Prophecies of Neferti,* conclude with a description of the actual recording:

> [His] majesty issued a command to the Hereditary Prince and Count, the Privy Councilor of the Palace, the Headman of the Entire Land, the Sealbearer of the king of Lower Egypt, the *Helmsman* of the Two Lands, the Leader, the Overseer of the Courtiers and [*Chief*] Treasurer, *the strong of arm,* Neshi: "Have everything which my majesty has done by strength put upon a stele which occupies its place in Karnak in the Theban Nome forever and ever." Then he said to his majesty: "I will act [*in conformance with*] that which [*my*] lord [*has commanded me*]."[46]

One other feature of these framing episodes is that they leave the time of the fulfillment of the prophecy open: the reader is told when the divine act took place, but it is left to the reader to discover when the end of the story will come. The connection between these texts and other popular forms of Egyptian literature helps to explain how this material survived: these tales were not simply products for the enjoyment of detached intellectuals. They were a part of the historical memory of the Egyptian people, a memory that depended upon storytellers rather than scribes to such an extent that even the historian Manetho, who could read hieroglyphics, chose to include them in his history when he does not seem to have bothered to include the accounts of royal deeds that could be found inscribed on the walls of temples.

The focus of the *Oracle of the Potter* is the history of Egypt rather than of the Roman empire. Despite its wide circulation, the same can be said of the vision of Asclepius, and the feeling that Egypt was a font of wisdom made this possible. This focus raises the further question as to whether such texts should also be seen, in their Egyptian context at least, as vehicles for the expression of cultural or national identity against the predominant, Hellenized culture of the time.[47] There is one explicitly anti-Greek outburst in another of the works attributed to Hermes (*CH* 16.1–2), but this is somewhat deceptive. After praising the superiority of Egyptian over Greek (in Greek), the author develops his work in full accord with the demands of Greek rhetoric, and the philosophic doctrines expounded are fully in accord with the milieu of Greek philosophy. The evocation of the Egyptian language may be no more here than a conceit born of the sort of cultural "orientalism" discussed at the beginning of this chapter. The author, who professes to be producing the words of Asclepius for king Ammon, seems to be doing nothing more than claiming legitimacy for his work as a piece of true Egyptian wisdom.[48] Otherwise the corpus is remarkably free of abuse, and this is particularly noticeable in the *Asclepius,* where the foes of civilization are from beyond the frontiers. In the age of the Ptolemies, Alexandria was the symbol of Greek culture, a new city founded by the side of Egypt, the symbol of foreign domination. There is nothing of the sort in these texts. In this, as in the nearly contemporary *Apocalypse of Elijah,* the description of chaos in Egypt has become detached from any overt political message; there is no individual to look out for, no savior on the horizon, no reason to scan other prophecies to see if they match up.[49] By this time as well, even a text like the *Oracle of the Potter* had become something other in the eyes of its readers than the political tract it was when it was first written.

Religion and prophecies could play an important role in revolts against Rome, but this does not mean that every oracle is by definition a "nationalistic" outburst. There were too many other reasons to read such books; the wisdom of pharaonic Egypt did not survive to the third century A.D. simply to encourage revolution or ethnic identity, especially when it was translated or composed in Greek. It could also survive because people found it interesting and instructive. This is presumably why a Coptic translation of the eschatological section of the *Asclepius* was bound in with other works of wisdom (including some sections of Plato's *Republic*) in one of the codices from Nag Hammadi, a collection that may have been connected with a monastery located near the find spot.[50]

THE REVELATION of Hermes Trismegistus to Asclepius and the extant versions of the *Oracle of the Potter* may be roughly contemporary, and they reveal the preservation of ancient Egyptian wisdom in the prophetic imagination of the Roman empire. At roughly the same period a series of texts going by the title of the *Chaldean Oracles* appeared on the scene.[51] These texts, while asserting a connection with the ancient traditions of Mesopotamia, are very different indeed from those written against the Egyptian background, and show how dangerous it is to assume that all eastern traditions exerted a similar influence upon the Roman world.

The *Chaldean Oracles* purport to offer a series of revelations by the gods about their essential nature and the nature of the universe. They seem to have promised that a new understanding of the gods could be gained through theurgy (god-working), and that this knowledge would keep the theurgist safe from the corruption of his body by demons, as well as guarantee him a special place in heaven. The books themselves (we don't know how many there were) were presented to the world as the work of a gentleman named Julianus, who claimed to be a Chaldean and to have discovered the theurgic art. In at least one place he claims to have spoken with the soul of Plato, who spoke through the body of Julianus' son, Julianus II. This may have been facilitated by Julianus' request of "The Connective of All," when he realized that he was going to have a son, that this son be given the soul of an archangel and that he be joined with "all the gods and with the soul of Plato, which dwelt with Apollo and Hermes."[52]

The purpose of this collection, much of which reads like a peculiar brand of reheated Middle Platonism in bad hexameter verse, is evidently to establish theurgy on a more respectable intellectual foundation, giving it a founder who could be placed in time, and who could be associated with a non-Platonic heritage.[53] The idea that it was possible to command the gods through a combination of stones and secret wisdom that is a significant feature of theurgy was anything but new when these texts first saw the light of day, but philosophic ingredient gave it fresh respectability. It may not be coincidental that the *Chaldean Oracles* were first taken up by Iamblichus very shortly after Porphyry suggested, in a work ostensibly addressed to an Egyptian priest named Anebo, that diviners and magicians were able to command demons through stones, herbs, and the like. Divine authority was better than human, and Chaldean wisdom was better than Porphyry's. By importing Chaldean wisdom on the basis of texts known best to himself, Iamblichus could stake out new ground in the competition for intellectual preeminence among the friends of Plotinus.[54] He could also set philosophy on a new course. A person was not limited to contact with inferior and malignant beings if that person understood the theurgic art. The difference between this doctrine and traditional Platonism is most succinctly brought out by the Byzantine scholar Michael Psellus in his commentary on the Chaldean oracles wherein he observes that "Plato makes us embrace the uncreated essence through reason and intuition; the Chaldeans, on the other hand, say that we are not able to approach the divine if we have not strengthened the chariot of our soul through material rites; he thinks the soul can be purified with stones, herbs, and incantations, to be well oiled for the ascension" (*Exegesis Orac. Chald.* 1132A 7–12). Psellus' language here looks as if it is borrowed from the oracles themselves, where "the light chariot of the soul" is evidently important, and where the "material rites" appear to have been described in some detail.[55] For Iamblichus, the oracles offered a route to intellectual primacy. To another Neoplatonist, Maximus of Ephesus, who exercised great influence over the emperor Julian, they seem to have offered a promise of the ability to alter the future by giving the practitioner the ability to command the gods.[56] To others, of course, they were simply magic tricks.[57]

It was just as Iamblichus was beginning to disseminate the *Chaldean Oracles* in Neoplatonic circles that the balance between east and west began to change, and Rome was reintroduced to Iranian Zoroastrianism. For the first two and a half centuries of Roman rule in the near east, the emperors of Rome looked alternately with fear and desire upon the realm of the Parthian kings. They sought to contain the threat that they felt Parthia could pose either by fomenting internal disorder within its boundaries or by seeking to control its western provinces. The relationship throughout remained fluid, with the Parthian kings sometimes posing as serious threats to the internal security of the eastern Roman provinces, and sometimes acting as little more than client princes. At all times there seems to have been considerable contact across the border, much of it connected with the trade in eastern luxury goods that flowed through the kingdom of Mesene in southern Mesopotamia, up the Tigris and across the desert under auspices of the merchants of the great desert city of Palmyra, which for most of this period was located in the Roman province of Syria. These years were, however, a period during which the influence of the followers of Zoroaster was insignificant within the power structure of the eastern kingdom. The Arsacid dynasts, who emerged from northern Iran, were not themselves Zoroastrians, and they evinced no discernible interest in Zoroaster's teachings. The Iranian center of Zoroastrianism remained the province of Fars, just beyond the normal reach of western traders until the second decade of the third century, when the Sassanid dynasts of that region, themselves devout believers, seized power from the Arsacids and inaugurated a new, far more violent, relationship with Rome that lasted until the Arab conquest in the seventh century.

Within the Roman empire, as we have seen, there were certainly relics of ancient, Achaemenid religious foundations, survivals that appear to have been cultivated with antiquarian enthusiasm into the second century. There was also Mithraism, a cult that may have arrived from the Crimea, where it arguably emerged under the Iranian dynasts of that region.[58] Mithraism may have offered its followers a watered-down version of Zoroastrian dualism in the guise of the worship of the Iranian god Mithras, a divinity who did not have a significant role in Achaemenid Zoroastrianism, but the surviving evidence does not permit any firm stand to be taken on this point. Throughout the empire this "barbarian wisdom" was subject to the influence of Greek thought; it was interesting because it could be made to conform to indigenous paradigms. Survivals of actual Zoroastrian doctrines were just that; as in the case of Persian influences that can be detected in Judaism, they contributed to continuing developments, detached from their roots and reformed in diverse local cults.[59] This kind of development could continue so long as "eastern wisdom" remained respectable. Such intellectual respectability was a function of the basic intellectual security of the inhabitants of the Roman world, who welcomed the ostensibly eastern because it could be domesticated and made to conform. When the empire was threatened from abroad in the third and fourth centuries, this attitude underwent a radical transformation as Persian wisdom that had not already been domesticated became anathema.

The Closing of the Roman Mind

Sometime in the year 100 a man named Elchesai is said to have written an account of a vision that he experienced in the Parthian city of Serae for a friend of his named Sobiai.[60] Elchesai told of seeing an extraordinarily large and well-proportioned angel in the company of his similarly proportioned heavenly female companion. The angel said that he was the son of God and that his associate was the holy spirit (Hipp. *Haer.* 9.8). He went on to say a number of interesting things about Christ (that he had a life on earth before the one that began with his birth to the Virgin Mary, and that he would be reborn periodically) and about how people ought to live their lives if they wanted to be saved (Hipp. *Haer* 9.8–11). In all likelihood, this book was originally written in Aramaic, although its contents are known primarily through hostile discussions of a later Greek version.[61]

Such a revelation was obviously too good to be shared with the world at large, and Elchesai therefore wrote that those privileged to read his account must "not recite this tale to all mortals, and guard these precepts carefully, because all men are not faithful, and all women are not straightforward" (Hipp. *Haer.* 9.12). These readers would no doubt have been particularly impressed in the years after 117 when they came to the section on astrology where Elchesai ordered that they

> take care not to commence your works on the third day after a
> Sabbath, since when three years of the reign of the emperor Trajan
> are completed from the time that he subjected the Persians to his
> sway—when, I say, three years have been completed, war rages be-
> tween the impious angels of the northern constellations; and on this
> account all kingdoms of impiety are in a state of confusion.   (Hipp.
> *Haer.* 9.11)

Such readers would know that Trajan had claimed suzerainty over Persia in 115 and that by 117 the eastern empire was being torn apart by a Jewish revolt that had broken out in Egypt and spread from there to Cyrenaica, Judaea, and Cyprus. Moreover, in 117 Abgar VII of Edessa had risen in revolt and destroyed a Roman army before being defeated by a second army under Lusius Quietus, who had followed up his success against Abgar by waging an extraordinarily brutal campaign against the Jews of Palestine.[62] In the same year, Trajan died and his successor renounced direct Roman government in Mesopotamia.[63]

This prophecy dates Elchesai's vision to precisely the period at the end of Trajan's reign (it would have been a quite extraordinary prophet who could have foreseen Trajan's Parthian war in 100, much less its initial success) and stands as an excellent example of the use of a post-eventum prophecy for contemporary social and political commentary, as well to validate the authority of a visionary.[64] If authentication was the intention, it worked. In the wake of the withdrawal of Roman armies from Mesopotamia, a community of followers of Elchesai grew up in lower Mesopotamia, and a century later Elchesai's book was discovered by a man named Alcibiades, who lived in the great cultural center of Apamea in central Syria. Sometime shortly after 222 he brought this book with him to Rome,[65] where it caused a tremendous stir in the Christian community, a community that was riven by controversy between two aspiring bishops, Callistus and Hippolytus. To those, like Callistus, who were inclined to believe in Elchesai, it was no doubt a remarkable new piece of eastern wisdom. To Hippolytus, who tried to discredit Callistus, it was simply a bit of derivative nonsense whose main points could be found in Greek philosophy or the books of the Egyptians (*Haer.* 9.12). This line of argument is particularly interesting in light of the fact that Alcibiades' book emerged from the world of Jewish Christianity, where heresy could be (and was) defined by adherence to "Greek doctrines," as the epistles of Paul were thought to be.[66]

At almost the same time that Alcibiades brought Elchesai's book to Rome, a member of the Elchesaite community in lower Mesopotamia began having some remarkable experiences.[67] At the age of twelve, Mani son of Pettikos met an angel who proved to be his heavenly double, and for the next few years he experienced many visions that he kept to himself.[68] He also began to talk to the local vegetation (it talked to him too) (*CMC* 5). At the same time he took service under the Great King Ardashir I. But on April 19, 240, when he was twenty-four, his companion appeared to him again and launched him on his career as the Apostle of Light (*CMC* 18–24). A year later he traveled to India, a natural choice for a young man from lower Mesopotamia, the region through which passed the sea trade between India and the west in a period when Persia and Rome were embroiled in war.[69] By 243 he seems to have returned to Persia, and he spent the rest of his life preaching his new gospel throughout the lands of the Persian king, with the support of no less a figure than Sapor I himself. It was in these years (probably) that he wrote the five books that were to provide the foundation of his faith in Aramaic, and one book summarizing his teachings for Sapor in Middle Persian.[70] After Sapor's death in 272, however, he soon fell victim to the politics of a new regime. Bahram I (273–276) had him imprisoned immediately after he came to the capital. On February 24, 274 (or 276), the Apostle of Light died in chains.[71]

Although Mani himself never seems to have traveled into the lands ruled by the emperors of Rome, his followers did set out in that direction during his lifetime, possibly even obtaining an interview with Zenobia of Palmyra in the few years after the capture of the Roman emperor Valerian by Sapor in 260, when her husband and she had made their city the political center of the Roman near east. It was certainly while Mani was still alive that the first Manichaean missionaries established themselves in Egypt.[72]

The popular reception of Mani's powerful new religion attests to the fervor of the missionaries, the power of their message, and the continuing interest in eastern wisdom.[73] But the followers of Mani's message soon found that the mystique of eastern wisdom was fading very fast. The three decades during which Manichaeism was first diffused across the Roman empire saw the beginning of a decisive shift in Roman openness to new eastern wisdom. For, while Elchesai's foe Hippolytus had tried to minimize the wonder of his message by showing that it was no more than reheated Greek philosophy, the enemies of Mani regarded the Persian origin of his doctrine as a decisive strike against it.

To the emperor Diocletian (284–305), who claimed to be the first man to restore the pristine order of the Roman empire against the barbarians, Manichaeism was a new and unexpected *prodigium* that had come into his realm from "the Persian race that is our enemy," to infect his subjects like the venom of a serpent through the execrable customs and savage laws of the Persians. He took this barbarism very seriously indeed, and on March 31, 302, he ordered the leaders of the Manichaean community in Egypt to be arrested and burnt at the stake along with their books.[74] For the bishop Eusebius of Caesarea, no great admirer of Diocletian, who followed up his persecution of the Manichaeans with a thoroughgoing persecution of the Christians in 304, the objections that could be raised to Mani's teachings were strikingly similar. According to Eusebius, "he [Mani] stitched together false and godless doctrines that he had collected from the countless, long-extinct, godless heresies and infected our empire with a deadly poison that came from the land of the Persians" (*HE* 7.31).[75]

The emperor, the bishop, and their colleagues and successors could not prevent the spread of Manichaeism, but their view of Persia as the source of corruption and evil illustrates a new phase in the relationship between the empire and the sages of the east. Rome had ceased to be the unquestioned ruler of the world: the walls of the "fortress" that was the imperial frontier system had been breached, armies had been defeated, an emperor had died in battle in 251, and another had been captured. It was only by dint of exceptionally hard work and good luck (the death of Sapor I in 272 and consequent lack of direction in Persian policy for the next two decades) that the emperors from Claudius II (268–270) to Diocletian had been able to recreate the image of Roman security. Those eastern sages who had already been accorded a membership in the club of the wise would not be expelled; Zoroaster remained a figure of considerable importance, as did Hermes Trismegistus and Julianus the Theurgist, but applications from aspiring members were no longer welcome.

There were also new doctrinal factors at work. The Christian apologists of the second and third centuries had created a canon of acceptable sages who could be quoted as examples of people who had dimly perceived the nature of the one God. According to one way of looking at things, they might not be correct because they lacked the essential ingredient for true knowledge (Christian belief), but they could still be used to prove that even polytheists had dimly perceived the truth before the birth of Christ. The history of the distant past could be valuable as proof that Christianity descended from a much more ancient tradition than did Greek religion: just as the books of Hebrew scripture contained knowledge from periods of human history that were earlier than any other, so Christianity, which replaced Hebrew revelation, had an ancient, respectable pedigree (neatly placed in the context of the early empires of the near east). On a more radical view, the Hebrew prophets themselves could be abandoned. Thus Lactantius wrote, "Let us leave aside the testimony of [Hebrew] prophets, lest a proof derived from those who are universally disbelieved should appear to be insufficient" (*DI* 1.5). Instead he turned to the works of classical poets, philosophers, and prophets. Hermes Trismegistus and sibyls take pride of place among the visionaries cited throughout the *Divine Institutes,* and at one point even the oracles of the gods are adduced to suggest the truth of Christian doctrine (*DI* 1.7). In the final book of the *Divine Institutes,* Lactantius combines themes to be found in Daniel, the book of Revelation, sibylline oracles, Hermes Trismegistus' *Perfect Discourse,* and the vision of Hydaspes. This last character, whom Lactantius describes as the father of Darius, reported a dream in which he interpreted the vision of an inspired boy (young boys were often used a mediums) before the war at Troy.[76] His work appears to have first come to the attention of Christians in the second century as a Persian equivalent to sibyls (his location before the Trojan War looks like an effort to place him in the same time span as one that was often used for the Erythraean Sibyl) and the Hebrew prophets. In other works it appears that he was a source for the wisdom of India as well, and generally he appears to have been a useful, fictional representative of the whole tradition of learning that was created by the intellectuals and pseudointellectuals of the Roman world for the peoples who lived beyond the eastern frontier.[77] The diversity of prophets enabled Lactantius to present his version of the end of the world as a truly ecumenical one.

By the beginning of the fourth century, there were already plenty of authors whose works could be plundered for quotations, and there was no need to add to their number. Moreover, from the second century onward, local bishops had been forced to contend with serious challenges to their authority raised by martyrs who might (and did) claim that their sufferings had brought them closer to God and new prophets claiming that they had the latest word from God.[78] In response, they had sought to strengthen their position by discouraging martyrdom and denying the validity of new revelation. Paul wrote on the value of active prophecy in a Christian community, "if all are uttering prophecies, the visitor, when he enters, hears from everyone something that searches his conscience and brings conviction, and the secrets of his heart are laid bare, so he will fall down and worship god, crying 'God is certainly among you'" (1 Cor. 14:24–5); but by the third century the ideal congregation came together to listen to the bishop rather than to the voice of god. New books of prophecy were therefore no more welcome than new prophets.

Finally, the advent of Christianity at the center of power in the fourth century changed the balance of wisdom between west and east. Christianity was a religion of the Roman world; emperors could (and did) see it as their duty to protect Christians beyond the frontiers and to support missionary efforts to convert the heathen. Now that the Roman state had Truth on its side there was much less interest in importing new ideas from the dangerous and corrupting powers of the east. Rome already had all the secret wisdom that it needed.

Epilogue: Power, Culture, and Communication

PROPHECY PROVIDED a crucial medium for the description of power in the Roman world. Prophecy of all sorts enabled people to understand their relationship with the immanent powers of the universe, and, because it was so important for describing this relationship, it became a vital force in the operation of other sorts of power. Prophecy was intimately involved in the history of communities; it helped spell out their relationship with the gods. It provided a means for expressing community identity; people kept, read, interpreted, and reinterpreted prophetic books as a way of finding out who they were, and what events beyond their control really meant to them. They consulted active sources of prophecy to answer questions that they were incapable of answering on their own. They could conceive the history of prophetic utterance as a touchstone for developments on earth.

The reading and use of prophecy were not, however, purely intellectual or emotional activities. Because prophecy could be used to describe relationships, it could also be used to help shape those relationships. Prophecy had a very real political role. Moreover, because it was so varied in its forms, it was open to all sorts of manipulation. People were readily aware of this possibility, and might well wait and see whether or not the prophecies that were presented to them seemed to be authentic; but if there was some reason to believe that they were, they could act as very powerful reinforcement to claims of political legitimacy. In such cases prophesies cannot be thought of as being either retrospective or prospective, for they were both proof that what had happened was divinely sanctioned and indications that the powers that controlled the earth had an interest in maintaining a situation that was therefore beyond human control.

The single most important development in the three centuries after Augustus was the growth of Christianity, a religion that was itself founded upon prophecies. In the Greco-Roman world, the variety of prophetic media was made possible by the infinite variety of cult, the numerous avenues that were opened between human and divine. The tradition of Christian prophecy owed a great deal to this world. The vivid experiences of Paul were not conditioned by the books of the faith that he read nearly so much as by the beliefs of the followers of traditional cults whom he encountered, and by the prophets, likewise influenced by external practice, who filled the Palestinian landscape during his lifetime.[1] Paul had visions of god; he spoke in tongues; he felt the divine spirit within him. He was a very dangerous man because he could rely upon his personal experience with the divine to guide him in changing the established rules of society.

With the passing of Paul and his generation, Christians had to begin to rethink the role that God could play on earth. The church that had been formed by Paul could not survive if it permitted others to have his access to God, and it was thus that in the second century Christians rediscovered the importance of canonical scripture, the necessity of a firm common ground for discussing the nature of Christ's revelation to the community as a whole. One reason for this was the need to be clear about just what Christ had said. In a world of many competing books, it was increasingly necessary to sort the wheat from the chaff, the nutty from the useful. There was also an increasing need to define appropriate lines of authority. Prophecy could no longer be concerned with the present; it had to become a purely historical phenomenon, a guide to the future and proof of past miracles.[2] Individual Christians could, and must, still have their own, personal experiences of God, but these experiences could no longer dictate the faith of their community.[3] So too, individual Christians or entire communities could have their own books in addition to those that were recognized as a part of the primary canon. Interest in these secondary, or local, canons is a fundamental feature of the phenomenon that is generally (and somewhat misleadingly) known as "apocalypticism," the seeking of additional revelation through books attributed to sages that were not accepted in the primary canon.[4] It is also a fundamental feature of the creation of a canon of acceptable polytheist prophets like the Sibyl, whose words could illuminate the secrets of the universe and confirm Christian doctrine. Within these secondary canons, there could be somewhat more diversity in prophetic type and form than in the primary canon: but it was generally the case that their revelations had to take second place. In the primary canon, accepted prophets had to look like the authority figures of the church: they had to be men; they also had to be dead so that they could not confuse a situation by offering their own views on what it was that they were saying. In this, the early church was blessed by its Jewish heritage, from which it inherited the idea of a sacred canon, male prophecy, and prophetic interpretation through the exegesis of texts.

In the Jewish tradition of exegetical prophecy, it was commonplace "to affirm that revelation is comprehensible only through the authoritative tradition of interpretation."[5] It was interpretation by teachers who worked within a literary tradition. Even a person like Josephus, who regarded himself as a true prophet, had to acknowledge that his personal revelations were not as important as those that occurred in the sacred books; and he also seems to have consciously modeled his behavior upon that of great figures of the past (chiefly Daniel and Jeremiah).[6] This style and mode of interpretation were manifestly different from those of traditional cult, in which revelation was comprehended by results or explicable through other revelations. This is precisely the process that we see at work in the successive editions of the *Oracle of the Potter*, in which interpretation was based upon other oracular texts, and in Roman augury, in which each successful interpretation provided a precedent for future analysis. These books were constantly being up-dated. The most important development of post-exilic Judaism, and the development that created Judaism out of ancient Israelite prac-tice, was the idea of a fixed primary canon that provided people with all they needed to know if they had the wit to understand it. The emergence of this canon was obviously a long process, and, as we can now see more clearly as a result of the discoveries around Qumran, it was certainly not complete to everyone's satisfaction in the lifetime of Christ, or even by the time of the great revolt against Rome that began in A.D. 65.[7] But by that time the idea, at least, that the interpretation of books must form the basis for under-standing divine action that was relevant to the community as a whole was firmly established, and it was to this idea that Christians returned (with some difficulty) in the course of the second century. As we have also seen, however, Christians could not permanently dispose of the alternative tradition.

The conflict between exegetical prophecy, prophecy on the basis of canonical books, and prophecy delivered by living people re-mained a problem of fundamental importance for religions based on books. They could not have the easy methods of acceptance or rejection that were open to their polytheist neighbors, but they also needed to be able to compete with the excitement generated by these new revelations. The creation of a canon and canonical tex-tual traditions gave Christianity and Judaism a stability that was crucial to their continuing success, but it did not mean that Chris-tians or Jews could simply ignore alternative sorts of prophecy. What it did mean was that new revelation had to be relegated to a readily definable second level, just as some books had also to be shelved in a second section.

To a devotee of traditional cult, the idea that a true revelation in one's own day was any less significant than a true revelation a thousand years before was inconceivable. Exegetical and living prophecy had to coexist, and the debate over the authentication of new wisdom was essentially concerned with the possibility that something new should be admitted to the cultural store of mar-velous events. The result was somewhat chaotic, but it was the chaos of human experience.

Notes

Index

Notes

1. Prophecy and Cult

1. For Plutarch's career see C. P. Jones, *Plutarch and Rome* (Oxford, 1971), 3–39, esp. p. 26 for his Delphic connections. S. Schröder, *Plutarchs Schrift de Pythiae Oraculis. Text, Einleitung und Kommentar* (Stuttgart, 1990), offers a superior analysis of one of Plutarch's Delphic dialogues. For Pausanias' cultural interests see C. Habicht, *Pausanias' Guide to Ancient Greece* (Berkeley, 1985), esp. 95–116 on Greek history and 117–140 on his attitude to Rome, suggesting that he regarded the Romans as outsiders; J. Elsner, "Pausanias: A Greek Pilgrim in the Roman World," *Past and Present* 32 (1992), 3–29, on the use of the past and, especially, the use of cult as a "defense mechanism" in the present.

2. Paus. 10.9.11–12 on Aegospotami; Plut. *De E apud Delph.* 386 C; *De Pyth. orac.* 407D, 408C; *De defect. orac.* 413B with Schröder, *Plutarchs Schrift de Pythiae Oraculis*, 10–15, 421.

3. For prophecy and divination see pages 10–15. For the problem apocalypticism see esp. M. Smith, "On the History of ΑΠΟΚΑΛΥΠΤΩ and ΑΠΟΚΑΛΥΨΙΣ," in D. Hellholm, ed., *Apocalypticism in the Mediterranean World and the Near East: Proceedings of the International Colloquium on Apocalypticism, Uppsala, August 12–17 (1979)* (Tübingen, 1983), 9–20; H. D. Betz, "The Problem of Apocalyptic Genre in Greek and Hellenistic Literature: The Case of the Oracle of Trophonius," ibid., 577–597. For

the modern problem of arriving at a definition of the genre see P. R. Davies, "The Social World of Apocalyptic writings," in R. E. Clements, ed., *The World of Ancient Israel: Sociological, Anthropological and Political Perspectives* (Cambridge, 1989), 254. The overall difficulty is also discussed usefully by L. Hartman, "Survey of the Problem of Apocalyptic Genre," in Hellholm, *Apocalypticism in the Mediterranean World,* 329–343. E. J. Bickerman, "Faux littéraires dans l'antiquité classique," *RFIC* 101 (1973) = *Studies in Jewish and Christian History* 3 (Leiden, 1986), 196–211, remains a crucial discussion of all these issues, as does J. Barton, *Oracles of God: Perceptions of Ancient Prophecy in Israel after Exile* (London, 1986), 129–130, 152–153. For the semantic problem connected with prophecy see his pp. 13–14. For a view of problems with the Jewish tradition of prophecy similar to the one taken here of the classical see R. Gray, *Prophetic Figures in Late Second Temple Jewish Palestine: The Evidence of Josephus* (Oxford, 1993), 6.

4. For the text see M. L. West, "Oracles of Apollo Kareios. A Revised text," *ZPE* 1 (1967), 184–185. For the procedure see C. A. Faraone, *Talismans and Trojan Horses: Guardian Statues in Ancient Greek Myth and Ritual* (Oxford, 1992), 61–64. For identification of the oracle as that of Apollo at Claros see F. Graf, "An Oracle against Pestilence from a Western Anatolian Town," *ZPE* 92 (1992), 271–272, restating the case that the plague is that which struck the empire in 165. This is the most likely solution, but see R. J. Lane Fox, *Pagans and Christians* (New York, 1986), 233–236, for the identification of the oracle as Delphic.

5. See particularly R. MacMullen, *Paganism in the Roman Empire* (New Haven, 1981); Lane Fox, *Pagans and Christians,* esp. 64–261; P. Chuvin, *The Chronicle of the Last Pagans* (Cambridge, Mass., 1990); K. W. Harl, "Sacrifice and Pagan Belief in Fifth- and Sixth-Century Byzantium," *Past and Present* 30 (1990), 7–27, is a useful survey of the continuity of pagan practice in the East; S. Mitchell, *Anatolia: Land, Men, and Gods in Asia Minor* 2 (Oxford, 1993), 117–118 and 122–150, on the world of Theodore of Syceon.

6. E. Gibbon, *The Decline and Fall of the Roman Empire,* chap. 28. For a survey of survivals and adaptations in western Europe after the collapse of the western empire see V. J. Flint, *The Rise of Magic in Early Medieval Europe* (Princeton, 1991); for survivals in Britain in the early modern period see K. Thomas, *Religion and the Decline of Magic* (New York, 1971), 25–50; and for the issue of different traditions' descending

from (and adapting) classical traditions see the lucid summary of the critiques of Thomas' work in S. J. Tambiah, *Magic, Science, Religion, and the Scope of Rationality* (Cambridge, 1990), 24–31.

7. The terminology used to describe the distinction between the complementary forms of religious experience adopted here seems preferable to "ritual" and "miracle" used by, for instance, M. Douglas, *Purity and Danger: An Analysis of the Concepts of Pollution and Taboo* (Oxford, 1966), 59, because her "ritual" is often used to obtain "miracle." The need that she sees to draw a distinction between two complementary varieties of religious experience without using the semantically overcharged word "magic" remains a crucial advance on earlier work. A similar semantic issue is addressed by R. Rappaport in "The Obvious Aspects of Ritual," in idem, *Ecology, Meaning, and Religion* (Berkeley, 1979), 173–221, who notes that ritual combines what he terms the "sacred," which is the product of language, and the "numinous" or "holy," the product of emotion. We are talking about the same problem, but his terminology somewhat occludes the different purposes of ritual actions. These semantic issues are important because the weight of post-Reformation religious discourse has so burdened certain terms, such as "magic," with doctrinally derived connotations as to render them virtually useless for analyzing non-Christian behaviors. I prefer my terminology precisely because it is free of doctrinal implication, even though I concede that the religious behavior that I term as intellectually passive often demands a good deal of personal activity.

8. For the recommendation to pay attention to existing cults in the context of the creation of a new one, and to send choirs to honor divinities in other cities, see now Graf, "An Oracle against Pestilence," 272.

9. Quoted in M. A. Wes, *Michael Rostovtzeff, Historian in Exile: Russian Roots in an American Context,* Historia Einzelscriften 65 (Stuttgart, 1990), 80.

10. See now T. G. Parkin, *Demography and Roman Society* (Baltimore, 1992), 67–91.

11. See Liddell and Scott s.v. ἱερεύς; Chantraine, *Dictionnaire étymologique de la langue grecque* (Paris, 1984) s.v., stressing the original meaning of "priest who sacrifices"; *OLD* s.vv. *flamen, sacerdos;* see also *fetialis.* It is interesting that Varro expressly connected with word with cult practice, saying that "because in Latium they always kept their heads covered and had their hair girt with a woolen *filum* 'band,' they were originally called

filamines," and that they took their names from the rites that they celebrated (*LL* 5.84). For the rather complicated history of these terms see G. Wissowa, *Religion und Kultus der Römer* (Munich, 1902), 413–414.

12. R. L. Gordon, "The Veil of Power: Emperors, Sacrificers, and Benefactors," in J. North and M. Beard, eds., *Pagan Priests: Religion and Power in the Ancient World* (Ithaca, 1990), 201–219.

13. M. Beagon, *Roman Nature: The Thought of Pliny the Elder* (Oxford, 1992), 26–54, is useful for a summary of ancient attitudes toward nature and divinity.

14. See the texts collected in D. S. Potter, *Prophecy and History in the Crisis of the Roman Empire: A Historical Commentary on the Thirteenth Sibylline Oracle* (Oxford, 1990), 242. For charges of cannibalism and incest against Christians, see Ter. *Apol.* 7–9; Eus. *HE* 5.1.7–10.

15. See L. B. Zaidman and P. Schmitt Pantel, *Religion in the Ancient Greek City,* trans. P. Cartledge (Cambridge, 1992), 8–15, on Greek notions of the sacred, pollution, purity, piety, and impiety; the best study of pollution in the Greek world remains R. Parker, *Miasma. Pollution and Purification in Early Greek Religion* (Oxford, 1983); for these concepts in the Roman world see J. Schied, *Religion et piété à Rome* (Paris, 1985), 17–57.

16. M. I. Rostovtzeff, *The Social and Economic History of the Roman Empire,* 2d ed. (Oxford, 1957), remains the classic study of the division of classical civilization between urban and rural cultures. G. E. M. de Ste. Croix, *The Class Struggle in the Ancient Greek World* (London, 1983), 9–19, offers a penetrating discussion of this point from a Marxist perspective.

17. For crop yields in antiquity see the evidence collected in R. P. Duncan-Jones, *The Economy of the Roman Empire. Quantitative Studies,* 2d ed. (Cambridge, 1982) 328; P. Garnsey, *Famine and Food Supply in the Graeco-Roman World* (Cambridge, 1988), 11–13.

18. I am indebted on this point to Karen Carr, whose Ph.D. dissertation, "Did Roman Government Matter" (University of Michigan, 1990), provides an extraordinarily nuanced discussion of this issue.

19. See Tambiah, *Magic, Science, Religion,* 11–83, for a lucid survey of the issue.

20. For the impact of such divisions, leading to serious failure to understand religious activity, see the cases discussed by T. Ranger, "The Local and Global in Southern African Religious History," in R. W.

Hefner, ed., *Conversion to Christianity: Historical and Anthropological Explanations on a Great Transformation* (Berkeley, 1993), 65–98.

21. *The Anchor Bible Dictionary* s.v. "prophecy"; *The Oxford English Dictionary* s.v. "prophecy," listing this as the most common usage, though also admitting "one who speaks for God or any deity as the inspired revealer or interpreter of his will, one who is held or (more loosely) who claims to have this function," "an inspired or quasi-inspired teacher," and "the spoken or especially the written utterance of a prophet or of the prophets."

22. E. Fascher, *ΠΡΟΦΗΤΗΣ. Eine sprach-und religionsgeschichtlische Untersuchung* (Giessen, 1927), 4–7, 9. He does not, however, pay sufficient attention to *theos* compounds. See also, more helpfully in some cases, the survey of the semantic formations connected with *mantis* and *chrēs–in* Chantraine, *Dictionnaire étymologique*.

23. Fascher, *ΠΡΟΦΗΤΗΣ,* 12.

24. Theocr. 22.116; see also Fascher, *ΠΡΟΦΗΤΗΣ,* 28–29, esp. 29 n. 1.

25. Fascher, *ΠΡΟΦΗΤΗΣ,* 68.

26. J. Robert and L. Robert, "Décret de Colophon pour un chresmologue de Smyrne appelé à diriger l'oracle de Claros," *BCH* 116 (1992), 279–291; Fascher, *ΠΡΟΦΗΤΗΣ,* 42 (Akraiphiai). See also *I. Hadrianoi* 24 for a man who says, "I Gauros received the true oracles of the prophets and I wrote about the victory of Caesar and the contests of the Gods, from which I received all that I prayed for from beginning to end and I pride myself in returning gifts freely." For the text see Mitchell, *Anatolia* 2:13 n. 23. The *prophetai* here do not seem to have been the actual dispensers of divine revelation, but rather the interpreters of the revelation; they seem to have changed annually, and the situation may be analogous to that at Claros (where the word *prophetes* is also used of the interpreter).

27. *On.* 3.21: *eudokimein en toi proagoreuein.* The list of practitioners who are to be trusted or distrusted (see note 36 below) suggests that he is thinking here of similar people, that is, other occupants of the predictive world in which he himself moved.

28. H. S. Versnel, "Some Reflections on the Relationship Magic-Religion," *Numen* 38 (1991), 177–197, provides a very useful overview of the discussion of this topic, although, as is clear from what follows in the text, I accept the views expressed by A. D. Nock in his brilliant and

lucid discussion of the use of the term *mageia* in "Paul and the Magus," in F. J. Foakes Jackson and K. Lake eds., *The Beginnings of Christianity* (London, 1933), pt. 1, vol. 5, 171–172 = *Essays on Religion in the Ancient World*, ed. Z. Stewart (Oxford, 1972), 315.

29. P. Brown, "Sorcery, Demons and the Rise of Christianity: From Late Antiquity to the Middle Ages," in M. Douglas, ed., *Witchcraft Confessions and Accusations*, Association of Social Anthropologists Monographs, 9 (London, 1970), 17–45 = *Religion and Society in the Age of Saint Augustine* (London, 1972), 119–146.

30. Aug. *Conf.* 4.2; for Libanius' problems see Brown, "Sorcery, Demons and the Rise of Christianity," 127; for Apuleius see *Apol.* passim.

31. For the use of *defixiones* see now the balanced and nuanced discussion in J. G. Gager, *Curse Tablets and Binding Spells from the Ancient World* (Oxford, 1992), 3–41.

32. *C. Th.* 9.16.3.

33. Tac. *Hist.* 2.2.2–4.2; for the method employed see L. Robert, "Sur un Apollon oraculaire à Chypre," *CRAI* (1978), 338–344 = *OMS* 5.640–646.

34. For Daphne see Y. Hajjar, "Divinités oraculaires et rites divinatoires en Syrie et en Phénicie à l'époque gréco-romaine," *ANRW* 18.4, 2283–84, 2294–98; 2258–62 for Atargitis and Myra, 2273–74 for Allat.

35. A. Bouché-Leclercq, *Histoire de la divination dans l'antiquité* 1 (Paris, 1879), 107–109, remains the fundamental discussion of this point for the classical world.

36. Art. *On.* 2.69. He does not fulfill his promise to discuss people who cast horoscopes at birth, but the division he makes here looks as if he is thinking along the same lines as Sextus Empiricus, who distinguishes between astrologers who talk about natural phenomena and those who claim to predict the future from horoscopes (*Adv. Math.* 5.1–2).

37. R. Merkelbach, "Das Epigramm aus Veleda," *ZPE* 43 (1981): 241; G. Walser, "Veleda," *RE* 1955, cols, 617–622.

38. Suet. *Vesp.* 5.6; Jos. *BJ* 3.399–405.

39. *PGM* IV.2446–49; A. D. Nock, "Greek Magical Papyri," *JEA* 15 (1929), 224–225 = Stewart, *Essays on Religion,* 183.

40. Luc. *Alex.* 48. For the chronology of the development of the cult see C. P. Jones, *Culture and Society in Lucian* (Cambridge, Mass., 1986), 133–140; for the later celebration of Glycon in the Balkans see D. S. Potter, review of *Pagans and Christians, JRA* 1 (1988), 210 n. 6; *ILS* 4080,

discussed there as evidence for Glycon, has been shown to refer to Alexander the Great and a Balkan snake cult; M. Š. Kos, "Draco and the Survival of the Snake Cult in the Central Balkans," *Tyche* 6 (1991), 187–188.

41. Dio 67.18, 77.18; Phil. *V. Apoll.* 1.4; cf. F. G. B. Millar, *A Study of Cassius Dio* (Oxford, 1964), 20.

42. See esp. Amm. 23.5.10–11, 13–14 with 23.5.5: *quoniam nulla vis humana vel virtus meruisse umquam potuit, ut quod praescripsit fatalis ordo non fiat.* For the conflict between traditional religious practices and Julian's own beliefs see J. F. Matthews, *The Roman Empire of Ammianus* (London, 1989), 115–129.

43. A. J. Festugière, *La révélation d'Hermès Trismégiste* 1 (Paris, 1950), 89. The discussion in the text relies heavily on this lucid exposition and on that provided by F. H. Cramer, *Astrology in Roman Law and Politics* (Philadelphia, 1954).

44. O. Neugebauer, *A History of Ancient Mathematical Astronomy* (Heidelberg, 1975) 1, 3–4. See also his publication of a second-to-third century papyrus showing the use of a Babylonian-style ephemeris, ("A Babylonian Lunar Ephemeris from Roman Egypt," in E. Leichty, M. Ellis, and P. Gerardi, *A Scientific Humanist: Studies in Memory of Abraham Sachs* [Philadelphia, 1988], 301–304). His conclusion (p. 302), "that astronomers in the Roman period in Egypt had access not only to a few period relations and some eclipse observations, but could study in detail the Babylonian numerical analysis of the lunar motion. Needless to say, this drastically changes modern discussions of transmission of Babylonian to Greek astronomy," is somewhat overstated. As he observes (p. 302), the great interest of this text is that it shows that "no preserved cuneiform text can be continued so as to give the numbers in the papyrus," which shows that his belief that Babylonian mathematics influenced developments in the Greek world is proved beyond doubt, but that subsequent developments are indigenous to the Mediterranean rather than the Mesopotamian world. The so-called *sphaera barbarica,* which is mentioned as an antiquarian curiosity in astronomical texts of the Roman empire, is therefore an invention of the Greek world; for it, see Cramer, *Astrology in Roman Law and Politics,* 25–26.

45. For formulae to determine the time of conception see O. Neugebauer and H. B. van Hoesen, *Greek Horoscopes* (Philadelphia, 1959), 28. For the importance of conception, as opposed to birth, see Ptol. *Tetr.* 3.1.

46. Cramer, *Astrology in Roman Law and Politics*, 11.

47. Neugebauer and van Hoesen, *Greek Horoscopes*, 125.

48. Ibid., 125–126.

49. D. Baccani, *Oroscopi greci. Documentazione papirologica* (Messina, 1991), 126 suggests that the *ep' agathoi* in line 10 of *P. Oxy.* 2556 may be no more than a formula. In this context, I doubt that she is correct here.

50. Sex. Emp. *Adv. math.* 5.43–8; compare Pliny *NH* 2.22–25; Cic. *De div.* 2.90–99; Cramer, *Astrology in Roman Law and Politics*, 70–71 (Cicero), 204–207 (Sextus); Beagon, *Roman Nature*, 28–29. See also Luc. *Astrol.* 27–28, the conclusion of a parody of praises of the art.

51. See S. R. F. Price, "The Future of Dreams: From Freud to Artemidorus," *Past and Present* 28 (1987), 9–31, for Artemidorus' place in ancient dream interpretation.

52. The role of the god in all of this is left somewhat ambiguous; see Price, "The Future of Dreams," 16–17.

53. For Artemidorus' attitudes see Lane Fox, *Pagans and Christians*, 155–158; M. P. Nilsson, *Geschichte der griechischen Religion*[3] 1 (Munich, 1967), 169, notes that prediction through dreams falls between "inductive" and "inspired" prophecy. It would be better to say that dreams could be used in either an "inductive" or an "inspired" context.

54. See also Macrob. *Comm in Som. Scip.* 3.1, listing five categories of dream; Iamb. *De myst.* 3.2 on mantic and nonmantic dreams, with no evidence of his having read Artemidorus.

55. See, for example, *PGM* 4.3172–3208 (dream-producing charm using three reeds), 7.222–249 (appeal to Besas), 664–685 (appeal to Hermes), 12.144–152, 190–192; *PDM* suppl. 1–130 (eight spells for procuring dreams).

56. For the contents of physiognomic works see now M. W. Gleason, "The Semiotics of Gender: Physiognomy and Self-Fashioning in the Second Century C.E.," in D. Halperin, J. Winkler and F. Zeitlin, *Before Sexuality: The Construction of Erotic Experience in the Ancient Greek World* (Princeton, 1990), 389–415.

57. I include the last two forms of divination under the heading "subjective" because they did not depend on organically derived information, but upon the divine action that caused the consultant to pick a certain number or to roll a certain number with dice. Cicero explicitly excludes this form of divination from his consideration of "inspired" prediction (*De div.* 1.34.18), which can be understood only as a reflection of the fact

that it was practiced by the poor, although he is willing to admit that well–established practitioners of this sort may in fact be legitimately considered as working through the action of the gods and that their prophecies are sanctioned by antiquity: *cuius generis oracula etiam habenda sunt, non ea, quae aequatis sortibus ducuntur, sed illa, quae instinctu divino afflatuque funduntur; etsi ipsa sors contemnenda non est, si auctoritatem habet vetustatis.*

58. E. E. Evans-Pritchard, *Witchcraft, Oracles and Magic among the Azande*, rev. ed. (Oxford, 1976), 164.

59. *CIL* XI.1. 1129 for Forum Novum, for Praeneste, Antium, Tibur, and Ostia see A. Riemann, "Praenestinae Sorores," *MDAI* (Rome) 94 (1987), 131–161.

60. P. Amandry, *La mantique apollinienne à Delphes. Essai sur le fonctionnement de l'Oracle* (Paris, 1950), 25–36; H. W. Parke and D. E. W. Wormell, *The Delphic Oracle* 1 (Oxford, 1956), 18–19. The inscription published by P. Amandry, "Convention religeuse conclue entre Delphes et Skiathos," *BCH* (1939), 195–200, which he argued mentioned a fee for the use of the lot oracle, does not in fact do so; see F. Sokolowski, "Sur un passage de la convention Delphes-Skiathos," *Revue archéologique* 31/32 (1949), 981–984; I. Malkin, *Religion and Colonization in Ancient Greece* (Leiden, 1987), 30–31. The textual evidence collected by Amandry is still sufficient to prove the existence of the lot oracle during the period at which the inspired oracle also worked.

61. P. Tannery, "Astrampsychos," *REG* 11 (1989), 96–97.

62. G. M. Browne, "The Composition of the *Sortes Astrampsychi*," *BICS* 17 (1970), 95; Tannery, "Astrampsychos," 97–105. For the papyri containing sections from the *sortes* see G. M. Browne, *The Papyri of the Sortes Astrampsychi* (Meisenheim am Glan, 1974).

63. G. M. Browne, "The Origin and Date of the *Sortes Astrampsychi*," *ICS* 1 (1976), 53–58.

64. Browne, "Composition of the *Sortes Astrampsychi*," 95.

65. Ibid., 96–98.

66. F. Hienevetter, *Würfel und Buchstabenorakel in Griechenland und Kleinasien* (Breslau, 1912); G. Björck, "Heidenische und christliche Orakel mit fertigen Antworten," *Symb. Osl.* 19 (1939), 86–98; J. Nollé, "Epigraphica Varia," *ZPE* 48 (1982), 274–282; idem, "Südkleinasiatische Losorakel in der römischen Kaiserzeit," *Antike Welt* 18.3 (1987), 41–49 esp. 43–45 on the location of the oracles. Nollé includes a number of superior photographs of the texts in context; T. Ritti, "Oraculi alfabetici

a Hieropolis di Frigia," *MRG* 14 (1989), 243–286 offers a re-edition of several texts based upon an alphabetic lot system. It is of some interest that several responses suggest consultation of another oracle (e.g., Hp I.18: the king of the immortals will save you through the oracles of [Apollo] Kareios). For the manufacture of some texts by extracting lines from different oracles see Plut. *De Pyth. orac.* 407C with Schröder, *Plutarchs Schrift de Pythiae Oraculis,* 399–400. *P. Oxy.* 3831 is a lot oracle based on lines from Homer with instructions on days and times when it could be consulted.

67. For a general discussion of these oracles in an Egyptian context see Amandry, *La mantique apollinienne,* 174–175; J. D. Ray, "Ancient Egypt," in M. Loewe and C. Blacker, eds., *Divination and Oracles* (London, 1981), 181; A. Heinrichs, "Zwei Orakelfragen," *ZPE* 11 (1973), 115–116.

68. A. S. Aly, "Eight Greek Oracle Questions in the West Berlin Collection," *ZPE* 68 (1987), 99–100. See also *P. Oxy.* 3799, an inquiry by a person who wanted to know if he should offer a higher bid for the contract on a tax.

69. H. C. Youtie, "Questions to a Christian Oracle," *ZPE* 18 (1975), 253–257; for Coptic texts in this form see H. de Nie, "Een koptisch-christelijke Orakalvraag," *Ex Oriente Lux* 8 (1942), 615–618; S. Donadoni, "Una domanda oracolare Christiana da Antinoe," *Rivista degli studi orientali* 29 (1954), 183–186.

70. See part. Paus. 8.2. the most influential work on this theme was Euhemerus of Messene's utopian novel the *Hiera Anagraphe,* on which see F. Jacoby, "Euemeros," *RE* 6 (1907), cols. 952–972, and his edition of the fragments as *FGrH* 63. See also P. M. Fraser, *Ptolemaic Alexandria* 1 (Oxford, 1972), 289–295.

71. See now J. Bousquet, "La stèle de Kyténien a Xanthos de Lycie," *REG* (1988), 29–32.

72. See especially Phil. *Heroicus* 8; Lane Fox, *Pagans and Christians,* 144–148.

73. For a new god on Aegina in the second century see L. Robert, *A travers de l'Asie mineure* (Paris, 1980), 400.

74. R. Lamberton, *Homer the Theologian* (Berkeley, 1986), 3–8.

75. H. C. Youtie, "Sambathis," *HTR* 37 (194), 212 n. 17.

76. Acts 13:6–12, 17:16–34, 18:12, 23:24, 24:27.

77. C. P. Jones, "A Martyria for Apollonius of Tyana," *Chiron* 12 (1982), 137–144.

78. R. R. R. Smith, "Late Roman Philosophers' Portraits from Aphrodisias," *JRS* 80 (1990), 141–144. E. L. Bowie, "Apollonius of Tyana: Tradition and Reality," *ANRW* ii/16, 1689–91, casts doubt on the work about sacrifices. However, M. Dzielska, *Apollonius of Tyana in Legend and History* (Rome, 1986), 139–148, argues convincingly that it might well be authentic, and even if "[w]e cannot prove with absolute certainty that *peri thysion* was written by Apollonius himself, yet we are positive that it originated before Philostratus and is closely connected with the historical Apollonius."

79. G. Dagron and D. Feissel, *Inscriptions de Cilicie* (Paris, 1987), no. 88; cf. D. S. Potter, "Recent Inscriptions from Flat Cilicia," *JRA* 2 (1989), 309–310; Dzielska, *Apollonius of Tyana*, 68, argues that it refers specifically to the talismans of Apollonius.

80. For Ammianus' views on Maximus and other philosophers see Matthews, *The Roman Empire of Ammianus*, 115–129, 432–435 (on this passage). For the distinction between traditional divination and that practiced by Maximus see Matthews, 126–127, 428–431.

81. For Sossianus see T. D. Barnes, "Sossianus Hierocles and the Antecedents of the Great Persecution," *HSCP* 80 (1976), 239–252; for Nicomachus cf. O. Seeck, "Virius Nicomachus Flavianus," *RE* 6, col. 2508; the only evidence is Sid. Apol. *Ep.* 8.3.1.

82. For the pagans see G. Fowden, "The Pagan Holy Man in Late Antique Society," *JHS* 102 (1982), 36–37; for the Christian tradition see the next note.

83. W. L. Dulière, "Protection permanante contre des animaux nuisibles assurée par Apollonius de Tyane dans Byzance et Antioche. Evolution de son mythe," *BZ* 63 (1970), 247–277; W. Speyer, "Zum Bild des Apollonius von Tyana bei Heiden und Christen," *Jbh. f. Antike und Christentum* 17 (1974), 56–63; Dzielska, *Apollonius of Tyana*, 85–127.

84. For Leo see *PLRE* II.662–663 (Leo 5); for Isidore of Pelusium see P. Brown, *Power and Persuasion in Late Antiquity: Towards a Christian Empire* (Madison, 1992), 139–140; Dzielska, *Apollonius of Tyana*, 102–103; for Apollonius as a prophet of Christ see Speyer, "Zum Bild," 63; Bickerman, "Faux littéraires dans l'antiquité classique," 202 n. 32. For the extensive Arabic tradition see Dzielska, *Apollonius of Tyana*, 112–22.

85. See also Dzielska, *Apollonius of Tyana,* 86–89.

86. D. H. Raynor, "Moeragenes and Philostratus: Two Views of Apollonius of Tyana," *CQ* n.s. 34 (1984), 222–226.

87. Ath. *Leg.* 26.4.5; cf. C. P. Jones, "Neryllinus," *CPh* 80 (1985), 40–45.

88. For Lucian's treatment see Jones, *Culture and Society,* 117–132. Tatian, a contemporary who was admittedly a hostile witness, described him as an extreme example of hypocrisy, probably while he was still alive; see *Orat. ad Graecos* 26.21–24.

89. Men. Rhet. 26.4.5; Amm. 29.1.39; see, in general, Jones, *Culture and Society,* 131–132, esp. p. 131 on the possible *Apologies of Peregrinus.*

90. L. Holford-Strevens, *Aulus Gellius* (London, 1988), 105, "Peregrinus was more complex than Gellius knew," considerably understates the point. *NA* 12.11.1: *Philosophum Peregrinum, cui postea cognomentum Protea factum est, virum gravem et constantem . . .*, especially *constantem,* shows that this was very probably written after the self-immolation in 165; see Jones, *Culture and Society,* 131 n. 72.

91. See note 40.

92. The attribution of the Greek life to Athanasius has been called into question by, above all, T. D. Barnes, "Angel of Light or Mystic Initiate? The Problem of *The Life of Anthony,*" *JTS* n.s. 37 (1986), 353–368 (with earlier bibliography). Athanasian authorship of the Greek version is reasserted by A. Louth, "St. Athanasius and the Greek *Life of Anthony,*" *JTS* n.s. 39 (1988), 504–509, although he accepts the possibility of a Coptic original.

93. P. Brown, "The Rise and Function of the Holy Man in Late Antiquity," *JRS* 61 (1971), 93 = idem, *Society and the Holy in Late Antiquity* (Berkeley, 1982), 139. The shrines of saints could become focal points for other sorts of divination; see P. Athanassiadi, "Dreams, Theurgy and Freelance Divination: The Testimony of Iamblichus," *JRS* 83 (1993), 124–127.

94. See Lane Fox, *Pagans and Christians,* 404–410, for the history of the movement, taking account of recent discoveries. P. Labriolle, *La crise montaniste* (Paris, 1913), remains extraordinarily useful for the literary sources. C. M. Robeck, *Prophecy in Carthage: Perpetua, Tertullian, and Cyprian* (Cleveland, 1992), 199–205, offers an important analysis of the impact of Montanism on Christian visions. For recent work on the Phrygian homeland of Montanism, see Mitchell, *Anatolia,* 2:39–40.

95. See Proph. *V. Plot.* 10 with *En.* 3.4.3; 6. I am indebted to Dr. M. J. Edwards for discussion on this point.

96. See J. Reiling, *Hermas and Christian Prophecy* (Leiden, 1973), 19, for the varieties of inspiration.

97. Amandry, *La mantique apollinienne,* 179–180.

98. Lane Fox, *Pagans and Christians,* 198–200.

99. *Milet* I.3.33f, g; 37b; see J. L. Fontenrose, *Didyma* (Berkeley, 1988), 181–183, for the enrollment of new citizens. For the building of the theater see W. H. Buckler, "Labour Disputes in the Province of Asia," in *Anatolian Studies Presented to Sir William Mitchell Ramsay* (Manchester, 1923), 35; Fontenrose, *Didyma,* 193–194.

100. *I. Did.* 496a; L. Robert, *Hellenica* 11/12 (Paris, 1960), 543–546; Fontenrose, *Didyma,* 196–197; Lane Fox, *Pagans and Christians,* 102–104.

101. P. Hermann, "Athena Polias in Milet," *Chiron* 1 (1971), 291–298; R. Merkelbach, "Ein Didymaeisches Orakel," *ZPE* 8 (1971), 93–95; T. Drew-Bear and W. D. Lebek, "An Oracle of Apollo at Miletus," *GRBS* (1973), 65–73; Fontenrose, *Didyma,* 199–202.

102. For accounts of consultations see further Parke and Wormell, *Delphic Oracle* 1:30–34.

103. Fontenrose, *Didyma,* 85; H. W. Parke, *The Oracles of Apollo in Asia Minor* (London, 1985), 216.

104. Parke, *Oracles of Apollo,* 216–217, rightly suggests that the *adyton* in Iamblichus' account might simply mean "all parts of the temple not normally open to the laity," and plausibly points out that it is not necessary to assume that the priestess slept in what must have been a most uncomfortable building for three days—on the other hand, the alternative is not impossible.

105. It remains an open question whether any consultant was allowed into the temple, although I find it hard to imagine that an important imperial official would be denied access. There is also some question as to just how visitors would be admitted; see Fontenrose, *Didyma,* 80–81; Parke, *Oracles of Apollo,* 214–215.

106. Iamb. *De myst.* 3.11; *I. Did.* 212; cf. Fontenrose, *Didyma,* 83–84; Parke, *Oracles of Apollo,* 212–214. Parke is surely correct to see that Iamblichus had heard a number of different things about what happened when the prophetess sat above the water and did not know what was correct; but this does not mean that it was impossible for anyone to get into the

temple and watch her, as Parke concludes. It simply means that Iamblichus was not very well informed.

107. L. Robert, "L'oracle de Claros," in *La civilization grecque de l'antiquité à nos jours* (Paris, 1967), 305; contra Parke, *Oracles of Apollo*, 221, who argues for the old view that the *prophetes* drank from the spring and that the *thespiodos* wrote the response. Robert's argument is based upon the fact that the *thespiodos* served for many years, while the *prophetes* changed annually. I am inclined to agree with Robert, not only because it makes more sense that the most important member of the technical staff should be the person who drank the water (and the person who was associated with the site for the longest period). This is also the view that emerges most readily from Tacitus' description of the oracle (*Ann.* 2.54.2–3), *relegit Asiam adpellitque Colophona, ut Clarii Apollonis oraculo uteretur. non femina, ut apud Delphos, sed certis e familiis et ferme Mileto accitus sacerdos numerum modo consultantium et nomina audit; tum in specum degressus, hausta fontis arcani aqua, ignarus plerumque litterarum et carminum edit responsa versibus compositis super rebus, quas quis mente concipit.* This jibes with Iamblichus' description, and it is clear that Tacitus thought that the person who drank the water produced the verses. Robert and Robert, "Décret de Colophon," 287–291, show that Tacitus is correct in stating that the people of Colophon brought in prophets of Ionian extraction from other cities.

108. H. D. Betz, "The Problem of Apocalyptic Genre in Greek and Hellenistic Literature: The Case of the Oracle of Trophonius," in Hellholm, *Apocalypticism in the Mediterranean World,* 577–597.

109. See also L. Radke, "Trophonios," *RE* vii A (1948), cols. 678–695, esp. cols. 682–691; R. J. Clark, "Trophonius: The Manner of His Revelation," *TAPA* 99 (1968), 63–75, for discussion of consultations; E. Waszink, "The Location of the Oracle of Trophonius at Lebadia," *BABesch* 43 (1968), 23–30, for the possible location of the shrine.

110. Jones, *Culture and Society,* 140–141.

111. *IGR* IV.1498; Robert, *A travers de l'Asie mineure,* 405–408; Jones, *Culture and Society,* 143. For Lucian on Alexander's sexual activity see *Alex.* 41–42.

112. For a thorough discussion of Plutarch's views see Schröder, *Plutarchs Schrift de Pythiae Oraculis,* 25–59, esp. 39–43 on the notion of the body as an instrument of the soul, a notion that runs from Plato to late antiquity.

113. For a different theory of "emanations" see Plut. *De defect. orac.* 432D–434B.

114. Wolff, p. 162; see also Iamb. *De myst.* 3.1, although he goes on to argue that the theurgist is capable of commanding the gods, see part. *De myst.* 4.2, where the argument that this is still in accord with nature is crafted to defend his position against the charge of magic. Needless to say, not everyone was convinced.

115. See also A. D. Nock, "Greek Religious Attitudes," *Proc. Amer. Philos. Soc.* 85 (1942), 474–477 = Stewart, *Essays on Religion,* 538–541.

116. This point has recently been argued at length; see M. Beard, "Cicero and Divination: The Formation of a Latin Discourse," *JRS* 76 (1986), 33–46; N. Denyer, "The Case against Divination: An Examination of Cicero's *De Divinatione,*" *PCPhS* 31 (1985), 1–10; M. Schofield, "Cicero for and against Divination," *JRS* 76 (1986), 47–65.

117. J. Nollé, "Ofellius Laetus, platonischer Philosoph," *ZPE* 41 (1981), 197–206; *BE* 1981 n. 481; G. W. Bowersock, "Plutarch and the Sublime Hymn of Ofellius Laetus," *GRBS* 23 (1982), 275–279.

118. This is particularly true of Stoicism; for an excellent survey of their views on divination see Rutherford, *The Meditations of Marcus Aurelius: A Study* (Oxford, 1989), 197.

119. J. L. Mackie, *The Miracle of Theism: Arguments for and against the Existence of God* (Oxford, 1982), 22–23.

120. For a more extensive analysis of Cicero's critique of divination see Denyer, "The Argument against Divination," 6–8, who argues that there are seven main points in Cicero's attack. These are: (1) some signs are trivial; (2) the connection between signs and what they portend is arbitrary; (3) divination is unsystematic; (4) there are national differences in divination; (5) when portents are not arbitrary, the point of contact is symbolic; (6) omens are ambiguous; and (7) the marvelous character of portents is subjective.

121. On the tragic coloring of Ammianus' account of Julian's campaign see Matthews, *The Roman Empire of Ammianus,* 125–129; 176–177.

122. For the date see J. Hammerstaedt, *Die Orakelkritik des Kynikers Oenomaeus* (Frankfurt, 1988), 1–28.

123. Ibid., 33–48, for the title of the work.

124. For a general discussion of Epicurus' views on god see A. A. Long and D. W. Sedley, *The Hellenistic Philosophers* (Cambridge, 1987), 144–149.

125. For a thorough discussion of the eschatological tradition in Pauline writings see W. A. Meeks, "Social Functions of Apocalyptic Language in Pauline Christianity," in Hellholm, *Apocalypticism in the Mediterranean World*, 687–705; M. N. A. Bockmuehl, *Revelation and Mystery* (Tübingen, 1990), 129–193. For the changing place of eschatology see also the excellent survey by P. Fredriksen, "Apocalypse and Redemption in Early Christianity from John of Patmos to Augustine of Hippo," *Vigiliae Christianae* 45 (1991), 151–183.

126. L. Thompson, *The Book of Revelation: Apocalypse and Empire* (New York, 1990), 178.

127. For the complicated history of Revelation in the evolving Christian canon, see B. M. Metzger, *The Canon of the New Testament. Its Origin, Development, and Significance* (Oxford, 1987), 104–105, 154–155, 198, 203–204.

128. For problems in the Jewish tradition see Bockmuehl, *Revelation and Mystery,* 104–126; Gray, *Prophetic Figures,* 34. For Jewish alternatives through exegetical prophecy see M. Fishbane, *Biblical Interpretation in Ancient Israel* (Oxford, 1985), 443–524.

2. Scholars, Poets, and Sibyls

1. A. J. Festugière, "L'expérience religieuse du médecin Thessalos," *RB* 48 (1939), 45–77; idem, *La révélation d'Hermès Trismégiste* 1 (Paris, 1950), 56–59. For the text see now H. V. Friedrich, *Thessalos von Tralles* (Meisenheim am Glan, 1968).

2. For the links between sophists and doctors see G. W. Bowersock, *Greek Sophists in the Roman Empire* (Oxford, 1969), 59–75.

3. This is particularly interesting because the Pharaoh Nectanebus occupied an important position in the pseudepigrapha of early Hellenistic Egypt; see especially P. M. Fraser, *Ptolemaic Alexandria* 1 (Oxford, 1972), 676–680; J. G. Griffiths, "Apocalyptic in the Hellenistic Era," in D. Hellholm, ed., *Apocalypticism in the Mediterranean World and the Near East: Proceedings of the International Colloquium on Apocalypticism, Uppsala, August 12–17 (1979)* (Tübingen, 1983), 273–279. Another important Nectanebus text is *The Dream of Nectanebo,* on which see L. Koenen, "The Dream of Nektanebos," *BASP* 22 (1985), 171–194.

4. Fraser, *Ptolemaic Alexandria* 1:454–455; M. Beagon, *Roman Nature: The Thought of Pliny the Elder* (Oxford, 1992), 8–11, with references to earlier literature.

5. The basic studies of this text remain E. Rohde, "Zu den Mirabilia des Phlegon," *RhM* 32 (1877) = *Kleine Schriften* 2 (Leipzig, 1901), 173–176; J. Mesk, "Über Phlegons Mirabilia I–III," *Philologus* 80 (1925), 298–311.

6. Mesk, "Über Phlegons Mirabilia," 305–307; for more on talking heads see J.-G. Gauger, "Phlegon von Tralles Mirab. III: Zu einem Dokument geistigen Widerstandes gegen Rom," *Chiron* 10 (1980), 231–232, although the proper reference to the story of Gabienus discussed there is Pliny *NH* 7.52.178–179. Note also Pliny's view at *NH* 7.52.178: *plena praeterea vita est his vaticiniis, sed non conferenda, cum saepius falsa sint, sicut ingenti exemplo docebimus;* it is not the events that Pliny questions, but the accuracy of prophecies given under such circumstances. Shortly after this he discusses resurrection as if it were a well-attested phenomenon, though one to be classified as a prodigy rather than as an act of nature (*NH* 7.52.179): *post sepulturam quoque visorum exempla sunt, nisi quod naturae opera, non prodigia, consestamur.*

7. The basic study of this text is now Gauger, "Phlegon von Tralles," 225–262.

8. For a useful summary of prophecies in Vergil (though one adopting a view that I would not necessarily agree with) see J. J. O'Hara, *Death and the Optimistic Prophecy in Vergil's Aeneid* (Princeton, 1990).

9. M. P. O. Morford, *The Poet Lucan: Studies in Rhetorical Epic* (Oxford, 1967), 59, noting that something like one-tenth of the poem is taken up with various prophetic actions. See also B. Dick, "The Technique of Prophecy in Lucan," *TAPA* 94 (1964), 37–49.

10. Morford, *The Poet Lucan,* 60.

11. F. Ahl, *Lucan: An Introduction* (Ithaca, 1976), 130.

12. D. T. W. Vessey, *Statius and the Thebaid* (London, 1973), 243.

13. Morford, *The Poet Lucan,* 73–74; compare also *Phars.* 2.285 with Fantham ad loc.

14. C. Santini, *Silius Italicus and His View of the Past,* trans. C. Whyte (Amsterdam, 1991), 5–6.

15. Vessey, *Statius and the Thebaid,* 250; see also the interesting discussion in F. Ahl, M. A. Davis and A. Pomeroy, "Silius Italicus," *ANRW* ii/32.4, 2548–53.

16. D. Feeney, *The Gods in Epic: Poets and Critics of the Classical Tradition* (Oxford, 1991), 345.

17. The point may have been made in an earlier work, the *Melam-*

podia, see D. W. T. C. Vessey, "Statius and Antimachus: A Review of the Evidence," *Philologus* 114 (1970), 137.

18. I am not certain that this sudden shift does not argue in favor of the so-called Barth scholium, now usually discounted as a forgery, which states that the scene is derived from Antimachus of Colophon. For the scholarship on this issue see Vessey, "Statius and Antimachus," 119–120; 136–137.

19. Vessey, *Statius and the Thebaid,* 252–257.

20. Tac. *Ann.* 2.28.2; for the theory see A. Bouché-Leclercq, *Histoire de la divination dans l'antiquité* 1 (Paris, 1879), 330–339 (still invaluable).

21. Bouché-Leclercq, *Histoire de la divination* 3:364–368; for discussion of an alleged *necromanteion* in Epirus see S. Dakaris, *The Antiquity of Epirus: The Acheron Necromanteion Ephyra-Pandosia-Cassiope* (Athens, n.d.) (I am indebted to Professor S. E. Alcock for calling this to my attention). It is notable that the Acheron *necromanteion* does not seem to have operated after the Roman conquest. This fact does not, however, rule out the efforts of certain individuals to communicate from beyond the grave, see L. Robert, *Etudes anatoliennes* (Paris, 1937), 129–133, on the epitaph of a priestess (of imperial date to judge from the letter forms) at Thyatira who promised to give oracles by day or night. He notes a similar text of the fourth century A.D. from Akmonia in Phrygia. See also the possibility of a private necromanteion in the Villa Farnese; T. Hopfner, "Nekro-mantie," *RE* 16, col. 2233. Many also believed that the dead could be contacted through the agency of a recently sacrificed boy (a variation on the use of boys as mediums). For charges of this sort see Phil. *V. Apoll.* 8.7 (discussing the view that human livers provided better information); Dio 73.16.5; Eus. *VC* 1.36 (a possible variation on the part of Maxentius in 312); for the more practical side, see Amm. Marc. 19.12.14 (charges of indulgence in forbidden acts brought against people accused of fre-quenting graveyards at night); *Sent. Pauli* 5.23.16 on human sacrifice and magic.

22. For a good summary of the scholarship on this work see Fraser, *Ptolemaic Alexandria* 1:619. The second-century date of this poem is now firmly established by P. M. Fraser, "Lycophron on Cyprus," *RDAC* (1979), 328–343, a case not altered by S. West's effort to argue for massive interpolation in "Lycophron Italicised," *JHS* 104 (1984), 127–151.

23. R. G. M. Nisbet, "Virgil's Fourth Eclogue: Easterners and West-erners," *BICS* 25 (1978), 59–78.

24. I argued this point in detail in "Horace *Odes* 1.2: Panegyric and Sibylline Prophecy," a paper delivered at the 1992 annual meeting of the Classical Association of the Midwest and South.

25. *FGrH* 257 fr. 36 X; H. Diels, *Sibyllinische Blätter* (Berlin, 1890), remains the basic study.

26. *FGrH* 257 fr. 37 V.2; for the oracle connected with the *ludi saeculares* see *FGrH* 257 fr. 37 V.4; Zos. 2.6.

27. D. S. Potter, *Prophecy and History in the Crisis of the Roman Empire: A Historical Commentary on the Thirteenth Sibylline Oracle* (Oxford, 1990), 116–117.

28. See H. Parke, *Sibyls and Sibylline Prophecy in Classical Antiquity* (London, 1988), 117.

29. For similar problems with Orpheus see M. West, *The Orphic Poems* (Oxford, 1983), esp. 1–38.

30. Rzach, *RE* 1923, cols. 2074–75; Parke, *Sibyls and Sibylline Prophecy*, p. 23. E. Rohde, *Psyche: Seelencult und Unterblichkeitsglaube der Griechen*[4], 2 (Tübingen, 1907), 64 n. 1, believed that it was a generic term for "prophetess," but this does not conform with the usage of the word in the earliest testimonia. These are *DK Heracleitus* fr. 92 (it is not clear how much of this should be attributed to Heracleitus; see M. Marcovich, *Heracleitus* [Merida, 1967], 405–406); Ar. *Eq.* 61; *Pax*. 1095, 1115–16. Rohde was correct when he pointed out that the name later came to be a generic term for an inspired prophetess, as Bakis came to be a generic name for prophets. F. Graf, *Nordionische Kulte. Religionsgeschichtliche und epigraphische Untersuchungen zu den Kulten von Chios, Erythrai, Klazomenai und Phokaia* (Rome, 1985), 277, 349–350, suggests a possible Anatolian background. I am somewhat skeptical of this in light of the fact that the first evidence for this style of prophecy is so late, and because there is no evidence for this sort of prophecy in Homer, a point that seems to me to be quite correctly stressed in Bouché-Leclercq, *Histoire de la divination* 2:141.

31. Parke, *Sibyls and Sibylline Prophecy*, 9.

32. Hdt. 7.6.3; Parke, *Sibyls and Sibylline Prophecy*, 9, 184–189; West, *The Orphic Poems*, 40.

33. Parke, *Sibyls and Sibylline Prophecy*, 51–67.

34. E. J. Bickerman, "Faux littéraires dans l'antiquité classique," *RFIC* 101 (1973), 35–37 = *Studies in Jewish and Christian History* 3 (1986), 207–209.

35. *FGrH* 70 fr. 134; Parke, *Sibyls and Sibylline Prophecy,* 72–73. For Naevius and Greek literature see S. Mariotti, *Il Bellum Poenicum e l'arte di Nevio* (Rome, 1955) (still an important work).

36. D. H. *Rom. Ant.* 6.17, apparently a genuine notice.

37. R. Bloch, "L'origine des Livres Sibyllins à Rome: Méthode de recherches et critique du récit des annalistes anciens," in E. C. Welskopf, ed., *Neue Beiträge zur Geschichte der alten Welt* 2 (Berlin, 1965), 281–292. The Roman practice should therefore not be confused with the Greek practice—attested for several cities and tyrants—of collecting books of prophecies so that their contents would remain secret and could not be used against the state. For the Greek custom see A. D. Nock, "Greek Religious Attitudes," *Proc. Amer. Philos. Soc.* 85 (1942), 477 = *Essays on Religion and the Ancient World,* ed. Z. Stewart (Oxford, 1972), 542.

38. Diels, *Sibyllinische Blätter,* remains the basic study.

39. Plin. *NH* 7.119; Val. Max. 8.15.12.

40. The annalist Piso, who wrote in the mid-second century, also mentioned the Cimmerian Sibyl (fr. 41 Peter), but this appears to be eccentric.

41. *FGrH* 570; this point is convincingly argued by Parke, *Sibyls and Sibylline Prophecy,* 78–79.

42. *FGrH* 257 fr. 2; for a possible example of this coin see *BMC Troad* "Gergis" 6.

43. This point is maintained on the basis of some lines in *Orac. Sib.* 3, where the notion that Hades will attend an "avenger" is thought to reflect the identification of Hades with Ahriman, the enemy of Ahura Mazda; see M. Boyce and F. Grenet, *A History of Zoroastrianism* 3 (Leiden, 1991), 13, 371–377. Not the least of the problems with this view is that, as it now stands, the *Third Sibylline Oracle* is preserved in a sixth-century Christian collection, and that we have no way to date its compilation. The belief that these lines are Hellenistic is no more than an act of faith prompted by the fragment of Nicanor. The Sibyl seems to have acquired her international significance as a spokesperson, as opposed to her local importance in the Troad and Italy, only after Rome's conquest of the eastern Mediterranean.

44. Contra Parke, *Sibyls and Sibylline Prophecy,* 144; V. Nikiprowetsky, *La troisième sibylle* (Paris, 1970), 17–19.

45. On this point see especially E. Bickerman, "The Septuagint as a

Translation," *Proceedings of the American Academy for Jewish Research* 28 (1959) = *Studies in Jewish and Christian History* 1 (1976), 167–200.

46. Lact. *DI* 1.6.8–12; Carduans fr. 56.

47. Parke, *Sibyls and Sibylline Prophecy,* 37–38; see Rzach, *RE* 1923, col. 2096.

48. *FGrH* 146. It is tempting to identify this man with one of the Nicanors on Alexander's staff. Reports of prophecies by a Babylonian prophet would fit best into the work of a contemporary who would have been interested, and only a contemporary would have been likely to pick up material of this sort for a history of Alexander the Great that others had missed. The most attractive candidate of the nine Nicanors listed by Berve (*Das Alexanderreich aus prosopographischer Grundlage* [Munich, 1926], nos. 553–561) is Nicanor of Stagira, nephew of Aristotle, who carried the Exiles' Decree to Olympia. It is not absurd to suspect such a man of literary pretensions, nor, given Callisthenes' record of oracles and transmission of information about the east to Aristotle (*FGrH* 124 T 3), that he would be interested in such things.

49. For different sibylline lists see Bouché-Leclercq, *Histoire de la divination* 2:166–167.

50. For the Erythraean coins that depict a seated Sibyl see *BMC Ionia* "Erythrae" nos. 272–273; for the Cymaean coins, which show only the head of "The Sibyl of the Cymaeans," see F. Imhoof-Blumer, "Zur Münzkunde des Pontus, von Paphlagonien, Tenedos, Aiolis und Lesbos," *ZN* 20 (1897), 279; idem, *Kleinasiatische Münzen* (Vienna, 1901) 47; B. V. Head, *Historia Numorum*[2] (Oxford, 1910), 554. For offerings to the Sibyl see *I. Eryth. u. Klaz.* no. 207.73.

51. Parke, *Sibyls and Sibylline Prophecy,* 41, suggests that Pausanias may have omitted to mention the cave; but his description of the visit is so different from that in the *Cohortatio* that Parke's explanation must be regarded as an unlikely one: the *Cohortatio* discusses the oracles of the Sibyl at Cumae (which Pausanias did not find), and the description of the storage of the remains of the Sibyl is different.

52. For details see S. Reinach, "La sanctuaire de la sibylle d'Erythrée," *REG* 4 (1891), 276–286; K. Buresch, "Die sibyllinsche Quellgrotte in Erythrae," *Ath. Mitt.* 17 (1892), 16–36; P. Corssen, "Die Erythraische Sibylle," *Ath. Mitt.* 38 (1913), 1–22.

53. *Chron. Pasc.* 1.201; for a later repair of the shrine see *I. Eryth u. Klaz.* no. 228.

54. Tac. *Ann.* 6.12.3: *quaesitis Samo Ilio Erythris, per Africam etiam ac Siciliam et Italicas colonias carminibus Sibyllae.* All three cities claimed to be the home of Herophile.

55. Ov. *Met.* 14.144–146; cf. *FGrH* 257 fr. 37 V.4–5; *I. Eryth. u. Klaz.* no. 224.9–10; for more on this see Potter, *Prophecy and History,* 116.

56. *FGrH* 257 fr. 37 V.7–10.

57. *I. Eryth u. Klaz.* no. 224.5–8.

58. Paus. 10.12.3; cf. 10.12.6.

59. *Orac. Sib.* 3.819–823; see further Potter, *Prophecy and History,* 181.

60. Ver. *Aen.* 6.56, 77, 100–101; Tib. 2.5; for the date of Tibullus' poem for Messalla see F. Cairns, *Tibullus: A Hellenistic Poet at Rome* (Cambridge, 1979), 85–86. In Vergil's case, it is also stated that the Sibyl wrote her responses on leaves. This notion otherwise appears in the extant texts only in the oracle preserved by Phlegon (*FGrH* 257 fr. 36 X.64–67).

61. *Orac. Sib.* 8.362, 373. Hdt. 1.47 = PW 52; J. L. Fontenrose, *The Delphic Oracle: Its Responses and Operations with a Catalogue of Responses* (Berkeley, 1978), 111–115; R. Crahay, *La littérature oraculaire chez Hérodote* (Paris, 1956), 193–197.

62. *Orac. Sib.* 11.163–171, 3.419–431.

63. *Orac. Sib.* 3.813–816; Nikiprowetzky, *La troisième sibylle,* 41–43. In addition, Varro says that Apollodorus of Erythrae said that the Erythraean Sibyl predicted that Homer would tell many lies about the Trojan War (see note 62 above and Parke, *Sibyls and Sibylline Prophecy,* 4–5, 109–110); and Pausanias said that she would precede Homer and predict the Trojan War (10.12.2). See also Diod. 4.66.6.

64. *Orac. Sib.* 3.363, 4.91–92, 8.165–166; the line was known to Tertullian, *De pal.* 2.3. For a similar case see S. Brock, "A Syriac Collection of Prophecies of the Pagan Philosophers," *Orientalia Loveniensia Periodica* 14 (1983), 240.

65. Zos. 2.36.2; see H. W. Parke, "The Attribution of the Oracle in Zosimus, *New History* 2, 37," *CQ* 32 (1982), 441–445, who argues that the text cited here was originally the product of Apollo Chresterios at Chalcedon.

66. Potter, *Prophecy and History,* 125–132.

67. *FGrH* 257 fr. 36 X; Zos. 2.6.

68. Ver. *Aen.* 6.9–155; *Vis.* 2.4.1. Petron. *Sat.* 48.

69. Plut. *De Pyth. orac.* 398E, *De Sera Num. Vind.* 566E; Paus. 10.12.5.

70. For the problems with this statement see Potter, "Sibyls in the Greek and Roman World," *JRA* 3 (1990), 472–474.

71. Lact. *DI* 7.24.12: *quae poeta secundum Cymeae Sibyllae carmina prolocutus est.*

72. Parke, *Sibyls and Sibylline Prophecy,* 152–173; B. McGinn, *"Teste David cum Sibylla:* The Significance of the Sibylline Tradition in the Middle Ages," in J. Kirshner and S. Wemple, eds., *Women of the Medieval World* (Oxford, 1985), 12–13, for a good summary of these developments.

73. See Chapter 5, note 76.

74. Theoph. *Ad Aut.* 2.3, 31, 36; Athen. *Leg.* 30.1.

75. Preserved only in F; on the tradition see E. Dekkers' discussion in the introduction to his edition of Tertullian's *Apology* in *Corpus Christianorum.*

76. For the date of *Orac. Sib.* 14, showing that it is the latest oracle in the collection as it stands, see W. Scott, "The Last Sibylline Oracle of Alexandria," *CQ* 9 (1915), 144–166, 207–228; *CQ* 10 (1916), 7–16; Rzach, *RE* 1923, col. 2164.

77. For this view of these texts and different views see Potter, *Prophecy and History,* 95–96, esp. 96 n. 6.

78. J. Geffcken, *Composition und Entstehungszeit der Oracula Sibyllina* (Leipzig, 1902), 1–17; J. J. Collins, *The Sibylline Oracles of Egyptian Judaism* (Missoula, 1974), 21–41; idem, "The Development of the Sibylline Tradition," *ANRW* ii/20.1, 430–436; Nikiprowetzky, *La troisième sibylle.* The most reasonable summary of the problems with this text appears in E. Schürer, *The History of the Jewish People in the Age of Jesus Christ*[2], ed. M. Goodman, F. Miller, and G. Vermes (Edinburgh, 1986), 3:632–639.

79. B. Thompson, "The Patristic Use of the Sibylline Oracles," *Review of Religion* 16 (1952), 115–136. He points out that around 800 lines are quoted in twenty-two patristic writings. By far the most extensive quotations appear in Lactantius' *Divine Institutes.* For a useful list of quotations see Thompson, 130–136.

80. Potter, *Prophecy and History,* 97–98.

81. Ibid., 98–99.

82. Geffcken, *Comp. u. Ent.,* 33–37; Collins, "Development," 449–451; Gager, "Some Attempts to Label the *Oracula Sibyllina,* Book 7," *HTR* 65 (1972), 91–97.

83. Potter, *Prophecy and History,* 99 n. 14.

84. Ibid., 100.

85. For further discussion see Geffcken, *Comp. u. Ent.,* 34–46; Collins, "Development," 446–448.

86. For problems with the texts of Augustine's version, that in *Orac. Sib.* 8 and the *Oratio ad sanctos,* see Potter, *Prophecy and History,* 100 n. 15.

87. W. Bulst, "Eine anglo-lateinische Übersetzung aus dem griechischen um 700," *Zeitschrift für deutsches Altertum und deutsche Literatur* 75 (1938), 105–114; B. Bischoff, "Die lateinischen Übersetzungen und Bearbeitungen aus den Oracula Sibyllina," in *Mélanges Joseph DeGhellinck* (Gembloux, 1951) = *Mittelalterliche Studien* 1 (1966), 154–163; McGinn, *"Teste David cum Sibylla,"* 17–18.

88. Bischoff, "Die lateinischen Übersetzungen," 164–171.

89. Parke, *Sibyls and Sibylline Prophecy,* 215 n. 44, for this event.

90. For the *haruspices* see Chapter 4. For the salvation of Narnia see Zos. 5.41 with Paschoud's extensive note ad loc. For the survival of traditional practices into the sixth century see E. Sackur, *Sibyllinische Texte und Forschungen* (Halle, 1898), 118–119.

91. P. J. Alexander, *The Oracle of Baalbek: The Tiburtine Sibyl in Greek Dress* (Washington, D.C., 1967), 64–65. His reconstruction is still to be preferred; see Potter, "Sibyls in the Greek and Roman World," 474 n. 7.

92. J. Baroin and J. Haffen, *La profétie de la Sibylle Tiburtine* (Paris, 1987), 118–119.

93. R. Y. Ebied and M. J. L. Young, "A Newly Discovered Version of the Arabic Sibylline Prophecy," *Oriens Christianus* 60 (1976), 85. This text is classified as Arabic 5 in accordance with the classification of these texts in J. Schleifer, *Die Erzählung der Sibylle. Ein Apokryph nach den karschunischen, arabischen und äthiopischen Handrscriften zu London, Oxford, Paris und Rome.* Denkschriften der kaiserlichen Akademie der Wissenschaften Philosophisch-Historisch Klasse 53 (Vienna, 1910), Abhandlung 1. Another text (Arabic four) is published from an eighteenth-century manuscript by E. Y. Ebied and M. J. L. Young, "An Unrecorded Arabic Version of a Sibylline Prophecy," *Orientalia Christiana Periodica* 43 (1977), 279–307. For a German tradition, which is not modeled on the Tiburtine Sibyl, see I. Neske, *Die spätmittelalterliche Deutsche Sibyllenweissagung. Untersuchungen und Edition* (Göttingen, 1985), esp. 5–30, 41–44, on the date

(mid-fourteenth century). For a sibylline text interpreted by the twelfth-century visionary Joachim of Fiore, see B. McGinn, "Joachim and the Sibyl," *Cîteaux* 24 (1973), 97–138. Joachim claimed the authority of Augustine; for further discussion of different traditions that begin to pick up in Latin in the twelfth century see ibid., 118–119. On Byzantine influences see esp. P. Alexander, "The Diffusion of Byzantine Apocalypses in the Medieval West and the Beginnings of Joachimism," in A. Williams, ed., *Prophecy and Millenarianism: Essays in Honor of Marjorie Reeves* (Burnt Hill, England, 1980), 53–106; idem, *The Byzantine Apocalyptic Tradition* (Berkeley, 1985).

94. W. V. Harris, *Ancient Literacy* (Cambridge, Mass., 1989), 329.

95. A. E. Hanson, "Ancient Illiteracy," *Literacy in the Roman World, Journal of Roman Archaeology* Supplement 2 (1992), 164–165.

96. K. Hopkins, "Conquest by Book," in *Literacy in the Ancient World,* 135.

97. E. A. Meyer, "Explaining the Epigraphic Habit in the Roman Empire: The Evidence of Epitaphs," *JRS* 80 (1990), 95.

98. I use this term for convenience, as it is the one most commonly used to describe purveyors of oracles, although the term is also used of people who interpret oracles and sometimes even seem to give them, see E. Fascher, *ΠΡΟΦΗΤΗΣ. Eine sprach-und religionsgeschichtlische Untersuchung* (Giessen, 1927), 25; J. Robert and L. Robert, "Décret de Colophon pour un chresmologue de Smyrne appelé à diriger l'oracle de Claros," *BCH* 116 (1992), 279–291.

99. For the policing of sacred books see pages 150–151.

100. Paus. 10.12,1; Plut. *De Pyth. orac.* 398C; P. Amandry, *La mantique apollonienne à Delphes. Essai sur le fonctionnement de l'Oracle* (Paris, 1950), 203–204; Orig. *Contra Cels.* 7.53; Lact. *DI* 1.6; Ath. *Leg.* 30.1.

101. Amm. Marc. 21.1.11; 23.1.7; 30.4.11; Paus. 10.12; *P. Oxy.* 3711.27; for Plutarch (aside from references to the collection at Rome) see *Thes.* 24.5; *Dem.* 19.1; *Mor.* 243B, 285A–B, 397A, 398C–E, 399A, 401B, 406A, 566D, 675A, 870A.

102. Ael. Arist. 45.12,14; Dio Chrys. 12.35–36, 18.2, 20.13.

3. *Prophecy and the Informed Public*

1. L. L. Thompson, *The Book of Revelation: Apocalypse and Empire* (Oxford, 1990), 174–185; R. MacMullen, *Enemies of the Roman Order:*

Treason, Unrest, and Alienation in the Empire (Cambridge, Mass., 1966), 146: "prophecy is one of the several literary shapes in which hopes can be cast and wishes fulfilled."

2. Dio 62.18.3–4. For other discussions of these texts see D. S. Potter, *Prophecy and History in the Crisis of the Roman Empire: A Historical Commentary on the Thirteenth Sibylline Oracle* (Oxford, 1990), 237 n. 107.

3. Potter, *Prophecy and History*, 239, with references to other literature. There may be a connection with Etruscan beliefs in a succession of *saecula*.

4. For different measurements see Cens. *De die natali* 17.5–6.

5. S. Weinstock, *Divus Julius* (Oxford, 1971), 191–197. At the time it might also have been connected with a prophecy attributed to Veiovis, on which see, at length, A. Alföldi, "Redeunt Saturnia regna II: An Iconographical Pattern Heralding the Return of the Golden Age in or around 139 B.C.," *Chiron* 3 (1973), 131–140; idem, "Redeunt Saturnia Regna III: Juppiter—Apollo und Veiovis," *Chiron* 2 (1972), 215–230.

6. S. Lieberman, "Palestine in the Third and Fourth Centuries," *JQR* 36 (1946), 39–40; see also the two different reckonings of the millennium in the panegyrics of 307 and 313 (both delivered at Trier before Constantine) at *Pan.* 7(6).2.5; 12(9).3.5.

7. MacMullen, *Enemies of the Roman Order*, 160, for a survey of various numerological schemes of this sort and pages 92–93 above for the Tiburtine Sibyl.

8. Potter, *Prophecy and History*, 238.

9. *Orac. Sib.* 12.229–236, line 232 is manifestly an interpolation. The original author was counting from Julius Caesar rather than from Augustus, as the author of this line thought. To get nineteen, he was also counting Lucius Verus as an emperor; the twentieth emperor, who is identified as being of the number 80 (the Greek letter *pi*), is Pertinax (line 238). In a less doctrinaire context see *P. Oxy* 35, a school exercise providing a list of emperors from Augustus to Decius that omits Caligula, Galba, Otho, Vitellius, Macrinus, and Elagabalus while combining the regnal years of Marcus and Commodus for a total of 268 years since Augustus (whose reign is dated from Actium). For other problems see Potter, *Prophecy and History*, 236 n. 103.

10. B. McGinn, "Symbolism in the Thought of Joachim of Fiore," in A. Williams, ed., *Prophecy and Millenarianism: Essays in Honor of Marjorie Reeves* (Burnt Hill, England, 1980), 148.

11. For the problems connected with the composition of this oracle see page 90 above.

12. Of these possibilities, which are obviously not mutually exclusive, an original connection with Hadrian seems preferable in light of his appearance as the fifteenth king in another context (*Orac. Sib.* 8.50–52) and the seeming consistency with which the emperors of 69 are all included. The reference to Vespasian and his sons may be influenced by acclamations of the sort recorded by Josephus at *BJ* 7.73.

13. Aug. *Haeres.* 106, where this point is made explicit. For the issue in general see H. Chadwick, "Oracles of the End in the Conflict of Paganism and Christianity in the Fourth Century," in E. Lucchesi and H. D. Saffrey, eds., *Mémorial André-Jean Festugière: Antiquité païenne et chrétienne* (Geneva, 1984), 125–129.

14. Chadwick, "Oracles of the End," 126–127; P. Brown, *Augustine of Hippo: A Biography* (Berkeley, 1967), 125.

15. Hippol. *Haer.* 7.14; Epiphanius *Pan.* 24.7, with the useful summary of the system in K. Rudolph, *Gnosis: The Nature and History of Gnosticism*[2], trans. R. McL. Wilson (Edinburgh, 1984), 311, suggesting that Abraxas or Abrasax may have originated as a secret paraphrase for the name of Yahweh, the numerical value of which is 365; see G. Ifrah, *From One to Zero: A Universal History of Numbers* (Harmondsworth, 1985), 365.

16. For the sentiments see G. E. M. de Ste. Croix, *The Class Struggle in the Ancient Greek World* (London, 1981), 325. For a rather different perspective compare the comments of the Reverend S. D. F. Salmond, translator of part of this work for volume 5 of *The Ante-Nicene Fathers,* p. 178 n. 5: "true in 1885. A very pregnant testimony to our own times." Comments of similar penetration may be found in K. Strobel, *Das Imperium Romanum im 3. Jahrhundert* (Stuttgart, 1993), 122–123. R. Landes, "Lest the Millennium Be Fulfilled: Apocalyptic Expectations and the Pattern of Western Chronology 100–800 CE," in W. Verbeke, D. Verhelst, and A. Welkenhuysen, eds., *The Use and Abuse of Eschatology in the Early Middle Ages* (Leuven, 1988), 141–149, provides an excellent and lucid explanation of Hippolytus' thought and of the development of sabbatical millenarian beliefs in early Christianity. The clearest explication of the theory appears in *The Epistle of Barnabas* 15:4a–5a (ed. Prigent), in which Barnabas argues that since God created the world in six days, and one of God's days was 1,000 years (an assertion based on Ps. 90:4), the human world would exist for 6,000 years.

17. Landes, "Lest the Millennium Be Fulfilled," 147.

18. *Gen. Rab.* 76.6 trans. J. Neusner, *Genesis Rabbah: The Judaic Commentary to the Book of Genesis. A New American Translation* (Atlanta, 1985), 111–112, though for the text see Lieberman, "Palestine in the Third and Fourth Centuries," 38; for the circumstances see Potter, *Prophecy and History,* 268–273, 343–346. S. Swain, "Macrianus as the 'Well-Horned Stag' in the *Thirteenth Sibylline Oracle,*" *GRBS* 33 (1992), 377–379, is derivative.

19. Potter, *Prophecy and History,* 303.

20. Dio 77.23.3–4 (Caracalla), *Orac. Sib.* 12.185–186 (Avidius Cassius).

21. For L. Equitius see Cic. *Pro Sest.* 101; Val. Max. 3.2.18, 9.7.2; [Victor] *De vir. ill.* 73; for pseudo-Marius see Z. Yavetz, *Plebs and Princeps* (Oxford, 1969), 61–63, 70–71.

22. Tac. *Ann.* 2.39–40 (Clemens); *Ann.* 5.10, 6.24 (false Drusus).

23. F. G. B. Millar, *A Study of Cassius Dio* (Oxford, 1964), 214–218, on false Neros and the false Caracalla (noting that he is imitating Caracalla's imitation of Alexander).

24. Potter, *Prophecy and History,* 45–46, 314–319.

25. Lact. *De mort. persec.* 12–13 without clear indication of the place, for which see Eus. *HE* 8.5; for Julian's *Misopogon* see Malalas 13.5 with M. Gleason, "Festive Satire: Julian's *Misopogon* and the New Year at Antioch," *JRS* 76 (1986), 106–119, on the circumstances.

26. R. Katzoff, "Prefectural Edicts and Letters," *ZPE* 48 (1982), 210, for a list of texts containing provisions for their publication.

27. F. G. B. Millar, *The Emperor in the Roman World*[2] (Ithaca, 1991), 256.

28. For the reception of imperial edicts see S. Lieberman, "Roman Legal Institutions in Early Rabbinics and in the *Acta Martyrum,*" *JQR* 35 (1944), 6–9 (I am grateful to John Matthews for pointing this study out to me); for the translation from the *Sifre* see R. Hammer, *Sifre: A Tannaitic Commentary on the Book of Deuteronomy* (New Haven, 1986), 62; Millar, *Emperor*[2], 641.

29. For the Greek texts from the Babatha archive see N. Lewis, *Judaean Desert Studies: The Documents from the Bar Kokhba Period in the Cave of the Letters, Greek Papyri* (Jerusalem, 1989); and G. W. Bowersock, "The Babatha Archive, Masada and Rome," *JRA* 4 (1990), 335–342.

30. Millar, *Emperor*[2], 254–256; see also S. Mitchell, "Maximinus and

the Christians in A.D. 312: A New Latin Inscription," *JRS* 78 (1988), 105–124.

31. Millar, *Emperor²*, 254; P. *Oxy.* 1407.

32. R. Duncan-Jones, *Structure and Scale in the Roman Economy* (Cambridge, 1990), 15.

33. Ibid., 26–27.

34. See, for instance, *ILS* 422.

35. For a negative reaction to this (which nonetheless reflects the ideological importance of what Severus was doing) see Dio 73.7.4. For Commodus and the dissemination of the new titulature (and calendar) in the last year of his life, see now the superior study of M. P. Speidel, "Commodus the God-Emperor and the Army," *JRS* 83 (1993), 109–114, esp. 114 on Severus' conduct.

36. *HA V. Sev.* 9.10–11; on which see Z. Rubin, *Civil War Propaganda and Historiography* (Brussels, 1980), 14.

37. See T. D. Barnes, *Constantine and Eusebius* (Cambridge, Mass., 1981), 32–37; T. Grünewald, *Constantinus Maximus Augustus. Herrschaftspropaganda in der zeitgenössischen Überlieferung* (Stuttgart, 1990), 46–50.

38. *Pan.* 6(7).2.2, to which *Price Edict* 5 should be compared, along with *Pan.* 7(6).8.4; 8(5).11.2 (the importance of being first). See also R. Syme, *Emperors and Biography* (Oxford, 1971), 204. It is interesting that this view was propagated by his sons (*ILS* 725, 730, 732). Julian seems to have believed that it was true; see *Caes.* 336b, where Zeus forgives Constantine his crimes on account of Claudius and Constantius I; see also G. W. Bowersock, "The Emperor Julian on His Predecessors," *YCS* 27 (1982), 163–164.

39. *Pan.* 6(7).4.1; 3.1.

40. *P. Geiss.* 40.3–4. The obscurity of the statement is perhaps best appreciated through F. G. B. Millar, "The Date of the Constitutio Antoniniana," *JEA* 48 (1962), 130–131, where it is argued that the peril referred to is a boating accident in the Hellespont. It is, however, now generally agreed that the edict refers to Caracalla's murder of Geta.

41. The text is further interesting because it appears to be a fourth-century copy; this fact suggests that it had been copied to use as a precedent.

42. For the edict against the Manichaeans see page 208, for the edict on taxation see *P. Cairo Isidore* 1 (a prefect's summary of the edict).

43. Millar, *Emperor*[2], 644–651, restating the thesis most forcefully set out on pp. 228–259.

44. *Pan.* 12(9).2,4,9,16,22,25,26. For the notion in general see J. H. W. G. Liebeschuetz, *Continuity and Change in Roman Religion* (Oxford, 1979), 277–291.

45. *ILS* 705; on the date and circumstances see J. Gascou, "Le rescript d'Hispellum," *MEFR* 79 (1967), 617–623.

46. R. J. Lane Fox, *Pagans and Christians* (New York, 1986), 70.

47. On the expressly Christian outbursts see T. D. Barnes, *Constantine and Eusebius* (Cambridge, Mass., 1981), 210–212 and 245, for the perception of Constantine as more radical in the east than in the west, and that the images differed in the two parts of the empire.

48. Tac. *Ann.* 16.22.4; B. Baldwin, "The Acta Diurna," *Chiron* 9 (1979), 189–203.

49. *P. Köln* VI, 249; *ILS* 212; J. H. Oliver and R. E. A. Palmer, "Minutes of an Act of the Roman Senate," *Hesperia* 24 (1955), 329–349.

50. W. Eck, "Das s.c. de Cn. Pisone patre und seine Publikation in der Baetica," *Cahiers du Centre G. Glotz* 4 (1993), 189–208. I am much indebted to Clifford Ando of the University of Michigan and to Andrew Meadows and Greg Rowe of Oxford University for their extensive discussions of this text with me.

51. For the *Tabula Siarensis* see J. González, "Tabula Siarensis, Fortunales Siarenses et Municipia Civium Romanorum," *ZPE* 55 (1984), 55–100; a portion of this text was already known from Heba in Etruria, see *E&J* 94a. See also note 79 below.

52. Despite specifications in these decrees as to how they were to be published, a great deal of latitude seems, in practice, to have been left to governors; see Eck, "Das s.c. de Cn. Pisone," 190, 205–206 on the uneven publication of texts.

53. W. Turpin, "Imperial Subscriptions and the Administration of Justice," *JRS* 81 (1991), 101–118.

54. See esp. Tac. *Ann.* 3.53–4.

55. S. M. Sherwin-White, "Ancient Archives: The Edict of Alexander to Priene, a Reappraisal," *JHS* 105 (1985), 74–75.

56. Ibid., 69–72.

57. *Insc. Magnesia* 16–64, 66–84, 87. I am indebted to Professor Geoffrey Sumi for discussion of these texts.

58. *ML* 12. It is a marble corner block, and the side of the block

retains traces of two other inscriptions. For another such display at Pessinus see B. Virgilio, *Il tempio stato di Pessinunte fra Pergamo e Roma nel II–I Secolo A.C.* (C. B. Welles, *Royal Corr. 55–61)* (Pisa, 1981).

59. J. Reynolds, *Aphrodisias and Rome,* Journal of Roman Studies Monograph 1 (London, 1982), 33–37, nos. 6–21; for refinements to Reynolds' analysis of the wall see G. W. Bowersock's review of the publication, *Gnomon* 56 (1984), 48–53. For the Cyrene texts see J. Reynolds, "Hadrian, Antoninus Pius and the Cyrenaican Cities," *JRS* 68 (1978), 111–121. Another marble stele at Cyrene was covered with five letters from the emperor Augustus. For these see J. H. Oliver, *Greek Constitutions of Early Roman Emperors from Inscriptions and Papyri,* Memoirs of the American Philosophical Society 178 (Philadelphia, 1989) nos. 8–12 with bibliography. A dossier relating to the privileges of the temple of Artemis of Ephesus was published by D. Knibbe, H. Engelmann, and B. İplikçloğlu, "Neue Inschriften aus Ephesos XII," *JöAI* (1993), 113–122.

60. Oliver, *Greek Constitutions,* nos. 108–18 with commentary and bibliography. For the inscriptions of unfavorable responses to other cities, which are also inscribed on the Aphrodisias wall (nos. 13, 14); no. 12 is a letter of Augustus to Ephesus ordering it to return a stolen statue of Eros that had originally been dedicated by Julius Caesar at Aphrodisias; in doing so he further notes that "Eros is not a suitable offering when given to Artemis," an interesting example of Augustus' concern for religious propriety (rather than a joke—*pace* Reynolds, *Aphrodisias and Rome* ad loc.).

61. *IGLS* 4028. For more on the site see now F. G. B. Millar, *The Roman Near East, 31* B.C.–A.D. 337 (Cambridge, Mass., 1993), 271–273.

62. Reynolds, "Hadrian, Antoninus Pius and the Cyrenaican Cities," 113–114, for the texts.

63. S. Mitchell, "Requisitioned Transport in the Roman Empire: A New Inscription from Pisidia," *JRS* 66 (1976), 109.

64. *IE* 296; *ILS* 430; see also *ILS* 429, the incident referred to may be the "conspiracy of Apronianus," on which see Dio 76.7.3–9.2. The case allegedly involved a dream of empire and magic.

65. Herod. 2.9.4; see also H. Bloch, "A Dream of Septimius Severus," *CW* 37 (1943), 31–32.

66. *IE* 302, 304, 4336, where different words are used to render the Latin *restitutor.*

67. *OGIS* 520; *ILS* 751; *IE* 313a; for Dulcitius see *PLRE,* p. 274.

68. Herod. 3.9.12. On the question of Herodian's use of these pic-

tures see G. Picard, "Les reliefs de l'arc de Septime Severe au forum romain," *CRAI* (1962), 13; Z. Rubin, "Dio, Herodian and Severus' Second Parthia War," *Chiron* 5 (1975), 428–430. Herodian's account of Caracalla's murder also seems to break down into four vignettes and may likewise be based upon paintings sent to Rome by Macrinus, see Herod. 4.13.3–7. Compare also *HA V. Car.* 9.6.

69. Herod. 7.2.8 with Whittaker's note ad loc.

70. *Orac. Sib.* 5.16 = 12.20.

71. R. R. R. Smith, "The Imperial Reliefs from the Sebasteion at Aphrodisias," *JRS* 77 (1987), 88–138, for publication of the imperial reliefs; idem, "*Simulacra Gentium:* The *Ethne* from the Sebasteion at Aphrodisias," *JRS* 78 (1988), 50–77, for a thorough discussion of the *imagines* of various peoples.

72. Potter, *Prophecy and History,* 135–137. The doubts expressed there about the connection between a festival on July 11 at Carnuntum and the Rain Miracle are confirmed by I. Piso, "Die Inschriften von Pfeffenberg und der Bereich der Canabae legionis," *Tyche* 6 (1991), 162–165, showing that the festival is connected with the organization of the province.

73. Compare, however, Lact. *DMP* 5.3.

74. For statements of two extreme positions on the question of the propagandistic value of coin types see A. H. M. Jones, "Numismatics and History," in *Essays in Roman Coinage Presented to Harold Mattingly* (Oxford, 1956), 13–33 = *The Roman Economy,* 61–81; C. H. V. Sutherland, "The Intelligibility of Roman Imperial Coin Types," *JRS* 49 (1959), 46–55. For a more sophisticated view, stressing the ways in which coins could reflect attitudes or representational styles that were "in the air," as well as efforts at communicating more specific ideas depending on the circumstances of minting, see J. D. Evans, *The Art of Persuasion: Political Propaganda from Aeneas to Brutus* (Ann Arbor, 1992), 1–32.

75. Dio 60.22.3; 65.6.1; 77.12.6; see also F. Vittinghoff, *Der Staatsfeind in der römischen Kaiserzeit. Untersuchungen zur damnatio memoriae* (Berlin, 1936), 35.

76. For Julian see Soc. *HE* 3.17; Soz. *HE* 5.19; Ephrem Nis. *Hymn contr. Jul.* 1:19; *RIC* 8, pp. 195, 229, 337, 380, 392, 423, 438, 462, 483, 500, 531, showing that they began to be issued by mints as they passed under Julian's direct control; for Constantine see Eus. *VC* 4.15.1; *RIC* 7, p. 33 n. 3. Compare also the impressions in the seventh century made by coins of Tiberius (John Eph. *HE* 3.14) and Heraclius (John of Nikiou

Chron. 116.3). For an analysis of Ephraem's treatment of Julian's coinage see S. H. Griffith, "Ephraem the Syrian's Hymns 'Against Julian': Meditations on History and Imperial Power," *Vigiliae Christianae* 41 (1987), 253–254.

77. See now C. J. Howgego, "The Supply and Use of Money in the Roman World 200 B.C. to A.D. 300," *JRS* 82 (1992), 11–16.

78. W. Eck, "Senatorial Self-Representation: Developments in the Augustan Period," in F. G. B. Millar and E. Segal, eds., *Caesar Augustus. Seven Aspects* (Oxford, 1984), 129–167; E. Rawson, "The Antiquarian Tradition: Spoils and Representations of Foreign Armour," in *Staat und Staatlichkeit in der frühen römischen Republik* (Stuttgart, 1990), 157–173 = idem, *Roman Culture and Society: Collected Papers* (Oxford, 1991), 582–598, a fascinating study of an often neglected aspect of aristocratic display.

79. J. Reynolds, M. Beard, and C. Roueché, "Roman Inscriptions 1981–5," *JRS* 76 (1986), 128–129; *TS* 1.9–11. For the text see W. D. Lebek, "Die drei Ehrenbögen für Germanicus: Tab. Siar. frg. I 9–34; *CIL* VI 31199a 2–17," *ZPE* 67 (1987), 133; D. S. Potter, "The *Tabula Siarensis,* Tiberius, the Senate, and the Eastern Boundary of the Roman Empire," *ZPE* 69 (1987), 269–276, on the placement of the arches. For the development of this style of honor see W. D. Lebek, "Ehrenbögen und Prinzentod: 9 v. Chr.–23 n. Chr.," *ZPE* 86 (1991), 47–78. H. G. Frenz, "The Honorary Arch at Mainz-Kastel," *JRA* 2 (1989), 120–125.

80. S. Mitchell, "Imperial Buildings in the Eastern Roman Provinces," *HSCP* 91 (1987), 333; see also R. MacMullen, "Roman Imperial Buildings in the Provinces," *HSCP* 64 (1959), 207–235.

81. Millar, *Emperor²,* 421–422; Mitchell, "Imperial Buildings," 343–349.

82. Potter, *Prophecy and History,* 251–252, for details with bibliography.

83. See note 79 above.

84. Brasidas: Ar. *EN* 1134b23; Thuc. 5.11.1; Euphron: Xen. *Hell.* 7.4.12. See also P. Gauthier, *Les cités grecques et leurs bienfaiteurs iv⁼–iᵉʳ siècle avant J.-C.* (Paris, 1985), 62–63; For the cult of individuals in the Hellenistic world see C. Habicht, "Samische Volksbeschlüsse der hellenistischen Zeit," *Ath. Mitt.* 72 (1957 [1959]) 156–164 n. 1; for Prepelaus see J. Robert and L. Robert, *Claros I. Décrets hellénistiques* 1 (Paris, 1989), Menippos col. 1, 22–23. For discussion of the location and significance of this monument see ibid., 77–85. As the Roberts point out, this text

would tend to confirm the view of C. Habicht, *Gottmenschentum und griescische Stadte*[2] (Munich, 1970). S. R. F. Price, *Rituals and Power: The Roman Imperial Cult in Asia Minor* (Cambridge, 1984), 47–51, 42 n. 86, for references to other gubernatorial cults.

85. E. H. Smith, "*Imagines* in Imperial Portraiture," *AJA* 27 (1923), 286–301; H. Kruse, *Studien zur offiziellen Geltung des Kaiserbilds im römischen Reich* (Padeborn, 1934), 14–16, 26–34; M. Stuart, "How Were Imperial Portraits Distributed?" *AJA* 43 (1939), 601–617.

86. Kruse, *Studien*, 34–50; S. MacCormack, *Art and Ceremony in Late Antiquity* (Berkeley, 1981), 67–73.

87. *SB* 490; for a valuable summary of all known edicts surviving on papyrus see *P. Oxy.* 3781.

88. E. Heitsch, *Die griechischen Dichterfragmente der römischen Kaiserzeit* (Gottingen, 1961), no. 12, for the performance; for other details see *P. Oxy.* 3781.

89. L. Robert, "Recherches épigraphiques," *REA* 62 (1960), 321–324.

90. D. S. Potter, "Martydom as Spectacle," in R. Scodel, ed., *Theater and Society in the Classical World* (Ann Arbor, 1993), 53–88.

91. See esp. C. Picard, "La villa du taureau à Silin (Tripolitaine)," *CRAI* (1985), 138.

92. Dio 55.10.7; Suet. *Claud.* 17, 21; Tac. *Ann.* 12.36.

93. Herod. 3.10.2; *P. Dura* 54.14–15; J. Reynolds, *Aphrodisias and Rome* (London, 1982), 17, 18; *I. Gr. Bulg.* 659.

94. Potter, *Prophecy and History,* 195–196.

95. For the reality of the situation see ibid., 192–193.

96. A. J. Spawforth and S. Walker, "The World of the Panhellenion. I. Athens and Eleusis," *JRS* 75 (1985), 78–104; idem, "The World of the Panhellenion. II. Three Dorian Cities," *JRS* 76 (1986), 88–105.

97. C. P. Jones, "A New Lycian Dossier Establishing an Artistic Contest and Festival in the Reign of Hadrian," *JRA* 3 (1990), 488.

98. For the historians described by Lucian see C. P. Jones, *Culture and Society in Lucian* (Cambridge, Mass., 1986), 65–67.

99. For Fronto's effort see E. J. Champlin, *Fronto and Antonine Rome* (Cambridge, 1980), 111–114. Champlin's observation that Fronto was called upon in part to answer charges about Lucius' conduct is significant. See pages 160–161 for other cases of court favorites trying to influence public opinion.

100. J. F. Matthews, *The Roman Empire of Ammianus* (London, 1989), 161–175. His view of the relationship between Ammianus and Eunapius has recently been challenged by C. W. Fornara, "Julian's Persian Expedition in Ammianus and Zosimus," *JHS* 101 (1991), 1–15; but Fornara's arguments are not compelling.

101. Compare Tac. *Ann.* 2.55.4, 58.2 with the text of the *senatus consultum* recording the disposition of the case, as discussed in Eck, "Das s.c. de Cn. Pisone Patre," 196.

102. Pliny *Ep.* 6.16, 20; 7.33.

103. Pliny *Ep.* 9.19.5.

104. Matthews, *The Roman Empire of Ammianus,* 25.

105. For a judicious survey of Dio's career with full references to modern scholarship see A. M. Gowing, *The Triumviral Narratives of Appian and Cassius Dio* (Ann Arbor, 1992), 19–21.

106. Dio 79.17.1; see also Millar, *Cassius Dio,* 163, Dio 79.30.2; see also G. W. Bowersock, "Herodian and Elagabalus," *YCS* 24 (1975), 231–4.

107. Dio 76.3.1.4, with E. Hohl, "Kaiser Pertinax und die Thronbesteigung seines Nachfolgers im Lichte der Herodiankritik," *SDAW* (1950), 2, 58; Millar, *Cassius Dio,* 145–146.

108. Dio 80.7.4; see also Millar, *Cassius Dio,* 168; Bowersock, "Herodian and Elagabalus," 230–231.

109. T. D. Barnes, "Ultimus Antoninorum," *BHAC 1968/9* (Bonn, 1970), 60. It is also interesting that Dio seems to have known very little indeed about the god Elagabal—not even that he took the form of a conical black stone or that the emperor had tried to arrange a marriage between him and Minerva, Herod. 5.6.3; *HA V. Elag.* 6.8–9; Bowersock, "Herodian and Elagabalus," 234–235; Barnes, "Ultimus Antoninorum," 68.

110. Bowersock, "Herodian and Elagabalus," 233–236; M. Frey, *Untersuchungen zur Religion und zur Religionspolitik des Kaisers Elagabal* (Stuttgart, 1989), 87–93.

111. Barnes, "Ultimus Antoninorum," 73–74.

112. I cannot see any reason, given the date of the evolution of the sibylline tradition (see Chapter 2), to attribute the adoption of this style of prophecy to the influence of the corpus of texts that go by the somewhat misleading name of "Akkadian Apocalypses" or "Akkadian Oracles." The one common point of all these texts is that they consist of a

number of prophecies set out as a sort of "prophetic narrative," although beyond this the differences among the individual texts seem to be greater than their similarities. For the texts see A. K. Grayson and W. O. Lambert, "Akkadian Prophecies," *JCS* 18 (1964), 7–30; R. Borger, "Gott Marduk und Gott-König Shulgi als Propheten Zwei prophetische Texte," *Bibliotheca Orientalis* 28 (1977), 3–24; R. D. Biggs, "More Babylonian 'Prophecies,' " *Iraq* 28 (1967), 117–132; H. Hunger and S. A. Kaufman, "A New Akkadian Prophecy Text," *JAOS* 95 (1975), 371–375. For problems see esp. Grayson and Lambert, "Akkadian Prophecies," 16–19; Biggs, "More Babylonian 'Prophecies,' " 117–118; idem, "The Babylonian Prophecies and the Astrological Traditions of Mesopotamia," *JCS* 37 (1985), 86–91.

113. *Contra* A. Wirth, "Das Vierzehnte Buch der Sibyllinen," *WS* 14 (1891), 41, who thought they could be Timesitheus and Gordian III, but this view is difficult to reconcile with the historical circumstances. H. Ewald, "Über den geschichtlichen Sinn des XIVten Sibyllinischen Buches," *Abhandlungen der Konig. Gesell. zu Gottingen* 8 (1858–59), 150, thought that they might be Theodosius and Gratian, as the text says "two kings will rule after him, one showing forth the number 300, the other three," but there is no reason to think that the author would have spelled their names in the Latin alphabet.

114. Wirth, "Das Vierzehnte Buch," 44, thought it might be Lucius Priscus or Licinius Valerian.

115. For Marcus Antonius' Dionysian fantasies see Plut. *Alex.* 24.4; 33.6–34.1; 50.6; 60.5; 75.4–5, with C. B. R. Pelling, *Plutarch: Life of Antony* (Cambridge, 1988) ad locc.

116. It is impossible to make claims about any oracle as a whole without careful investigation of each section, a section being defined as a grammatically and thematically coherent passage dealing with a single subject. It is also impossible to assume that because one passage seems to deal with matters from an Egyptian or Syrian perspective, the rest of the extant oracle must have done so as well.

117. *Orac. Sib.* 12.68–77, 48–67; compare *Orac. Sib.* 14.107–115.

118. *Orac. Sib.* 5.35–37, 8.131, page 104 above; *Orac. Sib.* 12.99–116, 5.42–45, 12.147–161.

119. *Orac. Sib.* 12.176–205 with page 122 above; 12.245–249; contrast *Orac. Sib.* 4.52–7.

120. Potter, *Prophecy and History,* 139.

121. *Orac. Sib.* 12.84–92, 5.30–31; Potter, *Prophecy and History,* 300–303. For Nero in Jewish legend see S. J. Batomsky, "The Emperor Nero in Talmudic Legend," *JQR* n.s. 59 (1969), 312–317.

122. For the appearance of the false Nero of 69 see Tac. *Hist.* 2.9 with G. Chilver, *A Historical Commentary on Tacitus' Histories I and II* (Oxford, 1979) ad loc.

123. *Orac. Sib.* 8.56–8 (Hadrian); 12.206, 210–211 (Commodus); 12.274 (Elagabalus).

124. *P. Oxy.* 3298 i. 2 with Rea's note ad loc.; and compare *P. Oxy.* 3299; H. Musurillo, *Acta Alexandrinarum* 4.2.8–9.

125. *Orac. Sib.* 8.131–136, 5.36–37; 12.99–104 (Vespasian); *Orac. Sib.* 8.56–8, 5.45–50, 12.162–175 (Hadrian).

126. For the composition of these texts see Potter, *Prophecy and History,* 125–132.

127. For the perspective of the author of the *Thirteenth Sibylline Oracle,* see ibid., 141–154.

128. For Marcus see page 122 above. For the Severan weather miracle see Z. Rubin, *Civil War Propaganda and Historiography* (Brussels, 1980); for Probus see Zon. 12.29.

129. *Orac. Sib.* 12.215–217; compare *HA V. Comm.* 16.2. For Severus see Herod. 2.9.4.

130. *Orac. Sib.* 12.55–57; 14.112–113. There were serious rains and a consequent flood of the Tiber in A.D. 15; see Tac. *Ann.* 1.76.1.

131. Potter, *Prophecy and History,* 187–189, 242, for these lists.

132. *Orac Sib.* 12.47; for his suffocation see Tac. *Ann.* 6.50.5; Suet. *Tib.* 73; Dio 58.28.2.

4. *Prophecy and Personal Power in the Roman Empire*

1. It is difficult to know his own views on this subject, but the variation in their expression with the rhetorical necessity of a given passage suggests that he tended toward the agnostic. If fate had charted the course of all mortals in advance, the historian of power would be out of a job. He would be better advised to study astrology rather than the impact of the imperial personality upon the state. See esp. *Ann.* 4.20.3; 6.22.1–3. R. H. Martin and A. J. Woodman, *Tacitus, Annals Book IV* (Cambridge, 1989) ad loc. In more general terms see the brilliant analysis by A. D.

Nock, "*A Diis Electa:* A Chapter in the Religious History of the Third Century," *HTR* 23 (1930), 264–270 = *Essays on Religion and the Ancient World*, ed. Z. Stewart (Oxford, 1972), 263–266.

2. R. Syme, "The Crisis of 2 B.C.," *Bayerische Akademie der Wissenschaften. Philosophisch-Historische Klasse. Sitzunsberichte* 7 (1974), 14 = *Roman Papers*, ed. A. Birley (Oxford, 1984), 3:921.

3. G. W. Bowersock, "The Pontificate of Augustus," in K. Raaflaub and M. Toher, eds., *Between Republic and Empire: Interpretations of Augustus and His Principate* (Berkeley, 1990), 385–386.

4. Suet. *Aug.* 94.12: *tantum mox fiduciam fati Augustus habuit, ut thema suum vulgaverit nummumque argenteum nota sideris Capricorni, quo natus est, percussit* (Suetonius' *quo natus* is in error, Augustus was born on 23 September 63 B.C.). For the imperial coinage see RIC^2, 49–50 nos. 124–129 and 53 no. 174; for the *cistophori* see C. H. V. Sutherland, *The Cistophori of Augustus* (London, 1970), 95. Dio 56.25.5 mentions the publication of the horoscope in his discussion of the edict restricting divination in A.D. 11, but as an example of Augustus' lack of personal concern in the matter, not as an event of that year. The connection is asserted incorrectly in F. H. Cramer, *Astrology in Roman Law and Politics* (Philadelphia, 1954), 250 (this work is otherwise a sane and valuable guide to the subject).

5. S. Weinstock, *Divus Julius* (Oxford, 1971), 98.

6. Ibid., 294.

7. App. *BC* 1.97; Plut. *Sulla* 34; Aug. *CD* 2.24 also offers an extensive summary of prophetic moments from Sulla's career that probably derived, through Livy, from Sulla's memoirs. For the name Felix see J. P. V. D. Balsdon, "Sulla Felix," *JRS* 41 (1951), 1–10.

8. D. Feeney, *The Gods in Epic: Poets and Critics of the Classical Tradition* (Oxford, 1991), 258–260.

9. Weinstock, *Divus Julius*, 98, for the possible earlier history of this text. Plut. *Sert.* 11 for Sertorius.

10. Dion. Hal. 4.62 = Carduans fr. 60; Tac. *Ann.* 6.12.3; Cic. *De div.* 2.111–112. The implications of this procedure are brilliantly analyzed by J. Scheid, *Religion at piété à Rome* (Paris, 1985), 43–57.

11. H. Parke, *Sibyls and Sibylline Prophecy* in *Classical Antiquity* ‾, 209–210.

7. G. Liebeschuetz, *Continuity and Change in Roman Religion*), 83.

13. For the evolution of the sibylline tradition around the time of Augustus see pages 81–83 above.

14. J. Linderski, "The Augural Law," *ANRW* ii/16.3, 2226.

15. For the technical issues here see ibid., 2204.

16. Ibid., 2196–97.

17. Ibid., 2295.

18. Ibid., 2241–56.

19. Livy 23.36.10; 25.16.3.

20. L. B. Van der Meer, *The Bronze Liver of Piacenza: Analysis of a Polytheistic Structure* (Amsterdam, 1987), 157–164.

21. J. F. Matthews, *The Roman Empire of Ammianus* (London, 1989), 127–128.

22. M. Torelli, *Elogia Tarquiniensia* (Firenze, 1975), 122–124, for a useful list of *haruspices*. The distinction between *haruspicium* and augury does not seem to have been felt as strongly in Etruria; see fr. 2 of the *fasti LX Haruspicum* (Torelli, *Elogia Tarquiniensa*, 108): *[fu]lmine pr[ocuravit ostenta suo] | [c]armine et augurales d[iviniationes] | complures fecit.*

23. E. Rawson, "Caesar, Etruria, and the *Disciplina Etrusca*," *JRS* 68 (1978), 132–152 = idem, *Roman Culture and Society: Collected Papers* (Oxford, 1991), 289–323.

24. J. Linderski, "Cicero and Divination," *La parola del passato* 202 (1982), 12–38.

25. Tac. *Ann.* 6.20.2–21; Suet. *Tib.* 14.4 for another story that does not necessarily contradict Tacitus.

26. Torelli, *Elogia Tarquiniensia,* 97, 122.

27. G. W. Bowersock, *Augustus and the Greek East* (Oxford, 1965), 77 n. 5.

28. R. Syme, *Tacitus* (Oxford, 1958), 508 n. 9 on the family.

29. For the circumstances surrounding Tiberius' return see G. W. Bowersock, "Augustus and the East: The Problem of the Succession," in F. G. B. Millar and E. Segal, eds., *Caesar Augustus: Seven Aspects* (Oxford, 1984), 180–183; for dinner with Augustus, see Suet. *Aug.* 98.4; for the prophecy concerning Tiberius' long life, see Dio 58.27.

30. Suet. *Galba* 4; Jos. *AJ* 18.216; Tac. *Ann.* 6.20.2; Dio 57.19.4.

31. T. D. Barnes, "The Horoscope of Licinius Sura," *Phoenix* 30 (1976), 76–79.

32. O. Neugebauer and H. B. Van Hoesen, *Greek Horoscopes* (Phila-

delphia, 1959) nos. L 60 Licinius Sura; L 76 (Hadrian); L 113 (Pedanius Fuscus).

33. Amm. Marc. 22.12.8; Soz. *HE* 5.19 for details of the consultation; for the technique see Y. Hajjar, "Divinités oraculaires et rites divinatoires en Syrie et en Phénicie à l'époque gréco-romaine," *ANRW* 18.4, 2283–84; 2294–98.

34. The material that went into panegyrics might, of course, be dictated by the palace, and it may be that Pliny was reminded of this incident by someone close to the emperor even though the specific evidence for this kind of communication is much later, see Lib. *Ep.* 610 Foerster (I am indebted to Cliff Ando for this reference) and P. Heather, *Goths and Romans 332–489* (Oxford, 1991), 80.

35. *Pan.* 6(7).23.1: *commendo liberos meos praecipueque illum iam summa fisci patronicia tractantem.* For the identification of the office see Gallatier's note ad loc. The point that I make here is questioned by C. E. V. Nixon in a number of places, most importantly in "Latin Panegyric in the Tetrarchic and Constantinian Period," in B. Croke and A. Emmett, eds., *History and Historians in Late Antiquity* (Oxford, 1983), 91–93, where he discusses the evidence for the careers of all the authors in this period. This evidence seems to me to suggest precisely that, although the speakers are not themselves members of the court, they are people with connections to it.

36. *Pan.* 6(7).21.5 with B. S. Rodgers, "Constantine's Pagan Vision," *Byzantion* 50 (1980), 270–278, suggesting a reference to portrayals of Augustus in the poetry of Vergil and Horace. The notion is intriguing (see too B. Muller-Rittig, *Der Panegyricus des Jahres 310 auf Konstantin den Grossen: Ubersetzung und historisch-philologischer Kommentar* [Stuttgart, 1990] ad loc.; T. Grünewald, *Constantinus Maximus Augustus. Herrschaftspropaganda in der zeitgenössischen Überlieferung* [Stuttgart, 1990], 51–52), especially as Vergil's *Fourth Eclogue* was treated as a sibylline oracle by other contemporaries, including Constantine and Lactantius (page 86 above).

37. *Pan.* 12(9).2.5: *habes profecto aliquod cum illa mente divina, Constantine, secretum . . .* For previous experience see *Pan.* 12(9)1.1: *qui semper res a numine tuo gestas praedicare solitus essem,* with E. Gallatier, *Panégyriques latins* 2 (Paris, 1952), 105–106; Nixon, "Latin Panegyric in the Tetrarchic and Constantinian Period," 89–92. For the language used at this time and an excellent summary of the "conversion problem" see Grünewald, *Constantinus Maximus Augustus,* 78–86.

38. *Pan.* 4(10)14. A heavenly army also showed up for the decisive battle; *Pan.* 4(10).29.1.

39. Eus. *VC* 1.28.2.

40. *HA. V. Sev.* 2.9; Suet. *Aug.* 94.12, the similarity is noted by Cramer, *Astrology in Roman Law and Politics,* 209; for Severus as the source for this event see A. R. Birley, *Septimius Severus: The African Emperor* (London, 1989), 41.

41. Dio 72.23.1; for the occasion in 193 see F. G. B. Millar, *A Study of Cassius Dio* (Oxford, 1964), 29.

42. For Dio's fatalism see A. Gowing, *The Triumviral Narratives of Appian and Cassius Dio* (Ann Arbor, 1992), 29–30.

43. Pliny *Ep.* 3.27.12–14; App. fr. 2.

44. Dio 78.10; Pliny *Ep.* 7.27.2–3; Tac. *Ann.* 11.21.1.

45. C. P. Jones, "An Oracle Given to Trajan," *Chiron* 5 (1975), 403–406; Tac. *Ann.* 2.54.2.

46. Macrob. *Sat.* 1.23.14–17.

47. Zos. 1.57–58 with Hajjar, "Divinités oraculaires et rites divinatoires," 2278–79, on the later site.

48. For the visit to Stratonicaea see *Insc. Strat.* no. 310, for the date see T. D. Barnes, *The New Empire of Diocletian and Constantine* (Cambridge, Mass., 1982), 66; and S. Mitchell, "Maximinus and the Christians," *JRS* 78 (1988), 119, on the shrine. It was still giving oracles in the mid-third century, and it would not be surprising if the god had spoken at this point as well.

49. Mitchell, "Maximinus and the Christians," 120.

50. Hajjar, "Divinités oraculaires et rites divinatoires," 2264.

51. See now P. Brunt, *Roman Imperial Themes* (Oxford, 1990), 483–487, on Druidic hostility to Rome. He is correct to point out that Druids no longer seem to have drawn members from the upper orders of Gaul, but probably underestimates their continuing influence.

52. E. Schürer, *A History of the Jewish People in the Age of Jesus Christ*², ed. G. Vermes and F. G. B. Millar (Edinburgh, 1973) 1:543–545.

53. S. Appelbaum, *Jews and Greeks in Ancient Cyrene* (Leiden, 1979), 251–260, on messianic elements in the revolt under Trajan, although much of the evidence that he cites comes from sibylline oracles, which will not support his contention (they cannot be shown to be either first/second century or Jewish in their present configurations; see pages 88–96 above); but there is enough other evidence to be suggestive, particularly

regarding the selection of a king (Eus. *HE* 4.2.4) and the evidence for the desecration of temples. See also M. Hengel, "Messianische Hoffnung und politischer Radikalismus in der jüdisch-hellenistischen Diaspora. Zur Frage der Voraussetzungen des jüdischen Aufstandes unter Trajan 115–117 n. Chr.," in D. Hellholm, ed., *Apocalypticism in the Mediterranean World and the Near East: Proceedings of the International Colloquium on Apocalypticism, Uppsala, August 12–17, 1979* (Tübingen, 1983), 655–686. For the Neronian revolt see now M. Goodman, *The Ruling Class of Judaea: The Origins of the Jewish Revolt against Rome A.D. 66–70* (Cambridge, 1987), esp. 90–91, with his sensible observation that messianic beliefs do not in and of themselves involve opposition to Rome (although in this case they do seem to have influenced some).

54. Dio 54.7.2–3 with G. W. Bowersock, "The Mechanics of Subversion in the Roman Provinces," in *Opposition et résistances a l'empire d'Auguste a Trajan* (Geneva, 1986), 298.

55. Caesar *BC* 3.105.5 (for Pergamon), Suet. *Cal.* 57.1 (Olympia) with Bowersock, "The Mechanics of Subversion," 294–295, 298.

56. G. W. Bowersock, *Julian the Apostate* (Cambridge, Mass., 1978), 89.

57. D. S. Potter, *Prophecy and History in the Crisis of the Roman Empire: A Historical Commentary on the Thirteenth Sibylline Oracle* (Oxford, 1990), 242, 253.

58. For Titus see pages 13; 173. For the prophecies connected with Vespasian see E. M. Sanford, "Nero and the East," *HSCP* 48 (1937), 75–103; A. Henrichs, "Vespasian's Visit to Alexandria," *ZPE* 3 (1968), 51–80.

59. Suet. *Vesp.* 5.7: *ac non multo post comitia secundi consulatus ineunte Galba statuam Divi Juli ad Orientem sponte conversam*—plainly the same event as that reported at Tac. *Hist.* 1.86.1: *statuam Divi Iulii in insula Tiberini amnis sereno et immoto die ab occidente in orientem conversam*. Vespasian's knowledge of the revolt against Nero is evident from the chronology of his operations in Judaea in the spring of 68: he stopped the operations before he could possibly have received news of Vindex's revolt; see J. Nicols, *Vespasian and the Partes Flavianae* (Wiesbaden, 1978), 55. For Titus see Tac. *Hist.* 2.1.1: *Titus Vespasianus, e Iudaea incolumi adhuc Galba missus a patre, causam profectionis officium erga principem et maturam petendis honoribus iuventam ferebat, sed volgus fingendi avidum disperserat accitum in adoptionem.*

60. Bowersock, "The Mechanics of Subversion," 297–299, on the role of local priests.

61. For known cases involving members of the upper classes (fourteen in all) between Augustus and the Severans see Cramer, *Astrology in Roman Law and Politics*, 251–270.

62. *Mos. et Rom. legum coll.* 2.1: *denique exstat senatus consultum Pomponio et Rufo coss. factum, quo cavetur, ut mathematicis, Chaldaeis, ariolis et ceteris, qui simile inceptum fecerint, aqua et igni interdicatur, omniaque bona eorum publicaretur: et si externarum gentium quis id fecerint, aqua et igni interdicatur, ut in eum animadvertatur.* Tac. *Ann.* 2.32.3; Dio 57.15. See also Cramer, *Astrology in Roman Law and Politics*, 238–240; 270–271.

63. Suet. *Tib.* 63.1: *haruspices secreto ac sine testibus consuli vetuit. Vicina vero urbi oracula etiam discere conatus est sed maiestate Praenestinarum sortium territus destitit, cum obsignatas devectasque Romam non repperisset in arca nisi relata rursus ad templum.*

64. Cramer, *Astrology in Roman Law and Politics*, 242.

65. Ibid., 243–244.

66. Ibid., 244–245.

67. Ibid., 245–247.

68. Translated in J. Rea, "A New Version of P. Yale Inv. 299," *ZPE* (1977), 153–154. For the original publication see G. M. Parássoglou, "Circular from a Prefect: Dileat Omnibus Perpetuo Divinandi Curiositas," in A. E. Hanson, ed., *Collectanea Papyrologica: Texts Published in Honor of H. C. Youtie*, pt. 1 (Bonn, 1976), 261–274.

69. For a different view see T. D. Barnes, *Constantine and Eusebius* (Cambridge, Mass., 1981), 52–53. For subsequent legislation against divination and sacrifice see ibid., 210–211. Eusebius mentions two measures. The first is an edict banning public participation in traditional cult by higher imperial officials (*VC* 2.44). The second is presented as a ban on the making of statues, divination, "other foolish practices," and sacrifice (*VC* 2.45). This is generally taken to be the law referred to by Constans in 341 (*C. Th.* 16.10.2). But is this a ban on all sacrifice and divination? The collocation of acts mentioned in *VC* 2.45 suggests that Constantine may have been concerned with magic; for a scandal in the reign of Constantine involving a man who seems to have been connected with divination and magic involving statues, see Eun. *V. Ph.* 463; Matthews, *The Roman Empire of Ammianus*, 126. Even in 359, Ammianus implies that the

emperor's primary concern was with inquiry about his fate. See esp. Amm. Marc. 19.12.12.

70. *C. Th.* 9.16.6; for Taurus, the addressee of this edict, see *PLRE* 879–880.

71. Amm. Marc. 21.1.6: *acuebat autem incendebatque eius cupiditatem, pacatis iam Galliis, incessere ultro Constantium, animus coniciens eum per vaticinandi praesagia multa (quae callebat) et somnia, e vita protinus excessurum;* Eunap. fr. 21 (Blockley). The contents of the story correspond to this point in the autumn of 360 in Ammianus' narative, for it was only then that Julian resolved to "end the tyranny of Constantius."

72. Amm. Marc. 28.8.8. The chronology is complicated: see Matthews, *The Roman Empire of Ammianus,* 210.

73. Eus. *VC* 3.54–58; Barnes, *Constantine and Eusebius,* 247.

74. *C. Th.* 16.10.2 with note 69 above.

75. G. W. Bowersock, *Hellenism in Late Antiquity* (Ann Arbor, 1990), 1–13.

76. Matthews, *The Roman Empire of Ammianus,* 219–225. For Ammianus' view that the question rather than the fact of consultation was usually the point at issue in such cases see 19.12.14, 29.2.5; compare also *HA V. Carac.* 5.7.

5. Eastern Wisdom in Roman Prophetic Books

1. A. Momigliano, *Alien Wisdom* (Cambridge, Mass., 1975), remains of fundamental importance on this point.

2. The opposite position has recently been argued with great power by F. G. B. Millar, *The Roman Near East, 31* B.C.–A.D. *337* (Cambridge, Mass., 1993). My reasons for disagreeing with this position should emerge later in the discussion, although I am in agreement with Millar's basic thesis that Rome's presence in the near east created a profoundly new cultural dynamic.

3. M. Boyce, "On the Antiquity of Zoroastrian Apocalyptic," *BSOAS* 47 (1984), 68, accepting the views of S. K. Eddy, *The King Is Dead* (Lincoln, Neb., 1961), 10. The discussion that follows is heavily dependent upon Boyce's analysis.

4. Translated in E. W. West, *Pahlavi Texts* (Oxford, 1880), 191–193 (with anglicized nomenclature for clarity, and translating *ahan-abar-gumext* as "unmixed iron" instead of "mixed up with iron," for which see Boyce, "Antiquity of Zoroastrian Apocalyptic," 71–72).

5. Boyce, "Antiquity of Zoroastrian Apocalyptic," 71–72.

6. Ibid., 71; *contra* J. Duschesne-Guillemin, "Apocalypse juive et apocalypse iranienne," in *La soteriologia dei culti orientali nell'imperio Romano,* ed. U. Bianchi and M. Vermaseren, (Leiden, 1982), 756.

7. R. Eisenman and M. Wise, *The Dead Sea Scrolls Uncovered* (Rockport, Mass., 1992), 71–73. The preliminary commentary provided by the authors does not take account of the Iranian parallel, but the contents of this volume certainly justify observations about the conduct of scholars who kept this material from the public for so long. For the connection with tree worship see M. Boyce and B. Grenet, *A History of Zoroastrianism* (Leiden, 1991), 3:385. For other prophetic traditions entering Daniel see G. Vermes, *The Dead Sea Scrolls in English*[2] (Harmondsworth, 1975), 229, for the prayer of Nabonidus. J. T. Milik, *Ten Years of Discovery in the Wilderness of Judaea* (London, 1959), 37, suggests that this is the original version of the story that appears in Dan. 4:18–37 and that Nabonidus was replaced in the tradition by Nebuchadnezzar, who was more famous. Despite the reservations of some (see M. Goodman in E. Schürer, *A History of the Jewish People in the Age of Jesus Christ*[2] 3.1, ed. G. Vermes, F. G. B. Millar, and M. Goodman [Edinburgh, 1986], 440), this seems a likely proposition. Such replacements, which reflect the development of general cultural memories of history rather than conscious scholarly effort, are commonplace. For the early date of the composition see R. G. Kratz, *Translatio Imperii. Untersuchungen zu den aramäischen Danielzählungen und ihrem theologiegeschichtlichen Umfelf* (Düsseldorf, 1987), 99–110; for the possibility of a later date (not likely, given the connection between *The Prayer of Nabonidus* and Neobabylonian texts) see Goodman's summary in *History of the Jewish People*[2], 441 n. 5. For another Daniel story see Eisenman and Wise, *The Dead Sea Scrolls Uncovered,* no. 11.

8. J. W. Swain, "The Theory of the Four Monarchies," *CPh* 35 (1940), 1–5.

9. Dion. Hal. *Ant. Rom.* 1.2.2–4 with E. Gabba, *Dionysius and the History of Archaic Rome* (Berkeley, 1991), 193 n. 7; for Trogus see Swain, "Theory of the Four Monarchies," 16–17.

10. App. *Praef.* 9 with Swain, "Theory of the Four Monarchies," 14.

11. *Orac. Sib.* 13.84 with the discussion in D. S. Potter, *Prophecy and History in the Crisis of the Roman Empire: A Historical Commentary on the Thirteenth Sibylline Oracle* (Oxford, 1990), 260. This pattern is also used, in a rather confused way, in an oracular text included in a collection of

sibylline oracles that may have been put together in the late fifth century. In that case, however, all that can be said with certainty is that it was acceptable to the Christian compiler and that the eschatological motifs used in it were thoroughly recognizable by that time; see page 89 above.

12. See, e.g., M. L. West, *Hesiod. Theogony* (Oxford, 1978), 176.

13. Boyce, "Antiquity of Zoroastrian Apocalyptic," 68.

14. Ibid., 70.

15. Ibid., 59. For a useful summary of the late sources for Zoroastrian prophecy see A. Hultgard, "Forms and Origins of Iranian Apocalypticism," in D. Hellholm, ed., *Apocalypticism in the Mediterranean World and the Near East: Proceedings of the International Colloquium on Apocalypticism, Uppsala, August 12–17, 1979* (Tübingen, 1983), 387–411. His view that "the explicit apocalyptic traditions are, however, found only in Middle Iranian and Pahlavi texts" is somewhat problematic in that several of the Gathas of Zoroaster (the earliest texts, probably composed by Zoroaster himself) contain accounts of Zoroaster's instruction by Ahura Mazda. The Gathic material is, quite properly, stressed in G. Widengren, "Leitende Ideen und Quellen der iranischer Apokalyptik," in Hellholm, *Apocalypticism in the Mediterranean World,* 77–80. For the Gathas see S. Insler, *The Gathas of Zoroaster.* Acta Iranica 8 (Leiden, 1975), where Zoroaster's accounts of his instruction are conveniently laid out.

16. G. Fowden, *Empire to Commonwealth: Consequences of Monotheism in Late Antiquity* (Princeton, 1993), 28–36, for a lucid account of the rise of Zoroastrianism under the Sassanids. It should be noted, however, that despite Sapor's obvious devotion to the faith, Kartir does not seem to have fully established himself at the center of power until after Sapor's death. This much is suggested by Mani's career while Sapor was still alive (see page 208). It is also interesting that Kartir himself seems to have thought that his co-religionists were in need of serious instruction as to what the faith actually consisted of, and that he claims to have had a vision in the reign of Sapor in which he learned the truth about the gods, see esp. *KNRm* 6, 75 fol. For his career see now D. N. MacKenzie in G. Herrmann, *The Sasanian Rock Reliefs at Naqsh-i Rustam* (Berlin, 1989), 29–30. The Avestan alphabet, which was invented to record the works of Zoroaster, was not developed until the fifth century (M. Boyce, *Textual Sources for the Study of Zoroastrianism* [Chicago, 1984], 1:113–114), although Iranian tradition suggests that written texts were available in the time of Ardashir and Sapor, when an edition was allegedly produced.

17. For a sensible summary, downplaying much earlier speculation that had unduly exalted the importance of Zoroastrian thought, see K. Rudolph, *Gnosis: The Nature and History of Gnosticism*[2] trans. R. McL. Wilson (Edinburgh, 1984), 282–285, although he appears to attribute too much possible "Iranian" influence to the *Hymn of the Pearl*, a section of the *Acts of Thomas* that appears to have been the product of Syriac Christianity of the early third century and was subsequently appropriated by the author of the original version of the life of Mani that survives in the Cologne Mani Codex. For a thorough analysis of this work see P.-H. Poirier, *L'hyme de la perle des Actes de Thomas* (Louvain-la-Neuve, 1981). For the impact of Zoroastrian thought on post exilic Judaism see M. Boyce, *A History of Zoroastrianism*[2] (Leiden, 1982), 191–195. For more on the evolution of Zoroastrian thought in the Hellenisitc world see H. Waldmann, *Der Kommagenische Mazdaismus* Istanbuler Mitteilungen Beiheft 37 (Tübingen, 1991).

18. *FGrH* 115 fr. 65. For the connection between this and Zurvanite thought see Widengren, "Leitende Ideen und Quellen der iranischer Apokalyptik," 127–133.

19. For this material see now the thorough discussion by R. Beck, "Thus Spake Not Zarathustra: Zoroastrian Pseudepigrapha of the Greco-Roman World," in Boyce and Grenet, *A History of Zoroastrianism*, 491–565. For the problems of Zostrianos and Zoroaster see M. J. Edwards, "How Many Zoroasters? Arnobius, *Adversus Gentes*, 1.52," *Vigiliae Christianae* 42 (1988), 284–285.

20. Phil. *V. Apoll.* 1.25.1: *e Babylon teteikistai men ogdoekonta kai tetra-kosia stadia* Cf. Hdt. 1.178.1: *houtoi stadioi tes periodou tes polios gignontai synapantes ogdoekonta kai tetrakosia . . .*

21. Beck, "Thus Spake Not Zarathustra," 511–521; A. D. Nock, "Paul and the Magus," in F. J. Foakes Jackson and K. Lake, ed., *The Beginnings of Christianity* (London, 1933), pt. 1, vol. 5, 164–82 = *Essays on Religion in the Ancient World*, ed. Z. Stewart (Oxford, 1972), 308–324.

22. A. Kuhrt, "Berossus' *Babyloniaka* and Seleucid Rule in Babylonia," in A. Kuhrt and S. M. Sherwin-White, eds., *Hellenism in the East: The Interaction of Greek and Non-Greek Civilizations from Syria to Central Asia after Alexander* (London, 1987), 32–56.

23. See also G. E. Sterling, *Historiography and Self-Definition: Josephus, Luke Acts, and Apologetic Historiography* (Leiden, 1992), 116–117.

24. Kuhrt, "Berossus' *Babyloniaka* and Seleucid Rule," 36–48.

25. B. P. Copenhaver, *Hermetica: The Greek Corpus Hermeticum and the Latin Asclepius in a New English Translation with Notes and Introduction* (Cambridge, 1992), 213–214. The most important recent contribution on the composition of this text remains G. Fowden, *The Egyptian Hermes: A Historical Approach to the Late Pagan Mind* (Cambridge, 1986), 39.

26. See the excellent discussion of W. Scott, *Hermetica* 3 (Oxford, 1926), 177–181.

27. Tac. *Ann.* 2.62 with Koestermann ad loc. The fact that the description differs significantly from Hdt. 2.102–104 makes it all the more likely that this is roughly the version that Germanicus received from an oral source. For tourism in Egypt and the invention of traditions about its antiquities, see esp. G. W. Bowersock, "The Miracle of Memnon," *BASOP* 21 (1984), 26–30.

28. For the preservation of Demotic popular literature in the Fayyum as the historical and cultural tradition of Egypt into the imperial period see E. A. E. Raymond, "Demotic Literary Works of Graeco-Roman Date," in *Papyrus Erzerhog Rainer* (Vienna, 1983), 46–53.

29. Scott, *Hermetica* 3:168, Copenhaver, *Hermetica,* 241.

30. See Potter, *Prophecy and History,* 196–197.

31. Possibly in a Greek version of an oracular text that was known to Callimachus see L. Koenen, "Die Adoptation ägyptischer Königsideologie am Ptolemäerhof," in *Egypt and the Hellenistic World: Proceedings of the International Colloquium Leuven—24–26 May 1982.* Studia Hellenistica 27 (Louvain, 1983), 182–186. The influence could, of course, have been the other way around. For an obscure tax collector of the imperial period who seems to have been a devoted reader of Callimachus and who used that poet as a source for the Greek names that he awarded Egyptians on the tax rolls, see H. C. Youtie, "Callimachus on the Tax Rolls," in D. Samuel, ed., *Proceedings of the Twelfth International Congress of Papyrology* (Toronto, 1970), 545–551 = H. C. Youtie, *Scriptunculae* 2 (Amsterdam, 1973), 1035–41. An unpublished, fragmentary Demotic text of the second half of the Ptolemaic period resembles the *Oracle of the Potter* in some regards; see Raymond, "Demotic Literary Works of Graeco-Roman Date," 50.

32. H. Frankfort, *Kingship and the Gods: A Study of Ancient Near Eastern Religion as the Integration of Society and Nature* (Chicago, 1948), 183.

33. D. L. Frankfurter, "Lest Egypt's City Be Deserted: Religion and

Ideology in the Egyptian Response to the Jewish Revolt (116–117 C.E.)," *JJS* 43 (1992), 203–220.

34. See now the useful and thorough analysis in D. L. Frankfurter, *Elijah in Upper Egypt: The Apocalypse of Elijah and Early Egyptian Christianity* (Minneapolis, 1993), 159–185.

35. The text translated at this point is a conjecture, the probability of which cannot be supported with confidence from the traces remaining on the papyrus, although it does seem to represent the meaning of the text; see L. Koenen, "A Supplementary Note on the Oracle of the Potter," *ZPE* 54 (1984), 11 n. 7. For the meaning of Zonophoroi see idem, "Die Prophezeiungen des 'Topfers,' " *ZPE* 2 (1968), 202.

36. For the text here see Koenen, "A Supplementary Note," 11.

37. Ibid., 11 n. 12; he now inclines to an earlier date, possibly as early as the late sixth or early fifth century B.C.

38. He seems to be known from other texts of the same period, see K.-T. Zauzich, "Der Schreiber der Weissagung des Lammes," *Enchoria* 6 (1976), 127–128.

39. Koenen, "Prophezeiungen des 'Topfers,' " 178–209. The three papyri are *P. Graf* 29787 (second century A.D.) = P_1; *P. Rainer G.* 19813 (third century) = P_2; *P. Oxy* 2332 (late third century) = P_3. As *P. Graf* 29787 preserves material not in the other two, and the texts of *P. Rainer G.* 19 813 and *P. Oxy* 2332 are different, in the discussion in the text I follow Koenen in referring to them as separate texts.

40. Koenen, "A Supplementary Note," 12.

41. For different modes of reading these texts see J. Barton, *Oracles of God: Perceptions of Ancient Prophecy in Israel after Exile* (London, 1986), 152–153.

42. See also *P. Teb. D.* 13, a text mentioning Memphis that appears to be oracular and is datable to the late first/early second century, and is thus, at present, the latest Demotic oracle. It is too fragmentary to say more about it than this. Nothing can be said with certainty about the "unpublished" Greek text in P. Trinity College Dublin 192 b, a transcription of which is given by C. H. Roberts in his edition of *P. Oxy.* 2332 (one of the texts of the *Oracle of the Potter*) in *P. Oxy.* 22, 92 n. 3.

43. M. Lichtheim, *Ancient Egyptian Literature* 1 (Berkeley, 1975), 134–135.

44. See also the stories contained in the Westcar papyrus, *P. Berlin*

3033 (translated in Lichtheim, *Ancient Egyptian Literature* 1:215–222. For the evil reputation of Khufu, the builder of the Great Pyramid, compare Hdt. 2. 124.1; see also B. J. Kemp, "Old Kingdom, Middle Kingdom and Second Intermediate Period," in B. G. Trigger, B. J. Kemp, D. O'Connor and A. B. Lloyd, eds., *Ancient Egypt: A Social History* (Cambridge, 1983), 77.

45. Lichtheim, *Ancient Egyptian Literature* 1:139–145.

46. *ANET*, p. 555. For this style see J. Van Seters, *In Search of History: Historiography in the Ancient World and the Origins of Biblical History* (New Haven, 1983), 146.

47. See Fowden, *The Egyptian Hermes*, 37–38, for an affirmative answer to this question.

48. A.-J. Festugière, *La révélation d'Hermès Trismégiste* 2 (Paris, 1949), 17–18.

49. Frankfurter, *Elijah in Upper Egypt*, 216–226, is very good on the lack of firm historical allusions in this text.

50. See J. M. Robinson, ed., *The Nag Hammadi Library in English* (New York, 1977), xiv, for the contents of this codex; and Rudolph, *Gnosis*[2], 42–52. For the problem of the connection between these books and a neighboring Pachomian monastery, see R. Bagnall, *Egypt in Late Antiquity* (Princeton, 1993), 304.

51. For this date see D. S. Potter, review of R. Majercik, *The Chaldaean Oracles, JRS* 81 (1991), 225–227. The works are ostensibly second century, but the traditions relating to their authorship are plainly fantasy, and we know of no readers before Porphyry and Iamblichus, since arguments connecting doctrines in the oracles with the second-century Platonist Numenius are unconvincing. The whole issue of the language of the Chaldeans during the Roman period is dealt with very well in Millar, *The Roman Near East*, 497–498, noting that the last evidence for the original language of the Chaldeans, Akkadian, dates to A.D. 74–75.

52. H. Lewy, *The Chaldaean Oracles and Theurgy*[2], ed. M. Tardieu (Paris, 1978), 224–225, 229.

53. For the Greek context (though accepting an earlier date than is assumed here) see S. I. Johnston, "Riders in the Sky: Cavalier Gods and Theurgic Salvation in the Second Century A.D.," *CPh* 87 (1992), 303–321.

54. H. D. Saffrey, "Abamon, pseudonyme de Jamblique," in *Philomathes: Studies and Essays in the Humanities in Memory of Philip Merlan,* ed.

R. B. Palmer and R. Hamerton-Kelly (The Hague, 1971), 227–239 = *Recherches sur le Néoplatonisme après Plotin* (Paris, 1990), 95–107, establishes both the priority of Iamblichus' use of the texts and his polemic purpose. I am indebted to Professor T. D. Barnes for calling this to my attention. P. Athanassiadi, "Dreams, Theurgy and Freelance Divination: The Testimony of Iamblichus," *JRS* 83 (1993), 118–121, acknowledges the differences between Iamblichus and Porphyry, though she takes a less confrontational view of their relationship.

55. Lewy, *Chaldaean Oracles and Theurgy*[2], 178–179; 230–233, drawing the appropriate parallel with rites described in the magical papyri.

56. J. F. Matthews, *The Roman Empire of Ammianus* (London, 1989), 127–128.

57. Potter, review of Majercik, *The Chaldaean Oracles*, 227.

58. For this view see P. Beskow, "The Routes of Early Mithraism," in *Etudes mithraiques. Actes du 2ieme Congrès International Téhéran, du 1er au 8 septembre 1975*, Acta Iranica 4 (Leiden, 1978), 7–18. It must be conceded that his view remains open to serious question.

59. See now the extensive and valuable discussion in Boyce and Grenet, *A History of Zoroastrianism*, 197–360.

60. G. P. Luttikhuizen, *The Revelation of Elchasai: Investigation into the Evidence for a Mesopotamian Jewish Apocalypse of the Second Century and Its Reception by Judaeo-Christian Propagandists* (Tübingen, 1985), 61. It is possible that Sobiai is not an individual, but rather a mistake for the plural passive participle of the Aramaic verb *sb*' meaning "the baptized."

61. Luttikhuizen, *The Revelation of Elchasai*, 192–194. I cite here only the version of Hippolytus because it appears to be closest to the original.

62. For the circumstances see D. S. Potter, "The Mysterious Arbaces," *AJP* 100 (1979), 541–542; T. D. Barnes, "Trajan and the Jews," *JJS* 40 (1989), 145–162.

63. D. S. Potter, "The Inscriptions on the Bronze Herakles from Mesene: Vologeses' War with Rome and the Date of Tacitus' *Annales*," *ZPE* (1991), 277–290.

64. Luttikhuizen, *The Revelation of Elchasai*, 192, suggesting the late autumn of 116 as the date.

65. The chronology is secured by Eus. *HE* 6.21; Hipp. *Haer.* 9.8.

66. See now S. N. C. Lieu, *Manichaeism in the Later Roman Empire and Medieval China* (Tübingen, 1992), 41–42.

67. The connection between the revelation of Elchesai and the com-

munity in which Mani grew up is challenged by Luttikhuizen, *The Revelation of Elchasai,* 220–224, not, I think, convincingly. The difference in the spelling of the founder's name between the Mani Codex and Hippolytus should not surprise anyone familiar with the codex (a translation from Coptic), and the similarities listed by A. Henrichs and L. Koenen, "Ein griechischer Mani-Codex (P. Colon. inv. nr. 4780," *ZPE* 5 (1970), 141–160, remain convincing. See also Lieu, *Manichaeism in the Later Roman Empire,* 40.

68. Rudolf, *Gnosis*[2], 329; for youthful visions see *CMC* 4–5. References to the Cologne Mani Codex are to codex pages.

69. For trade see Potter, "Inscriptions on the Bronze Herakles," with references to more detailed discussions; for the political circumstances, Potter, *Prophecy and History,* 35–37.

70. Lieu, *Manichaeism in the Later Roman Empire,* 8.

71. For the circumstances see ibid., 108–109.

72. Ibid., 103–106.

73. Ibid., 151–191.

74. T. D. Barnes, *Eusebius and Constantine* (Cambridge, Mass., 1981), 20.

75. It is interesting that Eusebius appears to have been familiar with the teachings of Elchesai, through the works of Origen, who regarded the Elchesites as a Christian heresy (*HE* 6.38). For the view of the language of Eusebius and Diocletian taken here see P. Brown, "The Diffusion of Manichaeism in the Roman Empire," *JRS* 59 (1969), 92–98; Lieu, *Manichaeism in the Later Roman Empire,* 121–125.

76. J. Bidez and F. Cumont, *Les mages hellénisés* (Paris, 1938), 1:215–223, with fragments collected in 2:361–377. They attempt to connect him with the Vistaspa of authentic Zoroastrian tradition, but, given the thoroughly confused and Hellenic context of his works, this seems a bit too optimistic. For a thorough and generally sensible discussion of the tradition see now Boyce and Grenet, *A History of Zoroastrianism*[3], 376–381, although their belief in "Persian Sibyllists" as an influence on this work is based on a thorough misunderstanding of the tradition. So too, the notion that the oracle was originally written in verse (377 n. 60) is without foundation.

77. Amm. Marc. 22.6.32 for the connection with India. For the tradition linking him with Darius and dating him to the period before the Trojan War see Lact. *DI* 7.15.19; for the connection between the Ery-

thraean Sibyl and the Trojan War see Potter, *Prophecy and History*, 119. The view of Hydaspes as a sort of Persian parallel to Sibyls and the Hebrew prophets appears in Lact. *Epit. Inst.* 68; Justin Mart. *Apol.* 1.20.1; 44.12; Clem. Alex. *Strom.* 6.5.

78. D. S. Potter, "Martyrdom as Spectacle," in R. Scodel, ed., *Theater and Society in the Classical World* (Ann Arbor, 1993), 54–56; R. J. Lane Fox, *Pagans and Christians* (New York, 1987), 404–410, on Montanism; and C. M. Robeck, *Prophecy in Carthage: Perpetua, Tertullian, and Cyprian* (Cleveland, 1992), on the issue of good and bad visions.

Epilogue

1. For this group see now R. Gray, *Prophetic Figures in Late Second Temple Jewish Palestine: The Evidence of Josephus* (Oxford, 1993), 112–63, although she does not seek to relate their methods to those in the non-Jewish world. For the possibility of a connection between Paul's visions and contemporary Jewish mysticism see now the thorough and convincing studies by C. R. A. Murray-Jones, "Paradise Revisited (2 Corinthians,. 12:1–12): The Jewish Mystical Background of Paul's Apostolate," *HTR* 86 (1993): 177–217, 265–292.

2. For the diverse influences on the development of the Christian canon see now the superior treatment of B. M. Metzger, *The Canon of the New Testament: Its Origin, Development, and Significance* (Oxford, 1992), 75–112, esp. 78–106.

3. See Chapter 1, note 94.

4. I am indebted to Professor Brian Schmidt for the terminology used here: he should not be held responsible for the way it is used.

5. M. Fishbane, *Biblical Interpretation in Ancient Israel* (Oxford, 1985), 2; Gray, *Prophetic Figures,* 110.

6. Gray, *Prophetic Figures,* 35–79.

7. The question seems to have been firmly settled by 90; see J. Barton, *Oracles of God: Perceptions of Ancient Prophecy in Israel after Exile* (London, 1986), 26–27; Metzger, *The Canon of the New Testament,* 110 with bibliography.

Index

Aelius Aristides (orator 2nd century AD): and dreams, 21; and oracle of Apollo at Claros, 39

Alexander of Abonuteichos (prophet 2nd century AD): and Marcus Aurelius, 16, 169; compared to Apollonius of Tyana, 34; physical appearance, 31; role in the cult of Glycon, 45; services rendered, 30. *See also* Glycon

Alexander the Great (king of Macedon 336–323 BC): cultural impact of his conquests, 185; oracles concerning, 75

Ammianus Marcellinus (historian 4th century AD): and Julian's Persian expedition, 17, 52; describes prosecutions for divination under Valentinian and Valens, 179–182; information problems, 131–133; on Apollonius of Tyana, 33; on the self-representation of Constantius II, 116; views on prophecy, 52, 182

Antichrist, 56, 109

Aphrodisias: history wall at, 118–119; Sebasteion at, 122

Aphrodite: in a lot oracle, 26; landing on Cyprus, 30; oracle of at Aphraca, 169; oracle of at Paphos, 13, 160

Apocalypticism, problem with as a concept, 3, 215

Apollo: and Erythraean Sibyl, 71; birth places of, 30; Clarian, 4–6, 15, 37; Lakeutes, 13. *See also* Apollonius of Tyana; Claros; Delphi; Didyma

Apollonius of Tyana (holy man 1st century AD): and Apollo, 39; and Ephesus, 32–33; as magician, 34; as Pythagorean, 33; at Babylon, 190; compared to Alexander of Abonuteichus, 34; maker of talismans, 34; physical appearance, 32; prophetic ability of, 165–166; Severan interest in, 17; traditions concerning, 33–34

Appian (historian 2nd century AD): saved by prophetic bird, 168; uses scheme of four kingdoms, 187

Ariolus, 11, 174

prophecy, 2, 9–10, 60–61; martyrdom, 211; readings of books by pagan prophets, 58, 184, 210–212; role of demons in pagan prophecy, 48, 55–57. *See also* Canon; Constantine I; Hippolytus; Montanism; Paul, Saint; Jesus Christ; *Oracula Sibyllina; Revelation*

Cicero (consul 63 BC): and *haruspicium*, 156–157; *Concerning Divination*, 22, 50–51, 233n116; views on lot oracles, 23

Claros, oracle of Apollo at, 4–6; consultation of, 39, 43; importance of in the Roman Empire, 37; thespiodos at, 43, 232n107. *See also* Germanicus Caesar

Claudius (emperor 41–54 AD): and *haruspices*, 157–158; games celebrating conquest of Britain, 129; in *Oracula Sibyllina*, 141, 143, 145; legislation against astrologers, 175

Coinage, and imperial propaganda, 124–125

Communication, speed of, 111

Constantine I (emperor 306–337 AD): adoption of Claudius Gothicus as an ancestor, 112–113, 163; alleged vision of Constantius I, 163; connected with Vergil, *Eclogue* 4, 163; conversion of, 114–115, 163; different image for Christians and pagans, 114–115; legislation against divination, 12, 178, 180; legislation against sacrifice, 181; on Sibylline Oracles, 83, 85, 109; propaganda compared with that of Diocletian, 113; vision of Apollo, 163

Constantius II (emperor 337–361 AD): personal prophetic power of, 164–165; edicts against divination, 178, 180

Cornelius Cethegus (conspirator with Catiline in 63 BC), and oracle concerning Cornelii, 149

Cornelius Lentulus (consul 49 BC), and oracle concerning Cornelii, 149

P. Cornelius Scipio Aemilianus (consul 147, 134 BC), and oracle of a Spanish woman, 148

P. Cornelius Scipio Africanus (consul 205, 194 BC), use of prophecies, 147–148

L. Cornelius Sulla. *See* Sulla

Corpus Hermeticum: Egyptian context, 201–203; imperial panegyric in, 98; *Perfect Discourse*, 192–194, 202; Zoroaster in, 190

Cult, civic: as "passive" form of religious experience, 5–6; interaction of with prophecy, 4–6, 57; as representation of community history, 7, 13; representation of a way of dealing with the natural world, 7–8; persistent change in, 4–6, 9

Cult, imperial, 128–129

Daniel: different interpretations of, 105–108; succession of kingdoms, 187; variant traditions, 263n7

Daphne, oracular spring at, 15; Hadrian's consultation of, in 117, 161; procedure, 161

Decius (emperor 249–251 AD): as Antichrist, 109; in *Oracula Sibyllina*, 109, 144, 188

Delphi: importance of in the Roman Empire, 38; in Phlegon of Tralles, 63; lot oracle at, 23; Plutarch and Pausanias on, 1–2; rites connected with consultations at, 40–41

Demography, and religion, 6–7

Dice. *See* Lot oracles

Didyma (Oracle of Apollo at): consultations, 41–42; importance of in the Roman Empire, 37. *See also* Diocletian; Trajan

Diocletian (emperor 284–305 AD): consults oracle at Didyma, 170; edicts against Christians, 110; edict

Iamblichus: on prophetic inspiration, 48; prophetic power of, 204; use of *Chaldean Oracles,* 204

Impiety, defined in terms of nature, 8. *See also* Magic

Imposters, of members of noble or imperial families, 109, 142

Instruction (or Wisdom) Literature, Egyptian, 194, 200–201

Jesus Christ: compared to Apollonius of Tyana, 34; imitation of, 56; on false prophets, 56

Josephus (historian 1st century AD): as prophet, 16, 52, 215; on *Daniel,* 106

Judaism: and prophecy, 56, 215–216; influence of Zoroastrianism upon, 189; role of prophecy in revolts against Rome, 171; unimportance of Sibyl to in the Hellenistic age, 77. *See also Daniel*

Julian (emperor 361–363 AD): and *haruspices,* 17, 156; attempts to rebuild temple at Jerusalem, 171; coins of, 125; in edicts of his officials, 120–121; *Misopogon,* 110; prophetic companions of, 179, 204; vision of the *genius populi Romani,* 160

C. Julius Caesar (Roman general/dictator 1st century BC): and *haruspices,* 158; and oracle concerning Scipios in Africa, 148; as first emperor, 104; his personal *haruspex,* 159

Kingdoms: as metals, 106–107, 186–188; theory of succession of, 89, 105, 186–188

Lactantius (Christian theologian 3rd-4th centuries AD): on Hebrew prophets, 210; on Hydaspes, 211; on Sibylline Oracles, 83, 85, 89

Lamb of Boccharis. See The Prophecy of the Lamb

Libanius (rhetorician 4th century AD): on Apollonius of Tyana, 34; prophetic inspiration of, 167

Licinius Sura (consul 97 (?), 102 AD): horoscope of, 161

Lot oracles: at Bura, 27; at Delphi, 23; at Patavium, 23; at Praeneste, 23, 175; Christian use of, 29; criticism of, 23, 26; Egyptian, 26; in southern Asia Minor, 26; techniques, 23–29. *See also Sortes Astrampsychi*

Lucan (poet 1st century AD), *Pharsalia,* prophecy in, 65–66

Lucian (satirist 2nd century AD): on Alexander of Abonuteichus, 34; on Apollonius of Tyana, 34; on Peregrinus, 35

Lycophron (poet 2nd century BC ?), *Alexandra,* 70

Magic: compared with theurgy, 204; contrasted with divination, 177, 180; defined as "unnatural" religious practice, 9, 12. *See also* Apollonius of Tyana; *Goeteia;* Necromancy

Magicians: Apollonius of Tyana as, 34–35; Thessalus and, 59

Magos/magi: connection with magic, 12, 184, 190

Mani (prophet 3rd century AD), career, 208

Manichaeism: spread of, 209. *See also* Diocletian; Eusebius

Mantis/mantike: at Paphos and Kition, 13; defined, 11; Libanius on, 167

Marcus Aurelius (emperor 161–180 AD): and Alexander of Abonuteichos, 16, 169; and Avidius Cassius, 109; in edict of Alexander Severus, 113; Rain Miracle connected with, 122, 141, 144–145

Maximin Daia (emperor 305–313 AD), consultation of oracles by, 170

Menander Rhetor (author of handbook on rhetoric, 3rd century AD): on Didyma, 41; on imperial panegyrics, 116, 129; on Peregrinus, 35

Metals. *See Daniel;* Hesiod; Zoroaster/ Zoroastrianism; Kingdoms

Millennium, sabbatical, 106

Mirabilia. See Paradoxography; Phlegon of Tralles; Prodigies

Montanism, and Christian prophecy, 36

Musáeus: cultural icon, 2; oracles of, 72–73

Nature: as paradigm of good and bad practice, 8–10; fluidity of paradigm, 7–8

Necromancy, 13, 16, 65–70, 236n21

Nectanebus (Egyptian Pharaoh/sage): Thessalus and, 58–59; texts concerning, 234n3

Nero (emperor 54–68 AD): and serpents, 16; expulsion of diviners, 175; in *Oracula Sibyllina,* 141–142; legend of return of, 90, 104, 108; oracles concerning, 100; prodigies connected with revolt against in 68 AD, 172–173. *See also* Imposters

Numbers (significant): name of Rome, 104; 365, 104–105

Oenomaeus the Cynic (philosopher 2nd century AD), as critic of oracles, 53–54

The Oracle of the Potter: date of, 198–199; discussed, 194–203; texts of, 197–198

Oracles: different techniques of obtaining, 13; "inspired," 37; civic records of, 4; 49; distinct from other forms of divination in some Christian thought, 180–181; geographic distribution of, 38; independence of, 170; obscurity of, 50; purpose of rituals connected with consultations of, 40, 46; reasons for consulting, 38–39; records of responses kept by, 45–46, 170; "theological" responses, 38. *See also* Lot oracles; Prophecies

Oracula Sibyllina: acrostic concerning Christ in, 90–91; collections of at Rome, 74, 149–151; extant collections, 88–91; *3,* 84, 86; *5,* 122, 138, 140; *8,* 83–84, 90, 103–104, 138, 142; *11,* 82; *12,* 102, 109, 122, 138, 140–143; *13,* 108–110, 138, 144, 188; *14,* 138–140. *See also* Sibyl; *Quindecimviri sacris faciundis*

Paradoxography, prophecy in, 61–64

Paul, Saint: and the Areopagus, 51; as prophet, 33, 214; in Jewish Christianity, 208; on prophecy, 55–56, 211

Pausanias (traveler 2nd century AD): experience at the oracle of Trophonius, 43–45; observes sites of *necromanteia,* 70; on ancient prophets, 58; on Delphi, 1–2; on lot oracle at Bura, 27; on Sibyls, 72, 75, 79–80, 85; words for prophecy, 11

Peregrinus (holy man/philosopher 2nd century AD), different views of, 35

Philostratus (man of letters 2nd-3rd centuries AD), on Apollonius of Tyana, 34–35, 165–166, 190

Phlegon of Tralles (paradoxographer, 2nd century AD): accounts of wonders, 61–64; on Sibyls, 70–71, 74

Physiognomy, 21–22

Pliny (the Elder, author of *Natural History,* 1st century AD): inspired to write history by a vision, 168; on

Berossus, 191; on prophecies, 167–168; on statues of Sibyls at Rome, 81; on Zoroaster, 189

Pliny (the Younger, 1st–2nd century AD): dream concerning personal peril, 168; on building projects, 126; on historians, 133. *See also* Silius Italicus; Trajan

Plotinus (philosopher 3rd century AD): prophetic power of, 166; thought of as a god by Porphyry, 37

Plutarch (man of letters 2nd century AD): on Delphi, 1–2; on prophetic inspiration, 38, 47–48; on Sibylline Oracles, 58–59; on Zoroastrianism, 189; story of prophet around the Red Sea, 32

Porphyry (philosopher 3rd century AD): on books of Zoroaster, 190; on inspired oracles, 38, 48, 57; on Plotinus, 37, 166

Priests, contrasted with prophets, 7–8

Prodigies: connected with the disaster of Varus (9 AD), 172; connected with Christian persecution, 172; observed, 63, 144, 235n6. *See also Haruspex; Mirabilia; Quindecimviri sacris faciundis*

Prophecies: authentication of, 83–87; changes in meaning of, 199, 202; composition of, 83–85, 93–97; "dynastic," 138, 253–254n112; historical reading of, 61–64, 99–110, 137–145, 199; importance of dating for interpretation, 64, 201, 207; perspectives in, 137–145; rewriting of, 169–170, 199. *See also* Hadrian; Septimius Severus; Sulla; Tiberius

Prophecies of Neferti, 200–201

Prophecy: authentication of, 30, 50, 52, 60, 83–87; concerned with the present, 2–3, 58–59, 183–184; connected with ideas about power, 2–3, 40, 49, 98, 213–214; connec-

tion with words for communication, 10–11; critics of, 50, 52–57; cultural value of, 2, 58, 183–186, 205–206, 210–212; errors, 38, 51–52; Greco-Roman definitions compared with modern, 10–11; hierarchy of techniques determined by individuals, 23; imperial legislation against, 174–181; importance of books in shaping attitudes towards, 60; inductive, 15–22; provides interpretative framework, 194, 207; subjective, 15, 22–47; theories of prophetic inspiration, 37–38, 47–51, 69; words for, 10–11. *See also* Canon; Christianity; Paradoxography

The Prophecy of the Lamb, 194–203; date of, 197

Prophet: at oracular shrines, 41–43; frauds, 16, 47, 50, 72; meaning of the word, 10–11; Palestinian, 31; spell to help, 30; special physical conditioning of, 32, 37, 165–166; women (other than Sibyls) as, 31, 41, 42, 148, 169. *See also* Alexander of Abonuteichos, Apollonius of Tyana; Elchesai; Plutarch; Sibyl; Veleda

Prophetes, 10–12

Prophetic power, as sign of moral excellence, 66, 164–167

Quindecimviri sacris faciundis: and prodigies, 149–150, 172; procedures, 150–151

Religion: active and passive, defined, 5; ancient definitions compared with modern, 9–10; seeking prophecy as an active experience, 45, 48

Revelation: and Christian traditions of prophecy, 56; omits emperors of 69 AD, 104

Sacrifice, and civic cult, 7. *See also* Constantine

Saeculum, 100–101

Scipio. *See* P. Cornelius Scipio Africanus; P. Cornelius Scipio Aemilianus

Scribonius Libo Drusus: accused of necromancy, 16, 69; investigation into his associates, 174

Ti. Sempronius Gracchus (consul 213 BC), and *haruspicium,* 157

Ti. Sempronius Gracchus (consul 163 BC): and augury, 152–153; and *haruspices,* 152, 157

Septimius Severus (emperor 193–211 AD): and astrology, 163–164; and oracle of Zeus Belus, 170; games commemorating victories, 129; in *Oracula Sibyllina,* 143–144; publicized predictions concerning his future greatness, 164; sends paintings of campaigns to Rome, 121; statues of as sources of information, 121; titulature of, 112

Sibyl: as cultural icon, 2; Babylonian, 75–77; Cimmerian, 73–74; connected with civic identity, 79–81, 86; Cumaean, in Vergil, *Eclogue* 4, 70, 163; Cumaean, in Vergil's *Aeneid,* 64; Cumaean, in Silius Italicus' *Punica,* 67; definition of, 72, 237n30; early traditions concerning Cumaean, 74; evolution of Christian traditions concerning, 87–93; evolution of pagan traditions concerning, 71–82; evolution of traditions concerning Cumaean, 74–75; evolution of traditions concerning Erythraean, 71–72, 75, 79–81; format of Sibylline Oracles, 73, 138; image of Cumaean, 81–82; inspiration of, 82–83; Jewish, 75–76; shrine of Cumaean, 80, 91; Tiburtine, 92–93; verses attributed to Erythraean, 71, 84. *See also Oracula*

sibyllina; Quindecimviri sacris faciundis; Terentius Varro

Silius Italicus (poet 1st century AD), *Punica,* prophecy in, 66–67

Sortes Astrampsychi: date of, 24–25; social status of users, 26; use of, 25–26

Statius, *Thebaid:* prophecy in, 67–69; and prophetic theory, 69

Sulla (dictator 1st century BC): oracles concerning, 148; personal *haruspex* of, 149

Tacitus (historian 2nd century AD): and prophecy, 16, 48; on predestination, 146; on rumor and inuendo, 132–133

Terentius Varro (scholar 1st century BC): on authenticating Sibylline Oracles, 83; list of Sibyls, 72, 78; story of Corfidius' prophecy, 167–168

Theodosius (emperor 379–395 AD), 36, 182

Thessalus (doctor 1st century AD), search for wisdom, 59–60

Theurgy, 203, 230n114

Thrasyllus (astrologer 1st century AD): and Caligula, 159; and Tiberius, 158–159; family of, 159

Tiberius (emperor 14–37 AD): and authentication of a Sibylline Oracle, 150; and Sibylline Oracle in 19 AD, 99; and the trial of Piso, 116; in documents of his subordinates, 120; in *Oracula Sibyllina,* 140–141, 145; legislation against divination, 174–175; prediction concerning Caligula, 52, 159; used lot oracle at Patavium, 27. *See also* Galba; Thrasyllus

Titus (emperor 79–81 AD): in *Oracula Sibyllina,* 145; visits Aphrodite at Paphos, 13, 173

Trajan (emperor 98–117 AD): consultation of the Oracle at Didyma, 169; consultation of the Oracle of Zeus Belus, 169; in edict of Alexander Severus, 113; in *Oracula Sibyllina*, 141; Parthian campaign and Elchesai, 207; prediction concerning in Pliny's panegyric, 162; titulature of, 112

Trebonianus Gallus (emperor 251–253 AD), in *Oracula Sibyllina*, 109–110, 144

Trophonius, dream oracle of at Lebadia, 43–45

Valens (emperor 364–378 AD). *See* Ammianus Marcellinus

Vates, 11

Veleda (German prophet 1st century AD): role in revolt against Rome, 171; Vespasian seeks oracle concerning, 16, 169

Vergil (poet 1st century BC):

Constantine connected with *Eclogues*, 163; prophecies in *Aeneid*, 65–65; Sibyl in *Eclogues*, 70

Vespasian (emperor 69–79 AD): and Josephus, 17, 52; expulsion of diviners, 175; in *Oracula Sibyllina*, 103–104, 141, 143, 145; use of prodigies in 68–69, 173. *See also* Veleda

Vitium, 153–154

Zenobia (ruler of Palmyra 268–272 AD): consults oracles, 169; and Manichaean missionaries, 208

Zeus: Belus, oracle of at Apamea in Syria, 169–170; Philios, oracle of at Antioch, 170

Zoroaster/Zoroastrianism: *Bahman Yasht*, 186–187; four metals as four ages, 186–187; in the Roman Empire, 189–190; Sassanian influence upon, 189, 205

REVEALING ANTIQUITY

G. W. Bowersock, General Editor